TAPESTRY

Reading 3

Linda Robinson Fellag

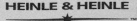

HEINLE & HEINLE

THOMSON LEARNING™

United States • Australia • Canada • Mexico • Singapore • Spain • United Kingdom

To Fodil, as always

Developmental Editors: Jennifer Monaghan, Jill Korey O'Sullivan
Sr. Production Coordinator: Maryellen E. Killeen
Market Development Director: Charlotte Sturdy
Sr. Manufacturing Coordinator: Mary Beth Hennebury
Interior Design: Julia Gecha
Illustrations: Pre-Press Company, Inc.
Photo Research: Martha Friedman

Cover Design: Ha Nguyen Design
Cover Images: PhotoDisc®
Composition/Production: Pre-Press Company, Inc.
Freelance Production Editor: Janet McCartney
Copyeditor: Timothy Lemire
Printer/Binder: Bawden

For permission to use material from this text, contact us:
web   www.thomsonrights.com
fax   1-800-730-2215
phone   1-800-730-2214

For photo credits, see page 235.

Heinle & Heinle Publishers
20 Park Plaza
Boston, MA 02116

UK/EUROPE/MIDDLE EAST:
Thomson Learning
Berkshire House
168-173 High Holborn
London, WC1V 7AA, United Kingdom

AUSTRALIA/NEW ZEALAND:
Nelson/Thomson Learning
102 Dodds Street
South Melbourne
Victoria 3205 Australia

CANADA:
Nelson/Thomson Learning
1120 Birchmount Road
Scarborough, Ontario
Canada M1K 5G4

LATIN AMERICA:
Thomson Learning
Seneca, 53
Colonia Polanco
11560 México D.F. México

ASIA (excluding Japan):
Thomson Learning
60 Albert Street #15-01
Albert Complex
Singapore 189969

JAPAN:
Thomson Learning
Palaceside Building, 5F
1-1-1 Hitotsubashi, Chiyoda-ku
Tokyo 100 0003, Japan

SPAIN:
Thomson Learning
Calle Magallanes, 25
28015-Madrid
España

Library of Congress Cataloging-in-Publication Data
Fellag, Linda Robinson.
    Tapestry reading 3 / Linda Robinson Fellag.
      p. cm.
    ISBN 0-8384-0050-7 (alk. paper)
    1. English language—Textbooks for foreign speakers. 2. Reading comprehension—Problems, exercises, etc.
3. College readers. I. Title: Tapestry reading three. II. Title.

PE1128 .F4243 2000
428.6'4—dc21   99-057628

 This book is printed on acid-free recycled paper.

Printed in the United States of America.
2 3 4 5 6 7 8 9 03 02 01 00

A VERY SPECIAL THANK YOU

The publisher and authors would like to thank the following coordinators and instructors who have offered many helpful insights and suggestions for change throughout the development of the new *Tapestry*.

Alicia Aguirre, *Cañada College*
Fred Allen, *Mission College*
Maya Alvarez-Galvan, *University of Southern California*
Geraldine Arbach, *Collège de l'Outaouais, Canada*
Dolores Avila, *Pasadena City College*
Sarah Bain, *Eastern Washington University*
Kate Baldus, *San Francisco State University*
Fe Baran, *Chabot College*
Gail Barta, *West Valley College*
Karen Bauman, *Biola University*
Liza Becker, *Mt. San Antonio College*
Leslie Biaggi, *Miami-Dade Community College*
Andrzej Bojarczak, *Pasadena City College*
Nancy Boyer, *Golden West College*
Glenda Bro, *Mt. San Antonio College*
Brooke Brummitt, *Palomar College*
Linda Caputo, *California State University, Fresno*
Alyce Campbell, *Mt. San Antonio College*
Barbara Campbell, *State University of New York, Buffalo*
Robin Carlson, *Cañada College*
Ellen Clegg, *Chapman College*
Karin Cintron, *Aspect ILS*
Diane Colvin, *Orange Coast College*
Martha Compton, *University of California, Irvine*
Nora Dawkins, *Miami-Dade Community College*
Beth Erickson, *University of California, Davis*
Charles Estus, *Eastern Michigan University*
Gail Feinstein Forman, *San Diego City College*
Jeffra Flaitz, *University of South Florida*
Kathleen Flynn, *Glendale Community College*
Ann Fontanella, *City College of San Francisco*
Sally Gearhart, *Santa Rosa Junior College*
Alice Gosak, *San José City College*
Kristina Grey, *Northern Virginia Community College*
Tammy Guy, *University of Washington*
Gail Hamilton, *Hunter College*
Patty Heiser, *University of Washington*
Virginia Heringer, *Pasadena City College*

Catherine Hirsch, *Mt. San Antonio College*
Helen Huntley, *West Virginia University*
Nina Ito, *California State University, Long Beach*
Patricia Jody, *University of South Florida*
Diana Jones, *Angloamericano, Mexico*
Loretta Joseph, *Irvine Valley College*
Christine Kawamura, *California State University, Long Beach*
Gregory Keech, *City College of San Francisco*
Kathleen Keesler, *Orange Coast College*
Daryl Kinney, *Los Angeles City College*
Maria Lerma, *Orange Coast College*
Mary March, *San José State University*
Heather McIntosh, *University of British Columbia, Canada*
Myra Medina, *Miami-Dade Community College*
Elizabeth Mejia, *Washington State University*
Cristi Mitchell, *Miami-Dade Community College*
Sylvette Morin, *Orange Coast College*
Blanca Moss, *El Paso Community College*
Karen O'Neill, *San José State University*
Bjarne Nielsen, *Central Piedmont Community College*
Katy Ordon, *Mission College*
Luis Quesada, *Miami-Dade Community College*
Gustavo Ramírez Toledo, *Colegio Cristóbol Colón, Mexico*
Nuha Salibi, *Orange Coast College*
Alice Savage, *North Harris College*
Dawn Schmid, *California State University, San Marcos*
Mary Kay Seales, *University of Washington*
Denise Selleck, *City College of San Francisco*
Gail Slater, *Brooklyn and Staten Island Superintendency*
Susanne Spangler, *East Los Angeles College*
Karen Stanley, *Central Piedmont Community College*
Sara Storm, *Orange Coast College*
Margaret Teske, *ELS Language Centers*
Maria Vargas-O'Neel, *Miami-Dade Community College*
James Wilson, *Mt. San Antonio College and Pasadena City College*
Karen Yoshihara, *Foothill College*

ACKNOWLEDGMENTS

Erik Gundersen, Rebecca Oxford, Maggie Sokolik, the other series editors, and the editorial team at Heinle & Heinle transformed the new *Tapestry* into a better organized, streamlined series. Jennifer Monaghan and Jill Korey O'Sullivan of Heinle vastly improved this manuscript with their thoughtful revisions.

Tapestry Reading 3: Contents

ACADEMIC POWER STRATEGIES	CNN VIDEO CLIPS	READING OPPORTUNITIES
Set your own goals in order to break down what may seem like an impossible learning task into smaller, more manageable parts.	"Adult Illiteracy" English learners depict the challenges and benefits of learning to read and write as adults.	Reading 1: a textbook excerpt about how reading for pleasure differs from reading for learning Reading 2: a quiz about the reading process Reading 3: a list of tips for reading college textbooks
Carry a small notebook to record vocabulary that you learn throughout the day, both inside and outside the class.	"Wireless Trends" Experts demonstrate a range of new products that use wireless technology, from hand-held computers to eye recognition software.	Reading 1: an excerpt from a book by Bill Gates about the future of communication technology Reading 2: an article about how the Internet works and tips for using it wisely Reading 3: an essay about how cyber-games may distort the player's sense of reality
Create a study schedule in order to handle a heavy academic load.	"Dog at Sea" A dog endures the challenges of the sea after he is left alone aboard his owners' motorboat.	Reading 1: a story of a young woman's survival at sea after an airplane crash Reading 2: an article describing the events leading up to the sinking of the Titanic Reading 3: a continuation of the article, describing the desperate last hours of the Titanic
Use government online and print resources as an easy, free source of information for college research and personal use.	"Anatomy of a Breakout" Members of a community suffer food poisoning after they eat tainted food at a church dinner.	Reading 1: an excerpt from a college textbook about food safety Reading 2: a quiz to determine the food safety level of your kitchen Reading 3: an article examining the safety of food sold from street vendors' carts
Recognize and use bibliographic citations in order to find and cite information.	"Working Women" A discussion of the differences in women's working conditions across the globe.	Reading 1: an essay exploring traditional gender-based roles and behavior Reading 2: an essay examining the changing roles of men and women in society and relationships Reading 3: a chart comparing earnings of men and women of different ethnic groups Reading 4: an excerpt from a textbook presenting facts about women attending colleges and universities

ACADEMIC POWER STRATEGIES	CNN VIDEO CLIPS	READING OPPORTUNITIES
Decide in advance how you want to participate in class discussions.	"Violent Teens" American teenagers and adults explore the factors that cause teen violence.	Reading 1: an essay describing the conflict in the United States over mass media content and control Reading 2: an excerpt from a textbook about how the media often portrays crime inaccurately Reading 3: the ratings lists for movies and TV in the United States Reading 4: a newspaper report about recent international films shown at the Cannes Film Festival
Communicate with your professors regularly in order to discuss your academic progress and obtain extra help.	"Consumer Credit" A couple manages their debts with assistance from a consumer help organization.	Reading 1: an article about the growing anti-consumer movement in the United States Reading 2: an article examining the effect of economic growth on personal happiness Reading 3: an article about the myth of the American Dream
Practice peer testing to prepare yourself and a study partner for examinations.	"Thanksgiving" Native Americans protest Thanksgiving celebrations in the United States.	Reading 1: an excerpt from a textbook exploring how the earliest migrants came to America Reading 2: an excerpt from a textbook describing changes that took place in the way of life of ancient Americans Reading 3: an excerpt from a textbook explaining how trading networks developed among ancient American cultures Reading 4: an excerpt from a textbook describing the way several native American cultures buried their dead
Cultivate a multicultural outlook to help you thrive in the college community—and in the world.	"Malaysia Aborigines" A discussion of the rights and problems of the aboriginal people of Malaysia.	Reading 1: an essay about the factors that bind ethnic groups and support ethnic identity Reading 2: an essay about identifying ethnic groups Reading 3: an excerpt from a textbook about the tensions that arise when sub-nationalities exist within nations Reading 4: an article which describes the stages of developing a multicultural worldview
Research the job market in order to predict the best careers for the future.	"Hot Jobs" Employment experts recommend majors that offer college graduates the best chances of getting good jobs.	Reading 1: an article about factors to consider when choosing a career Reading 2: an article predicting the future job market Reading 3: an article describing careers in the field of computers

Welcome to TAPESTRY!

Empower your students with the **Tapestry Reading** series!

••

Language learning can be seen as an ever-developing tapestry woven with many threads and colors. The elements of the tapestry are related to different language skills such as listening and speaking, reading, and writing; the characteristics of the teachers; the desires, needs, and backgrounds of the students; and the general second language development process. When all of these elements are working together harmoniously, the result is a colorful, continuously growing tapestry of language competence of which the student and the teacher can be proud.

Tapestry is built upon a framework of concepts that helps students become proficient in English and prepared for the academic and social challenges in college and beyond. The following principles underlie the instruction provided in all of the components of the **Tapestry** program:

◆ Empowering students to be responsible for their learning

◆ Using Language Learning Strategies and Academic Power Strategies to enhance one's learning, both in and out of the classroom

◆ Offering motivating activities that recognize a variety of learning styles

◆ Providing authentic and meaningful input to heighten learning and communication

◆ Learning to understand and value different cultures

◆ Integrating language skills to increase communicative competence

◆ Providing goals and ongoing self-assessment to monitor progress

Guide to **Tapestry Reading**

•••••••••••••••••••••••••••••••

Setting Goals focuses students' attention on the learning they will do in each chapter.

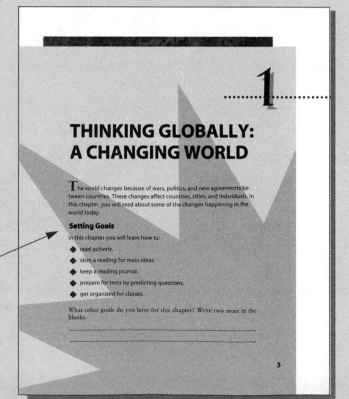

THINKING GLOBALLY: A CHANGING WORLD

The world changes because of wars, politics, and new agreements between countries. These changes affect countries, cities, and individuals. In this chapter, you will read about some of the changes happening in the world today.

Setting Goals

In this chapter you will learn how to:

◆ read actively.

◆ skim a reading for main ideas.

◆ keep a reading journal.

◆ prepare for tests by predicting questions.

◆ get organized for classes.

What other goals do you have for this chapter? Write two more in the blanks.

_____

_____

3

Stimulating reading selections from articles, stories, poems, interviews, essays, book excerpts, and more prepare students to read and comprehend a variety of academic texts.

Language Learning Strategies help students maximize their learning and become proficient in English.

Apply the Strategy activities encourage students to take charge of their learning and immediately use their new skills and strategies.

——— amnesty   ——— confession   ——— suffocation
——— apartheid   ——— reconciliation   ——— testimony
——— brink   ——— revenge

Read

Reading 2: The Search For Truth in South Africa

"Only the truth can put the past to rest."
—South African President Nelson Mandela

1 Jeffrey Benzien, a police captain in South Africa, stood before a crowd of his fellow citizens and motioned with his hands. He was demonstrating a method of torture that would take victims to the **brink** of **suffocation**. Benzien admitted that he used this torture on people arrested for opposing the government. According to **testimony** reported last summer by the South African Press Association, Benzien said he tortured people "to protect the government."

2 Among the people who gathered to hear Benzien's **confession** last summer were several of his victims, including Tony Yengeni. It was Yengeni who had asked Benzien to demonstrate the torture method. "I wanted to see it with my own eyes—what he did to me," Yengeni said. "What kind of human being could do that?"

A History Of Injustice

3 Benzien's tale is just one of thousands of stories of violence and abuse told during the past two years in South Africa. Judges, ministers, and lawyers listen to these stories and record them as part of their work for the country's Truth and **Reconciliation** Commission. Their goal: to learn the facts about South Africa's troubled past.

4 Europeans first settled in what is now South Africa in the 1600s. These colonists set up a government and lived apart from native Africans. Even after South Africa became a self-ruling country in 1910, white people remained firmly in control.

5 From 1948 to 1994, the nation was ruled under a system known as **apartheid** (uh-par-tide). Apartheid kept blacks and whites apart: separate schools, separate neighborhoods, separate rights. No black person had the right to vote or take part in the government. In a nation of 32 million black people and 6 million whites, no black person had a voice.

6 Black South Africans and others who tried to fight this system were silenced quickly and sometimes violently. Thousands were thrown in prison. Hundreds were tortured and murdered by the police. White South African leaders looked away, even though these acts were against the law. They wanted white people to stay in power.

An End To White Rule

7 Apartheid could not last forever. After a long struggle, South Africa held its first open election in 1994. Once black citizens had a voice, they used it. They elected Nelson Mandela the country's first black president. He had spent 27 years in prison for fi... for black equality.

8 As white rule ca... feared that blacks w... cruelties of aparthe... ment and Mandela... deal. People who h... against apartheid ... protection from pu... thing: tell the truth...

After You Read

Skimming: Getting the Main Ideas

After skimming the article, answer these questions:

1. What is the main idea of this reading?
2. What is the relationship of the United States and Europe, according to Mr. Havel?
3. What will happen if Europe becomes one, according to the reading?

Now read the article more closely. Remember to use the active reading strategies described at the beginning of the chapter.

LANGUAGE LEARNING STRATEGY

Keep a reading journal to help you keep track of your ideas and your learning. Keep your written responses to your readings together in a journal. This will help you to review your ideas, remember your reading, and more fully understand what you have read. You can keep your journal in a section of a notebook, a separate notebook, or on a computer disk. Use whatever is most convenient for you.

Apply the Strategy

Review your notes from the reading. What questions did you have? What ideas did you agree with or disagree with? Write a paragraph responding to the reading in your journal. In your response, you should discuss your own ideas and questions about the reading. Don't summarize it, but talk about your own reaction to it. You can also include questions about things you didn't understand.

Understanding and Communicating Ideas

A. Underline two passages in the reading that you found difficult to understand. Discuss those passages with a partner, and look up words you don't know. Then, rewrite those passages, putting them into your own words.

1. Paragraph number ——— New version: ———————
———————————————————————————
———————————————————————————

Tapestry Threads provide students with interesting facts and quotes that jumpstart classroom discussions.

CNN® video clips provide authentic input and expand the readings to further develop language skills.

Academic Power Strategies give students the knowledge and skills to become successful, independent learners.

 Getting Started

This chapter looks at food and dietary habits. Read these titles:

- "Do You Eat Smart?" a quiz from the *Los Angeles Times*
- "America Weighs In," a research article by Shannon Dortch
- "A Pyramid of Health," an article by Daniel Rogov

What is food to one man may be fierce poison to others.
—LUCRETIUS (95–55 B.C.E.),
DE RARUM NATURA

1. Based on these titles, predict the ideas this chapter will cover. List them here. _____
_____
_____

2. What do you already know about healthy eating? _____
_____
_____

3. What kind of diet does your home country have? _____
_____

4. Look ahead at the pictures and charts in this chapter. What do these tell you about the topic of the chapter? _____
_____

5. What do you want to learn from this chapter? Write down two questions you have about food and diet. _____
_____
_____

 **TUNING IN: "Istanbul Dining"**

Watch the CNN video about Istanbul dining. Discuss these questions with your class:

- What kinds of food are served in Istanbul?
- Describe what mealtimes are like in Istanbul.
- How does the Turkish style of eating compare with the style of eating in your native culture?

ACADEMIC POWER STRATEGY

Read newspapers and magazines to stay informed about current issues and arguments. Many students find they don't have enough time to keep up with current events. They stop reading newspapers and magazines when they go to college because they have so much reading to do for their courses. However, reading about current events can help you in your course work.

- Many problems in courses such as history, sociology, or psychology, have direct connections to current events. Knowing what those events are will help you to put your course reading into context.
- Reading newspapers and magazines provides you with reading practice.
- Reading about current events helps you to understand how people assemble their arguments.

Apply the Strategy

Find a weekly news magazine and bring it to class. Read one of the main news articles in it. Complete the following information, and discuss the article with your class:

Title: _____
Magazine: _____
Brief Summary: _____
_____

What controversies are there over this topic? _____
_____

What groups of people are involved? _____

What connections do you see to any of your college courses? _____
_____

Test-Taking Tips offer students practical steps for improving their test results.

Check Your Progress helps students monitor their own progress.

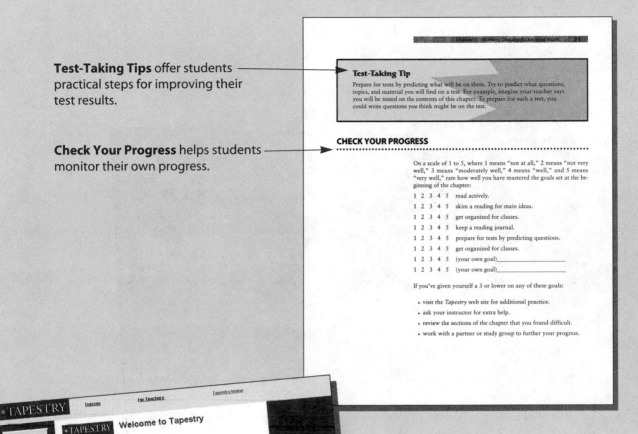

Test-Taking Tip

Prepare for tests by predicting what will be on them. Try to predict what questions, topics, and material you will find on a test. For example, imagine your teacher says you will be tested on the contents of this chapter. To prepare for such a test, you could write questions you think might be on the test.

CHECK YOUR PROGRESS

On a scale of 1 to 5, where 1 means "not at all," 2 means "not very well," 3 means "moderately well," 4 means "well," and 5 means "very well," rate how well you have mastered the goals set at the beginning of the chapter:

1 2 3 4 5   read actively.
1 2 3 4 5   skim a reading for main ideas.
1 2 3 4 5   get organized for classes.
1 2 3 4 5   keep a reading journal.
1 2 3 4 5   prepare for tests by predicting questions.
1 2 3 4 5   get organized for classes.
1 2 3 4 5   (your own goal)_____
1 2 3 4 5   (your own goal)_____

If you've given yourself a 3 or lower on any of these goals:

- visit the *Tapestry* web site for additional practice.
- ask your instructor for extra help.
- review the sections of the chapter that you found difficult.
- work with a partner or study group to further your progress.

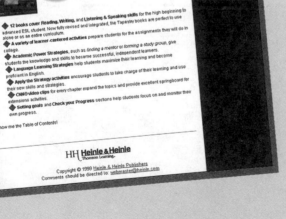

Expand your classroom at Tapestry Online
www.tapestry.heinle.com
- Online Quizzes
- Instructor's Manuals
- Opportunities to use and expand the Academic Power Strategies
- More!

For a well-integrated curriculum, try the **Tapestry Writing** series and the **Tapestry Listening & Speaking** series, also from Heinle & Heinle.

To learn more about the **Tapestry** principles, read *The Tapestry of Language Learning,* by Rebecca L. Oxford and Robin C. Scarcella, also from Heinle & Heinle Publishers. ISBN 0-8384-2359-0.

Look at the photo. Then discuss these questions with your classmates:

- How do you feel about reading in English?
- What makes you feel this way?
- Why is reading important?

A CAMPUS OF READERS

The ability to read college-level material is critical to your academic future. Indeed, educators estimate that 70 percent of your college success depends on how effectively you read. Chapter 1 presents some specific ideas to help you meet this challenge.

Setting Goals

In this chapter you will learn how to:

◆ set your own learning goals.

◆ express main ideas in readings.

◆ ask questions to focus your reading.

ACADEMIC POWER STRATEGY

*S*et *your own* goals in order to break down what may seem like an impossible learning task into smaller, more manageable parts. College-level learning requires you to set goals at many points—as you embark on a particular major, as you start a new course, as you manage an assignment, and as you begin to build the skills to succeed in your learning. Goals can concern learning English, becoming a better learner, and dealing more effectively with academic situations. You should set goals as you begin this course.

Apply the Strategy

Read the goals on page 3. What other goals do you have for this chapter? Write one or two of them here.

_____

_____

**Getting Started**

The writers in this chapter focus on three topics related to college reading. Look at the titles of the readings and answer the questions that follow.

Readings:

"Reading for Pleasure Versus Reading for Learning"

"What Do You Know about the Reading Process?"

"Ten Tips for Reading College Textbooks"

1. How do you think reading for pleasure differs from reading for learning?

_____

_____

_____

_____

_____

_____

_____

_____

2. What do you already know about how a person reads?

_____

_____

_____

_____

_____

_____

_____

_____

3. What good rules do you follow when you read a college textbook?

_____

_____

_____

_____

_____

_____

_____

_____

> 'Tis the good reader that makes the good book.
>
> —RALPH WALDO EMERSON

4. Preview the photos and illustrations in this chapter. What do these tell you about the topics of the readings?

_____

_____

_____

_____

_____

_____

_____

◆ **Getting Ready to Read**

A. Describe what you generally read. On the left side of the following chart, check the types of reading you do. Then talk to a classmate about the kind of reading he or she does and fill out the right side.

I Read	My Classmate Reads
_____ cookbooks	_____ cookbooks
_____ newspapers	_____ newspapers
_____ magazines	_____ magazines
_____ action-adventure stories	_____ action-adventure stories
_____ sports articles	_____ sports articles
_____ romance novels	_____ romance novels
_____ business letters	_____ business letters
_____ textbooks	_____ textbooks
_____ instruction manuals	_____ instruction manuals
(other) _____	(other) _____
(other) _____	(other) _____

B. Review the types of reading listed in **Part A**. Mark each type of reading as P (pleasure) or L (learning). Compare your answers with a classmate.

C. Predicting Ideas: Reading 1 discusses the differences in the way you read for *pleasure* and for *learning*. Think about how your reading behavior *changes* when you read for *pleasure* or for *learning*. With a classmate, brainstorm some of the activities you do when you read for these two different purposes. One example of typical reading behavior when a person reads for pleasure is provided.

WHEN I READ FOR PLEASURE . . .

I sometimes skip parts of the reading.

_____

_____

_____

WHEN I READ FOR LEARNING . . .

_____

_____

_____

_____

Vocabulary Check

The following words and phrases appear in the reading, "Reading for Pleasure Versus Reading for Learning." How many are familiar to you? Check them. Look up new words in a dictionary. Discuss the words with your classmates.

_____ retain

_____ long-term memory

_____ notion

_____ short-term memory

_____ retention

_____ cramming

_____ postponement

_____ cumulative

_____ opt

_____ troublesome

_____ extracting

_____ contemplating

_____ dawdle

(handwritten annotations:) total · extending a long period, lasting memory · an idea, belief · imediate, no long · ability to keep or retain st. · learn quickly · sự trì hoãn · to move st. to later time · to choose, decide · anoyance · to removing · to think about st. seriously · anticipate · waste time

 Read

Look over the ways that you predicted reading behavior changes when you read for pleasure versus reading for learning. As you read, confirm whether your predictions were accurate.

Reading 1: Reading for Pleasure Versus Reading for Learning

1 Maybe you already think you read pretty well. After all, you've been doing it for most of your life.

2 Or maybe you don't feel comfortable about reading. You prefer television to print. Or you think you get information better when someone tells it to you. Or you find English a hard language to follow.

3 Whatever your skills, *there are techniques to improve your reading abilities so that you can better handle subjects at the level of higher education.* Some of them I'll describe in this chapter. If you don't find what you need here (for example, you feel you need help in reading English as a second language), you can get assistance through your college's learning center or lab.

Two Types of Reading

4 Reading is principally of two types—for pleasure and for learning:

5 For pleasure: You can read action-adventure, romances, sports, and similar material just one time, for amusement. This is the kind of material that appears in many novels, magazines, and newspapers. You don't have to read it carefully, unless you want to.

6 For learning: Most of the other kind of reading you do is for learning of some sort, because you *have* to understand it and perhaps **retain** it. For instance, you certainly have to pay close attention when you're reading a cookbook or instructions on how to fix a car.

7 Reading for learning is something you will have to do all your life, whether it's studying to get a driver's license or finding out how much medicine to give an infant. Indeed, what many managers and administrators are doing all day, when they read reports, letters, and memos, is reading to learn.

8 But here's a difference between those kinds of reading for learning and reading textbooks: *In higher education, you'll often have to read the same material more than once.* The reason, of course, is that in higher education, you

(handwritten: keep, remember)

(handwritten at bottom:) bold = darking · italics : nghiên nghiêng

have to *understand and memorize* so much of what you read.

Reading to Feed Your *Long-Term Memory*

9 "Oh, boy," you may think. "You mean there's no way I can just read stuff once and **get it**[1] the first time?"

10 Perhaps you can if you're the sort who can memorize the code to a bicycle or locker combination with just one glance. Most people, however, need more practice than that.

11 This has to do with the **notion** of **short-term memory** versus long-term memory. The **retention** of information drops rapidly in the first 24 hours after you've been exposed to it (the "forgetting curve").

12 Some students might try to make these acts an argument for **cramming**—holding off until the last day before a test and then reading everything at once. However, there is no way such **postponement** can really be effective. Many instructors, for instance, have *cumulative* final exams. They test you not just on the new material you're supposed to have learned since the last exam. Rather, they test you on *all* the material back to the beginning of the course. If you **opt** for cramming, this puts you in the position of having to cram for the *whole course*. In sum, you need to do the kind of reading that will feed your long-term memory.

Treat Textbooks Seriously

13 Some students regard their textbooks as **troublesome** or uninteresting but unfortunately necessary (and expensive) parts of their instruction.

Or they think of the books as being perhaps useful but not vital (and so they try to avoid buying them).

14 There's a likelihood, however, that *half or more of your study time will be devoted to such books*. Thus, when you think about what your college education is, half of it is in your books. You need, then, to treat them as the tools of your trade (your trade being a student)—just as you would an instruction manual if your job required you, say, to tear down and fix motorcycles or to lead a tour group around your state.

15 With that in mind, here are a few tips for **extracting** some benefits from your textbooks:

16 *Look the text over before you take the course:* If you have any doubts about a course you're **contemplating** taking, take a look in the bookstore at the textbook(s) and any other reading materials that will be required for it. This way you can see what the course will cover and whether it is too advanced or too low-level in the light of your previous experience.

17 *Buy the books early:* In my first couple of semesters as a first-year student, I would **dawdle** as long as a week or 10 days before buying some of my books. Not a good idea. The school term flies by awfully fast, and I lost the advantage of a **head start**.[2] (Also, sometimes, when I waited too long the books were sold out.)

18 *Look the text over before the first class:* The reason, of course, is that in higher education, you have to understand and memorize so much of what you read. If you are familiar with the principal text before you walk into your first class, you will know what the course is going to cover and know how to use the book to help you. Taking a couple of minutes to go from front to back—from title page to index— will tell you what resources the book offers to help you study better.

---

[1]**get it:** understand (slang)

[2]**head start:** a start before others

After You Read

LANGUAGE LEARNING STRATEGY

Express the main ideas in readings to others in order to determine whether you have understood the most important idea. The main idea of a text generally appears at the beginning of the reading. In short texts, the main idea may appear in the first sentence; in longer readings, it can occur in the introductory paragraphs.

The main idea includes the *general topic* (what the reading is about) and its most important *specific points* (what is being said about the general topic).

Apply the Strategy

Read the following statements and choose the one that best expresses the main idea of Reading 1. Discuss your answer with classmates.

Statement 1: *There are techniques to improve your reading of college-level texts.*

Statement 2: *Reading for pleasure means you don't have to read a text twice.*

Statement 3: *Look over your textbook before the course begins.*

Vocabulary Building

A. Check your comprehension of the vocabulary words from the reading by combining the words and phrases in the three rows to make true sentences. Work with a classmate.

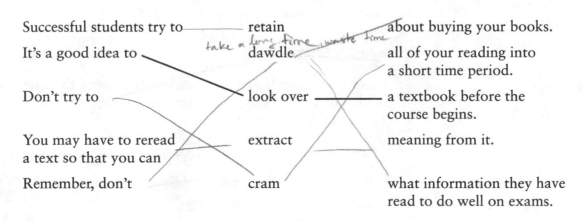

B. Write your own sentences using the following words and phrases.

short-term memory

_____

long-term memory

_____

cumulative

_____

troublesome

_____

head start

_____

Reading Journal

Keep a reading journal to keep track of your ideas and your thoughts about what you read. Write about this topic in your reading journal:

> Reading is (a) enjoyable (b) boring (c) difficult.

Select a response and explain your answer in your journal.

Getting Ready to Read

When reading, most students begin to lose concentration after 15 minutes.

Discuss the following questions with a group of your classmates before you read:

1. Do you use a dictionary when you read in English? How often?

2. What types of reading in English do you find the most difficult?

3. What types of reading do you find easier?

Vocabulary Check

Are these words familiar? Put a checkmark next to the words you already know. Use a dictionary to find the meanings of new words. Discuss them with your classmates.

_____ straightforward	_____ grasp	_____ sequence
~~gloomy~~ _dark & sad_ dreary	_____ transmit	_____ meaningless
_____ unique		

Read

Reading 2: What Do You Know about the Reading Process?

Perhaps you regard the reading of textbooks as a reasonably **straightforward** activity. Or perhaps you find the whole process **dreary** or mysterious or scary. Answer "True" or "False" depending on whether you agree or disagree with the following statements.

1. Reading makes unusual or **unique** demands on a reader.

   _____ True   ___✓___ False

2. Reading is a form of the thinking process. You read with your brain not your eyes.

   ___✓___ True   _____ False

3. Reading is a one-step process.

   _____ True   ___✓___ False

4. Effective readers constantly seek to bring meaning to the text.

   ___✓___ True   _____ False

5. Many comprehension problems are not just reading problems.

   ___✓___ True   _____ False

6. Good readers are sensitive to how the material they are reading is structured or organized.

   ___✓___ True   _____ False

7. Speed and comprehension are independent of each other.

   _____ True   ___✓___ False

Answers

1. *False.* Reading actually does not make unusual demands on a reader. The same mental processes you use to "read" people's faces or **grasp** the main idea of a situation you observe are used when you read.

2. *True.* Your eyes simply **transmit** images to the brain. Improving your reading means improving your thinking, not practicing moving your eyes faster or in a different way.

3. *False.* Reading includes three steps: (a) preparing yourself to read (thinking about what you already know about a subject and setting purposes for reading); (b) processing information; and (c) reacting to what you read.

4. *True.* When they are not comprehending, they take steps to correct the situation.

5. *True.* If you fail to understand something you are reading, it could be because it is poorly written. More likely, however, you lack the background information needed to comprehend—you wouldn't understand it even if someone read it aloud to you. Perhaps you need to read an easier book on the same subject first.

6. *True.* Good readers know the subject matter and main idea of each paragraph and understand how each paragraph is organized (for example, **sequence,** listing, cause and effect, comparison and contrast, and definition).

7. *False.* The more quickly you can understand something, the faster you can read it. However, "speed" without comprehension is **meaningless.** Reading is more than just allowing your eyes to pass over lines of print.

◆**After You Read**

A. Expressing the Main Idea: Tell a classmate the main idea of Reading 2 in one or two sentences. Include the *general topic* of the reading and *specific points* of the main idea. Use these sentences as a guide:

This reading is about <u>reading process</u>. It says/explains/tells us that
· *general topic*

<u>Reading is not one step process</u>.
specific points

B. Reactions: Discuss the following questions with classmates:

1. Which of the reading process questions did you answer incorrectly? Discuss each of these questions with classmates.

2. How do the author's ideas about the reading process compare with your own reading experiences?

 **Vocabulary Building**

Match the vocabulary words on the left with the definitions on the right. Check your answers with one or more classmates.

_c__ 1. unique *dug I*   a. to send

_e__ 2. grasp   b. order

_d__ 3. transmit   c. the only one of its kind

_b__ 4. sequence   d. direct

_f__ 5. meaningless   e. to understand or reach

_d__ 6. straightforward   f. without value or purpose

Reading Journal

Write about one or more of the seven points about the reading process from Reading 2. Based on the information you have learned from this reading, should you change your reading habits? If so, what types of changes should you make? If not, how does your experience as a reader "confirm" the author's ideas about the reading process?

TUNING IN: "Adult Illiteracy"

A. Pre-Viewing: Before you view the following CNN video segment titled "Adult Illiteracy," read and discuss the following questions:

1. What is the difference in meaning between these two words:

illiterate   literate   *illiterate is unable to read & write*
                          literate is able to read & write

2. List problems that you think an illiterate adult might have:

There are some problem for an illiterate adult might have : job, education, & they have to very hard to be a literate.

© CNN

1. helping children
*   applications*
*   writing checks.*
2. feel better

B. Discussion: After you view, discuss these questions with classmates:

1. What problems do the illiterate adults describe in the video clip? Compare your list with the ideas in the video.

2. What benefits do the adults receive after becoming literate?

3. How do the learning experiences of these adults compare to your learning of English? Are they similar? Different?

◆**Getting Ready to Read**

Complete the following activities with your classmates before reading "Ten Tips for Reading College Textbooks."

1. This reading is taken from a college textbook titled *College Study Skills: Becoming a Strategic Learner* by Dianna L. Van Blerkom. In this reading, the writer urges students to use a reading/study system. The list below describes the strategies in the reading/study systems mentioned in the reading. Read the list with your class. Do you understand each strategy? Are some of the strategies similar?

   Which of these strategies do you already use? Put a checkmark next to them.

   _____ **Preview:** Look at the title, headings, art, and the first paragraph(s) of a reading before reading.

   _____ **Survey:** Go through a reading quickly to look at headings and the final paragraph before you read.

   _____ **Examine:** Examine the reading for important information before you read. Formulate questions from the headings in the reading so that when you read, you will try to answer the questions.

   _____ **Question:** Ask yourself (or have someone else ask you) questions about the headings in a reading before you read to help you focus your reading.

   _____ **Read actively:** Mark a text and take notes about important ideas as you read.

   _____ **Notetaking:** Take notes in your notebook or in the margins of the reading about what you have read.

   _____ **Underline:** Underline important or unclear ideas in a reading.

   _____ **Review:** Read over, think about, and/or discuss a reading after you read in order to remember the main ideas.

   _____ **Recite:** Recite important information from a reading after you read to check your memory of the information.

   _____ **Prompt:** Prompt your memory to prevent forgetting important ideas in a reading—for example, by reciting important information.

2. On the next page is a list of the popular reading/study systems mentioned in the following reading. Discuss the differences between each system with your instructor and your classmates. Then with a group of classmates, discuss which of the following reading systems best describes the way you and your classmates read.

P2R   Preview, Read, and Review

PREP   Preview, Read actively, Examine, and Prompt

SQ3R   Survey, Question, Read, Recite, and Review

S-RUN   Survey, Read, Underline, Notetaking

LANGUAGE LEARNING STRATEGY

Ask questions before you read in order to focus your reading. Thinking about the content of a reading *before* you read is always a good strategy. Successful readers often do more than just preview the title, headings, and art accompanying a reading. They use the information they find through previewing to write questions about the reading. They write questions that they have about the topic, then look for the answers as they read. For example, the title of Reading 1, "Reading for Pleasure Versus Reading to Learn," may make a reader ask, "What are the major differences between these two types of reading?" or "Which type is more difficult?" Previewing and making up questions about reading content focuses your attention as you read because you are looking for answers to your questions. This strategy is especially useful for students, because the questions you ask and answer often appear on examinations based on reading.

Apply the Strategy

Consider the title of Reading 3, "Ten Tips for Reading College Textbooks." Make a list of three or more questions that you have about this topic. Compare your list with one or more of your classmates.

Vocabulary Check

Preview the following list of words taken from Reading 3. Are the words familiar? Check off those words you already know. Find the definitions of new words in a dictionary. Discuss the words with your classmates. Add new words to your Vocabulary Log.

_____ structure	_____ monitor	_____ prompt
_____ chunks	_____ intervals	_____ recall
_____ segments	_____ verbal	_____ recite
_____ glance		

Read

Reading 3: Ten Tips for Reading College Textbooks

bài giảng, thuyết trình

1. **Read the chapter before the lecture.** Reading the text chapter before the lecture will help you build background on the topic, learn the basic organizational **structure** of the material, and take better lecture notes.

2. **Divide the chapter into readable chunks.** A forty-page chapter is probably best read in four chunks of ten pages each. A twenty-page chapter may be read in two **chunks** of ten or in three chunks of seven, seven, and six pages. Dividing the chapter into smaller reading **segments** increases your comprehension and actually decreases the time you spend reading the chapter.

3. **List your reading assignment on a "To Do" list.**

4. **Space your reading.** Spread the ten-page chunks out over one or two days. Take breaks between sections or read one chunk in the morning, another in the evening, and the third chunk the next day.

5. **Preview the chapter before you read.** Read the title, introduction, and headings, **glance** at charts and pictures, and read the summary. A two- to five-minute preview reduces the total time you spend reading and increases your comprehension.

6. **Use a reading/study system.** Use a reading/study system such as P2R, PREP, SQ3R, or S-RUN, or develop your own system. Be sure you use some type of strategy before you read the chapter, while you read the chapter, and after you read the chapter.

7. **Mark the text or take notes as you read.** Highlight, underline, or take notes at the end of each section. Wait until you finish reading the paragraph of a "headed" section before you begin to mark your text.

8. *Monitor* **your comprehension.** Stop to check your understanding of the material at regular **intervals**. If the material is easy to understand, you may be able to wait until the end of each main division of the chapter to do a mental or **verbal** (reciting) check of your understanding. If the text is difficult, you may need to pause at the end of each paragraph.

9. **Review what you read.** After you complete your reading assignment, take five to ten minutes (or more) to review what you just read. Think about the main points that the author made in the chapter. Develop a **recall** column in your notebook or summarize the key information.

10. *Prompt* **your memory.** Use the headings of your textbook or your notes or use the recall words or questions to prompt your memory. **Recite** the information out loud or write it down.

 **After You Read**

A. Analysis: Look back at the 10 main points in Reading 3. Then, discuss the following questions with a group of your classmates.

1. Which of these steps do you already do?

2. Which are the most useful? Why?

3. Which are not important or useful to you? Why?

4. Are there any *other* useful tips that you use or might use to read college textbooks? Explain what they are and why they would be worthwile.

B. Sharing Ideas: Write 10 tips that *you* would give a student for reading college textbooks. Include your ideas and the author's tips. Share your advice with your classmates.

Vocabulary Building

Complete the following paragraph by filling in the blanks with each of the words listed below. Compare your answers with one or more of your classmates.

verbal	segments	monitor
glance	prompt	recite
intervals		

> On average, college students study two to three hours for every hour spent in class.

There are many useful tips for reading textbooks in "Ten Tips for Reading College Textbooks." One suggestion is that you divide a long reading into _segments_, or chunks, and read one part at a time. Another strategy is to _glance_ at the title of a reading, art or photographs, and headings before you read. It's also important to _monitor_ your comprehension in order to make sure that you understand what you read. Stop to check your comprehension at regular _intervals_. You can do this either with a mental (silent) or a _verbal_ check. Review the main ideas just after you read. Write the ideas down, or _recite_ them out loud. Both of these strategies will _prompt_ your memory so that you will not forget what you have read.

PUTTING IT ALL TOGETHER

• •

Comprehension

Check your comprehension of the chapter readings by marking the following statements as True (T) or False (F) based on information from the readings in this chapter.

_F_ 1. When you read for pleasure, you must read carefully.

_F_ 2. In college, you don't often have to read the same information more than once.

_T_ 3. You need your long-term memory when you read a college textbook.

_T_ 4. Most of college study time is spent on reading textbooks.

_T_ 5. You read with your brain, not just your eyes.

_F_ 6. Reading speed and comprehension are not connected with each other.

_F_ 7. If you read a complete textbook chapter at one time, you'll remember it better.

_F_ 8. It's not a good idea to mark a reading in a textbook.

_F_ 9. You should never pause at the end of each paragraph when reading a textbook, even if the reading is difficult.

_T_ 10. Asking yourself questions about what you have read will help you remember the ideas contained in a reading.

Score: 10 points for each correct answer

10 × _____ number of correct answers = _____ %

Analysis

Scan the chapter readings. Then, discuss the following questions with classmates.

1. How do the ideas in Reading 1 compare with the tips in Reading 3? Which ideas are the same or similar? Which ideas are different? Do you agree with all the ideas?

2. Look over the questions and answers in Reading 2. Which of the answers surprised you? Why? How do you think the information in this reading might affect the way you approach reading?

3. Which of the ideas in all the chapter readings do you find most useful? Explain why.

Final Project

With your study group or a partner, complete one of the following assignments in order to expand your knowledge about college reading.

Assignment 1: Describing a Textbook

Choose one of your college textbooks or a textbook that a student or instructor has given you. Review the textbook and make an oral presentation to classmates about the textbook. Use the following questions to organize your presentation. With your study group members, divide the questions so that each of you delivers part of the presentation. Be prepared to answer any questions that class-mates have about the book.

1. What is the title of the textbook?

2. When was it published?

3. How many chapters are in the text?
    About how long are the chapters?

4. Are the chapters grouped into units?
    How many units are there?

5. What type of introductory material begins each chapter?

6. How are the headings identified?

7. What types of study aids are found in the chapter?

8. Is there an index at the end of the chapter?
    A glossary?
    An answer key?

9. Does the textbook appear to be difficult to read?
    Why or why not?

10. Does the textbook appear to be interesting to read?
    Why or why not?

Assignment 2: Describing a Reading/Study System

In your college library, find a study skills book or reading book. Use it to find out more about one of the reading/study systems mentioned in "Ten Tips for Reading College Textbooks." With your study partners, make an oral presentation to your class about one of the systems. Use the blackboard to illustrate the main features of the system. Explain how this system might be used to study the main ideas in Chapter 1. Be prepared to answer questions.

Assignment 3: Interview on College Reading

With your study group partners, interview two to four students who are enrolled in a major that interests you or your partners. Ask the person these and/or other questions related to college-level reading:

1. How many classes are you taking?

2. How much reading do you do every night?

3. Which course requires the most reading? How much?

4. Which course has the most difficult reading? Why is it difficult?

5. How do you handle the amount and difficulty of college reading? What advice do you have for a new college student about reading?

Make an oral report on college reading based on your interviews. Be prepared to answer your classmates' questions.

Reading Journal

Answer these questions in your reading journal: What information have you learned that will make you a successful college reader? What steps will you take to handle the challenges of college reading?

Test-Taking Tip

Use summary files to prepare for mid-term and final examinations. In a course which includes a good deal of reading, an effective way of keeping track of the readings is to keep summaries of them as you complete them. These summaries don't need to be written in perfect English as they're for your own personal use. They should be brief and include only the most important information about the readings. You can keep these short summaries in a notebook, in a computer file, or on index cards kept in a box. These summaries will provide a simple, organized record of what you have read and will be a useful tool when reviewing for comprehensive tests such as mid-terms and finals.

CHECK YOUR PROGRESS

On a scale of 1 to 5, where 1 means "not at all," 2 means "not very well," 3 means "moderately well," 4 means "well," and 5 means "very well," rate how well you have mastered the goals set at the beginning of the chapter:

1 2 3 4 5   set your own learning goals.

1 2 3 4 5   express the main ideas in readings.

1 2 3 4 5   ask questions to focus your reading.

If you've given yourself a 3 or lower on any of these goals:

- visit the *Tapestry* web site for additional practice.
- ask your instructor for extra help.
- review the sections of the chapter that you found difficult.
- work with a partner or study group to further your progress.

L ook at the photo. Then discuss these questions with classmates:

- How and when do you use computers?
- How do you think you will use computers in the future?
- How much do you understand about computers?

THE ROAD AHEAD

N o other technological tool influences your life as much as the computer. In the new millennium, the way you communicate, have fun, work, and study will continue to be redefined by computers. What aspects of your daily life will computers have an impact on in the future? How can you use computers effectively? This chapter's readings explore these issues.

Setting Goals

In this chapter, you will learn how to:

◈ carry a small notebook to record vocabulary.

◈ identify a writer's audience and purpose.

◈ pay attention to how an author uses figurative language.

What other goals do you have for this chapter? Write one or two of them here.

_____

_____

 **Getting Started**

The writers in this chapter present three topics related to computers. Look at the titles of the readings and answer the questions that follow.

Readings:

"The Road Ahead" by William H. Gates

"Site Seeing on the Internet"

"Cyber-Worlds: How Real are They?"

1. In what new ways do you envision computers being used on the *road ahead* (in the future)?

   There is new ways I envision computers being used on the road ahead hight technology & far-reaching such as electricity.

2. In the computer world, what is a *site*? What is your definition of the *Internet*?

3. What might the term *cyber-world* mean? How does it differ from the real world?

4. Preview the photographs and charts in the chapter. What do these tell you about the topics of the readings?

 **Getting Ready to Read**

The first reading, an excerpt from *The Road Ahead*, was written by Bill Gates, founder of Microsoft Corporation. Discuss these questions with classmates before you read:

1. What do you know about Bill Gates? Why is he famous?

2. What computer products do you associate with Microsoft Corporation?

3. Gates writes about how the Internet will be used in the future. Do you use the Internet? If so, what for?

Vocabulary Check

Which of these words do you already know? Check them off. Work with a partner to find the meanings of new words.

_____ interactive

_____ far-reaching

_____ digital

_____ fiber

_____ wireless

_____ proliferation

_____ devices

_____ reshape

_____ evolves

_____ programmable

 Read

Reading 1: The Road Ahead

by William H. Gates

1 Information has become increasingly important to us, and indeed we're at the beginning of an information revolution. The cost of communications is beginning to drop. When communication gets inexpensive enough and is combined with other advances in technology, the influence of **interactive** information will be as real and as **far-reaching** as the effects of electricity.

2 At some point, a single wire running into each home will be able to send and receive all of a household's **digital** data. The wire might be **fiber,** which is what long-distance telephone calls are carried on now; or **coaxial cable,**[1] which currently brings us cable television signals; or the simple "twisted-pair" wire that connects telephones in homes to the local phone system. It may even be a **wireless** connection. If the **bits**[2] coming into the house are interpreted as voice calls, the phone will ring. If they're video images, they'll show up on the television set or a **PC.**[3] If they're news, they'll arrive as text and pictures on a screen.

[1]**coaxial cable:** telephone or TV cable with outer metal tube and protected center

[2]**bits:** in computer science, units of information

[3]**PC:** personal computer

3   In the years ahead, we'll see a **proliferation** of digital **devices** that will take on different forms and communicate at different speeds, enabling each of us to stay in touch over the net with other people as well as with information of all kinds. We'll use new versions of familiar tools—telephones, TVs, PCs, **white boards**,[4] notebooks, wallets—to take command of information and **reshape** the media that make up much of our daily life: books, magazines, newspapers, video, music, telephones, games, even the art on the walls. We don't know exactly what all of the successful appliances will look like, but we do know that as technology **evolves** an increasing number of the appliances will be general-purpose, **programmable** computers connected visibly or invisibly to the net.

After You Read

A. Comprehension: Discuss these questions with a small group of students to check your comprehension of ideas in the reading:

1. What does Gates predict will be the role of "interactive information" in the future?

2. According to the author, by what ways will information enter homes in the future?

3. Which "familiar tools" may be used in the future as computers?

B. Analysis: Discuss the following questions with a small group of classmates:

1. What do you think Gates means by the "information revolution"?

2. What does he mean by "interactive information"?

3. Is the author's explanation of how information will enter homes clear? Why or why not? If not, which parts are unclear?

4. Do Gates' ideas seem believable to you? Why or why not?

> In 1998, the fastest-growing Internet markets were in China and India, where users were expected to multiply 15-fold, to 5.5 million, at the beginning of the 21st century.
>
> —WORLD WATCH INSTITUTE, JANUARY 1999

ACADEMIC POWER STRATEGY

Carry a small notebook to record vocabulary that you learn throughout the day, both inside and outside the class. Keeping a vocabulary notebook, also called a "Vocabulary Log," will help you improve your vocabulary so that you can handle college-level reading and writing. This ability is essential to your college success.

[4]**white boards:** erasable white "blackboards"

Perhaps you already write down vocabulary words in your class notebooks. However, the vocabulary lists may get lost in your notes. A better strategy is to establish a separate place—a notebook with dividers, a pocket-sized notepad, or a set of notecards—as a Vocabulary Log. Divide the log into different sections for each of your classes, and include a separate section for words learned outside of class.

Apply the Strategy

Buy a separate notebook or use a set of notecards as a Vocabulary Log. Create one section in the log for this class. Organize the section by the chapters (Chapter 1, 2, etc.) or the chapter themes (Reading, Computers, etc.) in this textbook. Record at least 10 new words from each chapter that you want to learn. Write the word, its definition, and a sentence in which the word is used in the chapter readings.

Create a section in your Vocabulary Log for each of your other classes, too. Organize the log in a similar way for these classes. Write the word, its definition, and a sentence in which the word is used in the textbook or other materials or in your instructor's lecture.

Also, get into the habit of carrying the log around with you and adding words you learn throughout the day to the "words learned outside of class" section.

TUNING IN: "Wireless Trends"

A. Pre-Viewing: Discuss these questions with a group of classmates before viewing the CNN video clip "Wireless Trends":

1. What is a *wireless* technological device?

2. Are you familiar with these technological tools? Discuss them with your classmates.

cellular telephones	hand-held computers
pagers	voice recognition computer software
laptop computers	eye recognition software

3. Which of the above devices and tools interest you the most? Why?

B. Discussion: Read the following questions before you view the video clip. Discuss the questions with your classmates after viewing:

1. Which of the technological tools and devices listed on the previous page were discussed in the video clip? Put a check mark next to each one that was mentioned.

2. Which other technological products were discussed?

3. Which of the technological trends discussed is the most interesting to you? Why?

Getting Ready to Read

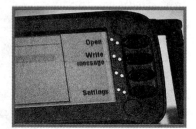

Discuss the following questions with classmates before you read "Site Seeing on the Internet":

1. Review your definition of *site* from the Getting Started activity on page 24. Do you understand the joke the writer has made with the phrase "site seeing"?

2. Is there a connection between "site seeing" and traveling? If so, what?

3. Have you used the Internet? If so, what for? What types of sites are your favorites?

Vocabulary Check

A. Are the following words familiar? Check the words you already know. Look up new words in your dictionary. In many cases, you will find more than one definition for a word. Discuss with a partner which definition might be the most appropriate for the subject of computers. Place new words and their definitions in your Vocabulary Log.

understand savvy   personalized _to swindle_ defrauded

dám, k° sợ venture   _quấy rầy_ _person_ nuisance _to move on_ navigate

far-reaching far-flung _scramble_ _trộn lẫn_ encrypt _conversation_ converse

a way access _easily understand_ foolproof _far away_ remote

_____ knowingly _enlarge_ _sống dài_ magnify _one that receive_ recipient

_____ linger   extent _có ác tâm_ maliciously

_____ tailored _notice_ conspicuously _____ disrupt

of unknown anonymous _to uncover_ expose _to get in_ retrieve

_____ unsolicited

B. Preview the list of computer terms titled "Cyberspeak—Learning the Language" on pages 31 to 32. Read the words and definitions. How many are already familiar to you? Write the new words and definitions in your Vocabulary Log. Discuss the words with classmates.

 Read

Reading 2: Site Seeing on the Internet

The *Savvy* Traveler

1 Millions of people are traveling the Internet (**a.k.a.**[1] Cyberspace). And as **going online**[2] gets easier and more affordable, even more will **venture** into Cyberspace. Because Cyberspace is an image on a computer screen, sometimes it is called a "virtual" world—not actually real. But travel anywhere has real risks and rewards. No matter where you go—even if you don't actually leave your home to get there—common sense and knowledge are your best travel companions.

Getting the Most From Your Travel

2 There is so much to do in Cyberspace and so many "sites" to see that you may wish you had a tour guide. Chances are your Internet service provider (ISP) offers a lot of information on its web site—from news to shopping to games—including links to other web sites. If you know where you want to go, you can simply type in the **URL**[3] and go there. Or, you can use a search engine to look among Web sites to find what you're looking for.

3   Travel Tip: A little planning goes a long way on the Internet. Try to identify the sites you want to visit or determine the subject areas you're interested in learning more about. It will help you save time, and if you pay for your on-line service by the hour, it will keep your charges under control. You might visit a famous museum, catch the latest news, enter a chat room to discuss a topic that interests you, learn about parenting, search for a travel bargain, purchase a book or CD, start a part-time business, or e-mail a letter to your **far-flung** family in a single step. Books, articles, friends, and people you work with can steer you to many interesting Web sites. Once you're on the road, your own curiosity and interests will lead you to even more sites.

Information—
The Currency of Cyberspace

4 Travel Tip: When you enter a Web site, look for a privacy policy that answers your questions about accuracy, **access**, security, and control of personal information, as well as how information will be used, and whether it will be provided to third parties. When you enter Cyberspace, you've arrived in a global marketplace stocked with products and services. But the Internet's major currency is information. You seek it from others. Others seek it from

[1] **a.k.a.:** short for "also known as"

[2] **going online:** connecting to the Internet (slang)

[3] **URL:** Uniform Resource Locator, or Internet "address"

you. Marketers, in particular, want to know as much about you and your buying habits as you are willing to tell. Since some information may be quite personal, you'll want to know how it is gathered, how it is used, and occasionally abused. Just as you might carry cash in a secret pouch when you go abroad, you may want to protect certain information when you go online.

5   Information is gathered on the Internet both directly and indirectly. When you enter a chat room discussion, leave a message on a bulletin board, register with a commercial site, enter a contest, or order a product, you directly and **knowingly** send information into Cyberspace. Often, a Web site may require information from you as the "toll" you pay to enter.

6   Data also can be gathered indirectly, without your knowledge. For example, your travels around a Web site can be tracked by a file called a "cookie" left on your computer's hard drive on your first visit to that site. When you revisit the site, it will open the cookie file and access the stored information so it will know how to greet you. You may even be welcomed by name. If you **linger** over a product or a subject that interests you, it will be noted. And soon, you may see ads on the site that look as if they've been custom **tailored** for you. As web sites gather information directly and indirectly, they can collect a complete data picture of you and your family. This kind of information is valuable to marketers because it helps them target their sales efforts.

Maintaining Privacy When You Travel
· · · · · · · · · · · · · · · · · · ·

7   It's difficult to be **anonymous** once you've ventured into Cyberspace. Expect to receive **unsolicited** advertising e-mail, even **personalized** ads that seem to know you. This so-called junk e-mail can be a **nuisance,** even a **scam.**[4] If it looks questionable, simply delete it. Check with your ISP or online service for ways to limit **unsolicited** e-mail.

8   Travel Tip: Know who you're "talking" to. Don't give out personal information to strangers. As anywhere, Cyberspace has its share of "**snoopers**"[5] and **con men.**[6] Guard your password. It's the key to your account. People who work for your service provider should never request your password. If they do, refuse the request and report the incident to your service provider immediately.

9   When shopping online, be very careful about revealing your Social Security or credit card number and shipping address. Many web sites scramble or **encrypt** information like that to ensure the safety of your personal data. Look at the privacy policy for information about how the web sites you visit scramble or encrypt your personal data. This technology is improving rapidly, but still is not **foolproof.**

10   Concerns about loss of privacy are not new. But the computer's ability to gather and sort vast amounts of data—and the Internet's ability to distribute it globally—**magnify** those concerns. To a large **extent**, privacy is up to you when you enter a web site. Look for a pri-

---

[4]**scam:** business deal designed to cheat people

[5]**"snoopers":** people who "snoop," or watch other people's private affairs (slang)

[6]**con men:** "confidence" men, people who cheat others (slang)

vacy statement. Sites that are most sensitive to your privacy concerns not only have privacy policies, but also display them clearly and **conspicuously,** offer you a choice to share your personal information or restrict its use, and explain how your information will be used.

Travel Insurance For Cyberspace

11 Experienced cybertravelers carry a little "travel insurance" when they enter Cyberspace. Here are some tips from the experts:

12 • Don't give out your account password to anyone, even someone claiming to be from your online service. Your account can be **hijacked,**[7] and you can find unexpected charges on your bill.

13 • People aren't always who they seem to be in Cyberspace. Be careful about giving out your credit card number. The same applies to your Social Security number, phone number, and home address.

14 • Be aware that when you enter a chat room, others can know you are there and can even e-mail you once you start chatting. To remain anonymous, you may want to use a nickname for your screen name.

15 • E-mail is relatively private—but not completely. Don't put anything into an electronic message that you wouldn't want to see posted on a neighborhood bulletin board.

16 • Check your online service for ways to reduce unsolicited commercial e-mail. Learn to recognize junk e-mail, and delete it. Don't even read it first. Never **download**[8] an e-mail attachment from an unknown source. Opening a file could **expose** your system to a virus.

17 • You can be **defrauded** online. If an offer is too hard to believe, don't believe it. Credit rights and other consumer protection laws apply to Internet transactions. If you have a problem, tell a law enforcement agency.

18 • Teach your children to check with you before giving out personal—or family—information and to look for privacy policies when they enter a web site that asks for information about them. Many kids' sites now insist on a parent's approval before they gather information from a child. Still, some openly admit they will use the information any way they please.

Cyberspeak—Learning the Language

19 You don't have to be a computer expert to book a trip into Cyberspace, but it certainly helps to know a few words of cyber-speak. Before long, you'll sound like a native and get around like an experienced traveler.

20   BOOKMARK—an online function that lets you access your favorite web sites quickly.

21   BROWSER—special software that allows you to **navigate** several areas of the Internet and view a web site.

22   BULLETIN BOARD/NEWSGROUP—places to leave an electronic message or share news that anyone can read and respond to. Marketers or others can get your e-mail address from bulletin boards and newsgroups.

23   CHAT ROOM—a place for people to **converse** online by typing messages to each other. (Once you're in a chat room, others can contact you by e-mail. Some online services monitor their chat rooms and encourage children to report offensive chatter. Some allow parents to deny access to chat rooms altogether.)

flame : fighter, yelling .

[7]**hijacked:** stolen and taken over by others (slang)

[8]**download:** copy data from one computer to another

24   CHATTING—a way for a group of people to converse online in real-time by typing messages to each other.

25   COOKIE—when you visit a site, a notation may be fed to a file known as a "cookie" in your computer for future reference. If you revisit the site, the "cookie" file allows the web site to identify you as a "return" guest—and offer you products tailored to your interests or tastes.

26   CYBERSPACE—another name for the Internet.

27   DOWNLOAD—the transfer of files or software from a **remote** computer to your computer.

28   E-MAIL—computer-to-computer messages between one or more individuals via the Internet.

29   FILTER—software you can buy that lets you block access to web sites and content that you may find unsuitable.

30   INTERNET—the universal network that allows computers to talk to other computers in words, text, graphics, and sound, anywhere in the world.

31   ISP (Internet Service Provider)—a service that allows you to connect to the Internet. When you sign up (it takes special software and a modem), you'll be asked to enter a screen name, a secret password, and your credit card number. Usually, online charges are billed to your credit card.

32   JUNK E-MAIL—unsolicited commercial e-mail; also known as "spam." Usually junk e-mail doesn't contain the **recipient**'s address on the "To" line. Instead, the addressee is a made-up name, such as "friend@public.com."

33   KEYWORD—a word you enter into a search engine to begin the search for specific information or web sites.

34   LINKS—highlighted words on a web site that allow you to connect to other parts of the same web site or to other web sites.

35   LISTSERV—an online mailing list that allows individuals or organizations to send e-mail to groups of people at one time.

36   MODEM—an internal or external device that connects your computer to a phone line and, if you wish, to a company that can link you to the Internet.

37   PASSWORD—a personal code that you use to access your account with your ISP.

38   SCREEN NAME—the name you call yourself when you communicate online. You may want to abbreviate your name or make up a name. Your ISP may allow you to use several screen names.

39   SEARCH ENGINE—a function that lets you search for information and web sites. Using a search engine is like accessing the main card file in a library, only easier. A few keywords can lead you almost anywhere on the Internet. You can find search engines or a search function on many web sites.

40   VIRUS—a file **maliciously** planted in your computer that can damage files and **disrupt** your system.

41   WEB SITE—An Internet destination where you can look at and **retrieve** data. All the web sites in the world, linked together, make up the World Wide Web or the "Web."

◆**After You Read**

Expressing the Main Idea: Which of the following statements best expresses the main idea of the reading? Remember that the main idea sentence should include the *topic* and *what the reading says about the topic*. It should represent "the big idea" of the text, not a small detail. Choose one statement, and discuss your answer with a partner.

A. Internet service providers offer a lot of information on their web sites.

B. Use common sense and knowledge when you use the Internet.

C. The Internet is a universal network that allows computers to talk to other computers anywhere in the world.

D. Teach children not to give out personal information about the family when they go online.

LANGUAGE LEARNING STRATEGY

Identify a writer's audience and purpose so that you can better understand why a writer includes certain information and presents it in a certain way. Good writers consider their audience (the people they are writing to) and their purpose (the reason or reasons for writing). A writer's audience is evident by the language or content that the writer uses. For example, a children's book on men's and women's roles in families will contain simpler language and ideas than a college anthropology textbook article on the same subject because it is written for different audiences. Writers also have different purposes. They may want to *inform* their readers, or *persuade* them to change their minds or take certain actions. Other times, writers may want to *produce a certain emotional response*—for instance, to make their readers smile or laugh, or make them sad. Writers can have more than one purpose in one piece of writing. If a writer wants to inform you, the language and content should be *objective* (containing no opinion). If a writer wants to persuade you or produce an emotional response, as in humorous writing, the language and content will be *subjective* (reflecting the writer's opinion).

Apply the Strategy

Discuss the following questions with classmates:

1. Reread paragraph 1 of "Site Seeing on the Internet." Who is the writer's audience or audiences? Make a list of possible audiences.

2. What does paragraph 1 tell you about the writer's purpose? In other words, why has the writer written this?

3. "Site Seeing on the Internet" is a U.S. government publication. Does this information help you identify the audience(s) and purpose(s) of the publication? How?

LANGUAGE LEARNING STRATEGY

Pay attention to how an author uses figurative language to express important ideas by creating a mental image in a reader's mind. Noticing how figurative language is used will help you identify the writer's meaning.

Writers commonly use figurative language in their writing. Figurative language is language used to compare objects that are not usually compared to one another. The purpose of using figurative language is to create a mental image in the reader's mind. For example, in the reading *The Road Ahead*, the writer gives his audience a mental picture of a long road stretching ahead. This is figurative language because the writer is comparing the future of computers to a road. Gates wants his readers to see computer technology as a long road that people will travel. Recognizing figurative language like this helps you figure out the writer's meaning more easily.

Apply the Strategy

Answer these questions with a partner. Discuss your answers with classmates.

1. Reread paragraph 1 of Reading 2. Circle all the figurative language used to compare the Internet to traveling.

2. Find five other examples of figurative language in the reading. Write down the word or words and the paragraph numbers in which they appear.

3. Did the writer use figurative language effectively in this reading? In other words, did the writer's comparison of the Internet to traveling create mental pictures in your mind? Explain.

Reading Journal

Write a journal entry on this topic: Computer technology is often called "the information highway." People often joke that the technology changes so quickly that getting on the highway is like trying to jump into a fast-moving vehicle. Is this a good way to describe computer technology? Would you describe computer technology by comparing it to something else? Explain.

◆ Getting Ready to Read

Before you read, discuss the following questions with a group of classmates:

1. What is a "cyber-world"? *That is mean about computer world.*

2. Have you played computer games? What kinds? *yes, I have. driven.*

3. Do computer games make a person feel like he or she is in a different "world"? Why?
Yes, they do. Because It make you feel more exciting and interesting.

Vocabulary Check

Are these words familiar? Look over the list, and check the words that you already know. Look up new words and write them in your Vocabulary Log. Discuss any confusing words with your instructor and classmates. Add new words to your Vocabulary Log.

> In January 1998, the number of Internet "hosts" (computers with permanent Web addresses) numbered more than 30 million.
>
> —*COMPUTER UNDERGROUND DIGEST*

_____ ornate   *to manege* manipulated

_____ scanning   *indispensable* essentially

_____ chugs   _____ distort *to reproduce*

_____ simulation, simulated   _____ detonate *to explode with sudden violence*

_____ assumes   _____ infancy *very early childhood*

_____ interacting   *to tell* foretell

_____ virtual   *to withdraw* retreat

_____ instinctively   _____ dominant *ruling*

_____ dispose *to put in order*   _____ inept *aptitude*

_____ wave   _____ blur *(v) to make*

◆ Read

Reading 3: Cyber-Worlds—How Real Are They?

1 A young American, Tyler Whitney, stands on the steps of an **ornate sleeping car**[1] of the **Orient Express**,[2] **scanning** the Paris train station for someone. Worriedly, he watches as police officers stand guard. Moments later, when the person he is looking for does not arrive, the train departs on a 2,000-mile journey to Constantinople (Istanbul) via Belgrade. The year is 1914.

2   Twenty minutes later, the train **chugs** through the French countryside. Suddenly, a motorcycle approaches alongside the train. Robert Cath jumps off the cycle and onto the moving train. He boards the Green Car

[1]**sleeping car:** railroad car with sleeping accommodations

[2]**Orient Express:** train route which traveled from Paris to Constantinople (Istanbul)

decorations : trang tri

of the Orient Express with only two items in his possession: a telegram from his old friend Tyler Whitney, and a newspaper clipping about a runaway murderer. He makes his way to Tyler's **compartment**[3] without delay, only to find his friend dead on the floor.

3   These people are not real, and their adventures did not happen. They exist in *The Last Express,* a computer **simulation** game. The computer user *thinks* of the characters and story as real, however, because he or she **assumes** the role of a cyber-person, **interacting** with other **virtual** characters and taking part in the story. Indeed, the moment that Robert Cath boards the train, *you* become him. *You* must figure out where your friend Tyler is. When *you* find his dead body, **instinctively**, you know *you* must **dispose** of it. But how? And when *you* are attacked by **Serbian**[4] rebels, what else can you do but fight for *your* life?

4   *The Last Express* is one of a **wave** of popular computer games in which the user becomes a player in a **simulated** activity. "Simulated flying, simulated pinball, simulated chess—simulated checkbooks, typewriters, and drawing pads; the computer provides a space where models of reality can be **manipulated**," reports science fiction writer David Gerrold.

5   Games like these may seem like harmless entertainment. However, when does the simulation become so important in users' lives that we should stop and take note? The popularity of the Japanese love simulation game, Tokimeki Memorial ("Tokimemo," for short), indicates that that time may already have come. In the game, the user must persuade one of 12 female cyber-characters to fall in love with him. The player converses with the cyber-characters to learn their likes and dislikes. The real-world players of the cyber-world game have become so inter-

ested in the cyber-girls that a popular magazine, *Virtual Idol,* publishes articles about the hobbies and life stories of the imaginary characters. One of the cyber-girls recently released a music CD.

6   "It's not just the software that simulates. It's the user too. When we disappear into our machines, we become simulations of ourselves," warns Gerrold.

7   Konami Corporation's creators of Tokimemo explain the responsibilities of assuming a role in a simulation game: "You are responsible for managing every aspect of this character's life. You are also responsible for this character's relationships, and your personal management decisions affect your relationships. **Essentially,** you assume the life of someone else."

8   Role-playing in a simulation game may **distort** a user's view of reality in other ways. In *The Last Express,* for example, the user may be stabbed to death repeatedly by an opponent or fail to **detonate** a bomb, but, in cyberspace, that poses no problem. Simply rewind the game and replay the events until the player takes the correct actions. Playing the game makes a user feel that she can "rewind" and replay her own life.

9   Indeed, cyberspace has become increasingly interactive in its **infancy,** which may **foretell** its future. Now, cyberspace is a comfortable **retreat** from reality, but in the future, it could become the **dominant** means of communication and entertainment. As people spend more and more time in cyberspace and become increasingly sheltered in cyber-worlds, they may likewise become socially **inept** in the real world. The lines between cyber-worlds and the real world have already begun to **blur.** In the future, if people become increasingly isolated from the real world by their dependence on cyber-communication, they may lose touch with reality.

---

[3]**compartment:** passenger's separate room on a train

[4]**Serbian:** ethnic group of Serbia and Yugoslavia

After You Read

A. Expressing the Main Idea: What is the main idea of Reading 3? Write one sentence to express the main idea. Include the *topic* of the essay and *what the writer says about the topic*. Compare your statement with classmates'.

B. Analysis: Discuss the following questions with classmates:

1. Reread the description of *The Last Express* computer simulation game in paragraphs 1–3. How does the writer make this game sound to you? Circle the best words in the group:

   exciting   dull   challenging   scary   simple

2. Reread the list of examples of computer simulations mentioned in paragraph 4. What makes these activities *simulations*? For example, why is playing chess on the computer a *simulation?*

3. Which of the simulations listed in paragraph 4 are you familiar with? Explain to your group the type of *simulation* programs that you know about.

4. What is the main idea in paragraph 5?

5. What is the main point of paragraph 7?

6. What is the main idea of the last paragraph?

C. Reactions: Discuss this question in your group:

Do you agree with the writer's main idea about computer simulation games? Why?

> In January 1998, more than half of the Internet's users–62 million people–lived in the United States.
>
> —*NEW YORK TIMES,* TECHNOLOGY AND SCIENCE SECTION

PUTTING IT ALL TOGETHER

Vocabulary Building

Complete the following statements about computers with the correct word or expression from the list below, taken from this chapter's readings. Use each word or expression only once. Look back at the readings to check your word choice.

filters   digital   retreat

assume   simulation   far-reaching

anonymous   isolated

In Reading 1, Bill Gates said that in the future "the influence of interactive information will be as real and as _assume_ as the effects of electricity." He described different ways that we will send and receive _____ data in our homes: through telephones, TVs, computers, and other tools. The author of Reading 2 described many ways that people currently use the Internet as a source of information. The writer warned that users should always check a Web site's privacy policy in order to be secure and remain _____, if you wish. It's also a good idea to place _____ on your Internet to make certain Web sites off limits to children. Computer _____ games were described in Reading 3. Computer games are a comfortable _____ from the reality. However, the author suggested that when users _____ the role of a cyber-character, they may become _____ from the real world.

Final Project

Research one of the following topics with a group of classmates to expand your knowledge about computers:

A. Conduct an Internet search on one of the following topics or another topic of your group's choice related to computers. Consult the guide, "Using the Internet as a Reading Source" in Appendix B on page 227. Find two articles. Read them and identify the main ideas.

1. basic parts of a computer

2. word processing software

3. buying products on the Internet

4. privacy on the Internet

5. children's use of the Internet

6. computer simulation games (in general, or by specific title)

7. Bill Gates, Microsoft Corporation chairman

B. If Internet access is unavailable, conduct the same research using print resources from a library. Use your library's databases to search for magazine or journal articles or books. Consult your instructor for information about using your college library. Find two articles. Read them and find the main ideas.

Reactions

Share the information that you gained from your research in a brief presentation to classmates. Answer the following questions about your classmates' reports:

1. What is your reaction to the information from the readings?
2. What did you learn from this presentation?

Test-Taking Tip

Catch up on unread material in order to prepare for a test. Preview any material that you have not yet read and decide what parts you feel you can just skim, and what parts you need to read carefully. It is important to at least skim all materials so you will have at least looked at everything before the test. Take notes on important ideas as you read.

CHECK YOUR PROGRESS

On a scale of 1 to 5, rate how well you have mastered the goals set at the beginning of the chapter:

1 2 3 4 5   carry a small notebook to record vocabulary.

1 2 3 4 5   identify a writer's audience and purpose.

1 2 3 4 5   pay attention to how an author uses figurative language.

If you've given yourself a 3 or lower on any of these goals:

- visit the *Tapestry* web site for additional practice.
- ask your instructor for extra help.
- review the sections of the chapter that you found difficult.
- work with a partner or study group to further your progress.

Look at the photo. Then discuss these questions with your classmates:

• How do you feel about water? Do you love it or fear it? Why?

• Have you ever been involved in or heard a story about an accident or adventure at sea?

TALES OF THE SEA

truyện kể?, truyện tưởng tượng

Some of history's most exciting adventures have occurred at sea. In Chapter 3, people who survived ocean dangers share their dramatic stories. You will read a personal account by a teenager who survived a plane crash over the Caribbean Sea. In addition, in two readings, you will relive the dramatic events that occurred before the famous sinking of the *Titanic*.

Setting Goals

In this chapter, you will learn how to:

◈ build up your reading rate in order to handle a heavy academic reading load.

◈ create a study schedule.

◈ synthesize material from different sources.

What other goals do you have for this chapter? Write one or two of them here.

_____

_____

◆ **Getting Started**

The writers in this chapter tell three stories about the dangers of the sea. Look at the titles of the readings and answer the questions that follow.

Readings:

"Survival at Sea" by Ariane Randall

The Story of the Titanic: "A Night to Remember" by Gary Arnold

The Story of the Titanic: "Abandon Ship" by Gary Arnold

1. What does "survival at sea" mean? What kind of situations does this phrase bring to mind?

   That is mean people who are still alive after storm.

2. What do you know about the *Titanic*?

   Titanic is story about the famous ship. It broken and sanked in the Ocean.

3. What happens when people "abandon ship"?

   The ship is flooding or shipwreck

4. Preview the photos and illustrations in this chapter. What do these tell you about the topics of the readings?

   storm in the Ocean & the ship going to sink

◆ **Getting Ready to Read**

A. What are the *dangers* of sea travel? What are the *exciting aspects* of sea travel? In the following list, mark those aspects that make sea travel dangerous (D) or exciting (E) to you. Add your own *dangerous* or *exciting* aspects to the list. Compare your list with classmates.

   ___✓___ high waves

   _____ limited communication with outside people

   ___✓___ far distance from other vessels

   ___✓___ far distance from land

   _____ closeness with nature

   ___✓___ sea animals

   ___✓___ wind and rain

_____ silence

_____ hard work

_____ possibility of shipwreck

___✓___ fresh fish every day

___✓___ using survival skills in case of a crisis

_____

_____

_____

B. The readings in this chapter relate stories in which people survive or perish at sea. Make a list of factors that might aid in a person's survival in the ocean and write them under the following headings:

Factors That Could Aid Survival at Sea	
Abilities	Tools
Weather windy , rain , wave ,	Other Factors

Vocabulary Check

The following words and phrases appear in Reading 1, "Survival at Sea." How many are familiar to you? Put a checkmark next to familiar words, and write unfamiliar words and their definitions in your Vocabulary Log. Discuss these words with a classmate and look them up in a dictionary, if necessary. Write an original sentence using each word.

U.S. pilot Amelia Earhart was on an around-the-world flight in 1937 when her plane disappeared over the Pacific Ocean.

to come, assemble congregated _a long, deep wound or cut_ gash _illusion_ hallucinate

death doomed _floating on the water_ afloat _Ocean_ brine

not clearly determined indefinitely _to distress greatly_ horrifying _loud, sharp_ shriek

disturbance, turmoil unrest _vô thức_ unconsciousness _to determine_ destined

small & unimpressive (adj) dinky _float (v)_ drift _to better, severely_ clobber

not willing reluctant _without feeling_ numb _rarely encounter_ scarcely

downward or slope descent _situation_ matted

LANGUAGE LEARNING STRATEGY

Build up your reading rate in order to handle a heavy academic reading load. One of the most common complaints of ESL college students is that professors assign too much reading over a short time. One strategy for managing the heavy volume of college reading is to build up reading speed. Here are three tips for reading faster: **preview**, **skim**, and **cluster**. To **preview** a reading, read the first two paragraphs, the first sentence of the remaining paragraphs, and the entire last two paragraphs of a reading. **Skimming**—moving your eyes quickly across the page and reading only a few keys words per line—will also build up speed. Finally, read **clusters** of three to four words, rather than one word at a time. Time your reading as you practice each of these techniques. Push yourself to move your eyes more quickly. Also practice with your class. Your instructor or another student can keep time and encourage you to read a certain amount within a time limit. Try to read 150 words per minute—an ideal rate.

Apply the Strategy

Before you read "Survival at Sea," use the preview technique. Read the first two paragraphs of the story. Next, read the first sentence of each paragraph. Then read the entire last two paragraphs. Does this reading technique give you an idea about the main events in this story? Discuss the main events with your classmates.

 Read

Reading 1: Survival at Sea

by Ariane Randall   Starting Time: _____ : _____

PART ONE
. . . .

1 My trip to a resort in Haiti began at New York's La Guardia Airport, two weeks after my fourteenth birthday. All the people going to the resort had **congregated** around the check-in counter. While waiting around, I met Anna Rivera and Delia Clarke, who would be passengers on the **doomed** plane, and Delia's daughter, Krista. Anna was concerned about how she could get **malaria**[1] pills.

[1]**malaria:** an infectious disease caused by a mosquito bite

2   I had a great time during my week in Haiti, waterskiing, snorkeling, swimming and suntanning—things I don't get to do much in New York City. During the week, the Haitians went on strike a number of times to protest against the government. At the end of the week, American Airlines, on which we were supposed to fly, canceled all flights to and from Haiti **indefinitely** because of the political **unrest**.

3   The resort gave those of us who were supposed to fly home Saturday a choice: either stay in the village for free until the airline restored service, or go by chartered airplane to Santo Domingo, in the Dominican Republic, and catch a connecting flight from there. I wanted to stay since I was having such a good time and there would be a July Fourth celebration, but my father decided that we should get out of the country while we still could. This story proves that all parents should listen to their children.

4   The next day, July 4, twelve guests gathered to wait for the bus. As it turned out, we wouldn't be leaving for another two hours, so I took the opportunity to sunbathe and go for a last dip in the pool. Finally the bus arrived, and I said goodbye to the friends I'd made.

5   At the airport the plane never came, due to engine trouble. Finally, the resort chartered four small planes, and a few hours later, four of us—Delia Clarke, Anna Rivera, my father, and I—boarded the last of them. It was a **dinky**-looking plane, a Cessna, with only three rows of seats. My father and Anna sat backward in the second row, and Delia and I faced them in the third row. Delia was slim and pretty with short brown hair. She told me she'd lost seventy pounds a few years before. (Later I guessed that kind of will power helped give her strength after we crashed.) Anna was also nice-looking. She was going home to New York.

6   We took off at 8:36 p.m. It was soon after that my dad looked out the window and noticed the stars were all wrong. From the location of the Big Dipper and other stars, he could tell that we were going west, toward Cuba, as opposed to east, toward Santo Domingo. He asked Anna, who spoke Spanish, to ask the pilot why we were going in the wrong direction, but she was **reluctant**. She didn't want to question authority. I don't know why I didn't use my Spanish to question him myself. The plane was getting cold, but I went to sleep for two hours, during which time, I have been told, we continued going 180 degrees in the wrong direction.

7   When I woke up, I noticed that we were over water, with no land in sight. The lights on the wings were not functioning properly. They started and stopped—and then stopped altogether. Most of the instruments on the dashboard were not lit up. This was something I hadn't paid too much attention to before but now scared me. The pilot was not getting a response on his radio,

and Anna noticed we were running out of gas. The next thing I knew the pilot was saying, "Mayday! Mayday!" into the radio. Anna cried, "We're going to crash!" I started looking desperately for my life jacket behind and under the seat, but I couldn't find it. Anna found hers. Delia did not. The last thing I saw the pilot doing was tossing his life jacket to my father, who gave it to me and then pulled me on his lap. The plane circled three times around an oil tanker and began the swift **descent**, gliding toward the sea.

Ending Time: _____ : _____

Total Number of Minutes: _____

Total Number of Words: 711

_____ Words/Minute

Expressing the Main Idea

On a piece of paper, write one or two sentences that express the main idea of Part One of "Survival at Sea." Compare your sentences with classmates.

Record your starting and ending time as you read Part Two of the reading. As you read, practice the clustering technique to build up your reading rate. Record your rate in the chart on page 226.

PART TWO   Starting Time: _____ : _____
....

8 We hit the water, and there is a terrible crashing sound as my side of the plane breaks off and water rushes in. I climb out onto the wing. As I stand there, I realize my glasses are gone. I fish around in the water and come up with half the frame. I toss it away. The plane is sinking, and my father comes out with the two ladies but no pilot. We swim away from the wreck as the tail disappears beneath the water. Now we are four people and two life jackets in the vast, dark Caribbean Sea. The pilot is nowhere to be seen.

9   The water is warm, and we swim together, realizing it's the safe thing to do and it's comforting. I am the least hurt, having received a blow to the head, probably from my dad's chin. He has a **gash** on his chin and is bleeding heavily. (Later, we found out he'd lost a quart of blood.) And he has bruises, especially on his legs. Delia seems to have broken her nose, and there is blood coming from it. She is not in pain, though. Anna has several cuts about her face, a broken arm, and a **concussion**[1] that has caused partial

[1]**concussion:** injury of the head

amnesia[2]. She keeps asking what has happened, and we tell her that the airplane has crashed. She will ask again the next minute.

10   Anna and I have inflated our life jackets. They have lights on them that shine brightly. We all hold on to each other, mainly so that the two without life jackets can remain **afloat,** but partly for security. I'm wearing boxer shorts, a T-shirt over my new red bikini, and Chinese slippers, which I keep on the whole time. My father's pants and shoes are bogging him down, so he takes them off.

11   We think we see a boat light, but it soon disappears. I wonder if we will ever be rescued. The thought of floating out here until I die is **horrifying.** I think about sharks and ask Anna and Delia not to splash about so much because it will attract "the wrong kind of fish." Sharks can smell blood a mile away, and three of us are bleeding. There is a silent agreement not to mention the pilot or sharks.

12   Pretty soon, we are all telling each other how glad we are to be together and how much we love each other. We talk about ourselves. Anna is single. (We find out later she has a sister.) She works with bilingual children and has a new job waiting for her on Monday. She is worried that the job won't be kept for her if we are not rescued soon. Delia has two boys back in Connecticut, where she works in a real estate office. She's happy that her daughter, Krista, was not on our flight. My father, Francis, a Russian history professor, will be teaching in the fall. I'll be a sophomore in high school, and if I make it back, I'll have the best what-did-you-do-for-your-summer-vacation essay to hit my teachers in a long time.

13   All of a sudden, a light appears. It looks like a boat light, and we are filled with hope. It appears to be coming steadily toward us. Delia is the only one who can really see, since both my father and I have lost our glasses and Anna is fading toward **unconsciousness.** Anna's injuries are so serious I think she's going to die, but she seems to get better as time goes on. After a half hour (I have my waterproof watch on) the boat light starts to fade. If no boat comes, I decide that I'll swim for land in the morning . . . if there's land anywhere in sight.

14   We think we see another boat light, but it turns out to be the planet Venus. I feel sick and throw up a lot, which makes me feel better. I **drift** off into something like sleep. Around 4:30 a.m., Delia spots something that looks like land but might be mist. We wait for dawn to be certain.

15   When dawn comes, we see it is definitely land. We talk about what to do. Delia and Anna cannot swim well, if at all. If we all go at their pace, there is no way we will reach shore by night. We must make a decision: If my father and I swim for shore, it seems likely we'll make it and be able to tell the Coast Guard where to find Anna and

[2]**amnesia:** loss of memory

Delia. Or my father might be able to find a boat and come back him-self, and in the meantime, they could continue to swim. The alterna-tive is to stick together and hope for rescue. My father and I think that splitting up will increase our collective chances of survival. Anna and Delia are reluctant—they feel safer in a group—but they acknowl-edge that splitting up would be better. Anna and Delia have the bet-ter life jacket. We separate, not really saying good-bye because we expect to see each other again soon. Even after we swim far away and can't see them, we hear their voices carrying over the waves.

Ending Time: _____ : _____

Total Number of Minutes: _____

Total Number of Words: 883

_____ Words/Minute

Predicting Ideas

What do you think will happen in Part Three? What will happen to Ariane and her father? What will happen to Anna and Delia? Com-pare your predictions with classmates.

As you read Part Three, try the skimming technique. Read only the key words on each line. The second time you read Part Three, record your starting time and time your reading rate. Use the clus-tering technique. Compute your reading rate and record it in the chart on page 226.

PART THREE   Starting Time: _____ : _____
. . . .

16 I keep my father posted on the time. Hours pass, and the nearer we get, the more we realize that we still have many miles to cover. We stop every twenty minutes or so for a rest break, dur-ing which I float on my back, which is not so hard to do with a life jacket. I'm not feeling very strong, and I hold on to my dad's shirttails and kick or just let him pull me.

17   It is noon, and we are still a good distance from land. I no longer hear the voices of Delia and Anna. Every now and then my father tells me he loves me a million, trillion times. I say I will tell him how much I love him when we get to land. I'm too tired to speak just now.

18   It is two o'clock. I have more energy now and a determination to get to land before dark. My dad is getting weaker but still pushes on. I get salt in my mouth all the time, and my tongue is

numb from it. It also gets in my eyes, but I have learned to open them quickly afterward, and for some reason this gets rid of the sting. My hair is all **matted**. We have not had water or food in thirteen hours, but I'm not hungry or thirsty.

19   It is three o'clock, and I'm starting to **hallucinate.** I see dolphins, seals, an occasional shark or two, sailboats, and buoys. I say to my dad, "We can do it." And he says, "Yes . . . we can do it." We keep telling each other "I love you" and that we'll make it to shore. I'm guiding my father now, because he keeps his eyes closed most of the time because of the **brine** and starts to go in the wrong direction unless I correct him. Two pieces of sugarcane float by us, and like the twig brought back to Noah's Ark, they seem like a sign of hope. I think I see palm trees behind me, but they are not really there. At six o'clock, we are maybe a mile from shore and feel certain we will make it before nightfall.

20   But an hour later, with the shore in sight, the sky has become gray with thunderclouds. We think we see thousands of tiny sailboats, and my dad yells for me to swim fast to them. I try hard as the wind blows and it gets stormier. I look back. I can't see my dad. "Daddy! Where are you?" I scream. No one answers, and I'm crying for the first time. "Help! Somebody please help! Daddy, where are you?" The rain is coming down hard and fast. I stick my tongue out to see if I can get some. It doesn't work too well. I fight with the waves to keep moving toward land. I ask God why He has put this test before me. I tell Him it won't work: I will come through this with flying colors; I'll ace this test.

21   When the storm passes, I just want to sleep. The problem is that I then drift with the current, which seems to be going out to sea. Sea snails are biting my legs, but I don't have the strength to brush them off. I don't know what has happened to my father. I try the signal we planned—a high **shriek**—in case we got separated, but he doesn't answer. I fight to keep awake but slowly drift off.

22   All the girls I hung out with at the resort are inside my head telling me to swim this way or that. I'm trying to swim toward a hotel, where I can go to sleep. I just want to relax, but I can't because I'll drown. The straps of my life jacket are cutting into me, so I take it off and let it float away. My mouth is burning from the salt—I don't want to die now—if I have to die, can't I at least have a Coke to drink?—something nice-tasting before I drown.

23   I dream I am **destined** to drown. Everyone says so, but I'm still trying to find a way out. I dream I inhaled something that burned out my lungs and throat. Then I'm being pulled. I'm being pulled out of the water into a dugout canoe. By two men. Are they capturing me? I must get out. I pick up a piece of wood from the bottom of the boat and try to **clobber** one of them with it. But he stops me and hits me back.

24   What a nice way for me to greet my Haitian rescuers—for that's who they were. I saw that they had picked up my dad, too, in another canoe. I heard my dad asking them to start a search for Anna and Delia. The villagers of Bariadelle fed us mangoes and fresh water and crowded around us to watch. They were trying to talk to us in **Creole**.[1] I could **scarcely** talk and was confused, but I did manage a *merci beaucoup*.[2]

25   From Bariadelle, we were driven to Dame Marie and deposited in a French Canadian mission station. By this time, my body had gone into shock. I had a high fever, a severe sunburn, and a throat infection that made it difficult to swallow anything without coughing. We were taken to a doctor, but by morning my fever was gone. I found out that I'd lost three pounds. (What a crash diet!) My father had lost fifteen. We were driven to a hospital in Anse d'Hainault and eventually, passing through fourteen roadblocks and over sixty miles of bumpy mountain roads, to the city of Jeremie. There, my father was able to phone my mother and brother and tell them that we were all right. There was still no news of Anna and Delia.

26   Back in New York, the phone never stops ringing. People call to find out if all this really happened to us. Sometimes I ask myself the same question. But what about Anna and Delia? I think of their voices over the waves as we swam away. What happened to them? What will happen to their families?

27   It is a miracle my father and I survived. When people ask me what I feel about the whole experience, I say that when you've almost missed life, you see it differently. To be with my family and friends, just to be able to go shopping to replace my lost clothes, each day seems like an amazingly good thing.

28   Shortly after Ariane Randall and her father were rescued, the U.S. Coast Guard began the search for the two missing women and the pilot. The search continued for three days, but Delia Clarke, Anna Rivera, and the pilot, Elia Katime, were never found.

Ending Time: _____ : _____

Total Number of Minutes: _____

Total Number of Words: 1170

_____ Words/Minute

[1]**Creole:** a French dialect

[2]*merci beaucoup:* French for "thank you very much"

 **After You Read**

Confirming Predictions: What *did* happen to the passengers of the crashed plane? Were your predictions accurate? Were you surprised by the events? Why or why not? Discuss your answers with classmates.

ACADEMIC POWER STRATEGY

Create a study schedule in order to handle a heavy academic load. Many students feel overwhelmed by work, family, and school responsibilities, so in order to be successful, they must find a way to balance the different areas of their lives. On average, you need to study about two to three hours for every hour you spend in class. To ensure that you leave enough time for studying, it's a good idea to create a study schedule. For a five-hour per week class, you'll need at least 10 hours study time. Consider study time one of your fixed responsibilities, just like your work, class, and/or family time.

Apply the Strategy

Use a weekly calendar to mark your fixed responsibilities: class times, work hours, and family responsibility times. Then, reserve two to three hours per week of study time for each class hour. On your weekly schedule, indicate which hours and days you will study for each class. Mark your schedule clearly with the names of the classes. Be realistic in creating your schedule. Leave enough time for sleep and for leisure time. When you finish making your schedule, discuss it with a group of your classmates.

Reading Journal

Think back on the article, "Survival at Sea," which you have just read. Were you successful in comprehending the main events when you used the reading techniques to build speed? How did using these techniques affect your reading ability? Did your reading rate increase from Parts One to Three? Which of the techniques worked the best for you? Answer these questions in your journal.

TUNING IN: "Dog at Sea"

© CNN

A. Pre-Viewing: Discuss the following questions with classmates before you view "Dog at Sea," a CNN video clip:

1. How might a dog become lost at sea?
2. How do the following words and phrases relate to the sea?

   castaway   seafarer   on board   tread water   Coast Guard

B. Discussion: After you view, discuss these questions with classmates:

1. What happened to the dog's owners at sea?
2. How was the dog rescued?
3. What is your reaction to this news story? Does it seem that too much effort is spent on rescuing the dog? Explain why or why not.

In the 13th and 14th centuries, Arab mathematicians drew charts of oceans and coasts. Previously, sailors had navigated their ships by the stars.

The *Titanic*

Vocabulary Check

Reading 2 contains many vocabulary words related to ships. The following words have been grouped in categories. Which of these words are familiar to you? Discuss the ones you don't know with classmates.

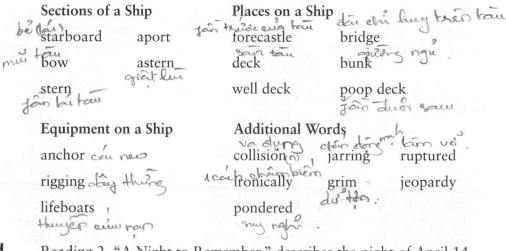

Sections of a Ship

bể (lái)
starboard   aport

mũi tầu
bow   astern
                   giạt lui

stern
jần bả tàu

Places on a Ship

jần trước của tàu   đầu chỉ huy trên tàu
forecastle   bridge

sản tàu   giường ngủ
deck   bunk

well deck   poop deck
                    jần dưới sau

Equipment on a Ship

anchor cái neo

rigging dây thừng

lifeboats
thuyền cứu nạn

Additional Words

va đụng   chấn động mạnh   làm vỡ
collision (n)   jarring   ruptured

1 cách châm biến
ironically   grim   jeopardy
                du tạo

pondered
suy nghĩ

Getting Ready to Read

Reading 2, "A Night to Remember," describes the night of April 14, 1912, when the ocean liner *Titanic* sank in the Atlantic Ocean. Use the skimming technique to read the article quickly to find the main ideas. Read the first two paragraphs of the article, then read the first sentence of each paragraph. Read the entire last two paragraphs. Then, answer these questions.

1. What did the *Titanic* hit? Titanic hit the iceberg

2. What time did the collision occur? The collision occur at 11:40 pm

3. What sounds occurred when the ship hit the iceberg?

4. What damage did the ship suffer? the ship ruptured.

5. How many passengers were aboard? 15,000

6. Who was aware that the ship was sinking? Murdoch

Read

Reading 2: *The Story of the Titanic:* "A Night to Remember"

by Gary Arnold

1 What happened the next few minutes after the *Titanic* hit the iceberg will forever remain in history. First Officer Murdoch, who was the officer of the watch at that time, was responsible for the navigation of the *Titanic*. We will probably never know what thoughts flashed through his mind as the wall of ice passed along the **starboard** side of the bow, pieces of it falling onto the **forecastle** and **well deck**.

2 Murdoch ordered "hard **aport**," when the bow began to swing, his intentions to bring the **stern** away from the iceberg, but it was too late. He immediately rang the watertight-door alarm and then threw the switch that closed the doors.

3 The **collision** occurred at 11:40 p.m., a collision which could have, perhaps, been avoided. Murdoch had ordered the engines reversed, which had, **ironically**, sealed the *Titanic's* doom. Like all ships, the *Titanic* turned more quickly the greater her forward motion. Had the *Titanic* proceeded ahead and turned, it is most likely that she would have avoided hitting the iceberg all together.

4   Moments later, Captain Smith rushed onto the **bridge**.

5   "What have we struck?" he queried.

6   "An iceberg, sir," was Murdoch's quick reply. "I put her hard a' starboard and run the engines full **astern**, but it was too close. She hit it. I intended to port around it, but she hit before I could do anymore."

7   "Close the watertight doors," Smith ordered.

8   "The watertight doors are closed, sir."

9   Captain Smith **pondered** the situation. He was now faced with the fact that his ship had been damaged, how seriously was uncertain yet. Furthermore, he had not been present on the bridge at what was the most critical part of the voyage.

10   Aside from the men on the bridge and those closest to the impact, few realized that anything had happened. George Symons, a lookout, was lying in his **bunk** and thought that the **anchor** had dropped and the scraping sound he had heard was the chain running out of the ship. Henry Sleeper Harper, of the American publishing family, sat up in his bed and saw the iceberg pass his window, pieces of it crumbling as it went by.

11   Almost everyone in the first-class smoking room stood up from their seats when the **jarring** motion disturbed the room. Quartermaster George Rowe, located on the **poop deck** at the very stern of the ship, felt the jarring motion and, seeing the iceberg, walked to the rail to watch it pass.

12   After days of steady rhythm from the engines, the *Titanic* was suddenly quiet. The wake trailing behind the ship, the wind blowing through its **rigging**, all were slowly dying away. Soon there were a number of off-duty crewmen milling around on the forward well deck, trying to find out what had happened.

13   Meanwhile, a very worried Captain Smith directed Fourth Officer Boxhall to inspect the ship for damage. Boxhall worked his way deep into the **bow** of the *Titanic* but could not find any sign of damage. He returned to the bridge with his report to the captain. Smith then ordered Boxhall to go and find the carpenter and to get him to **sound the ship**.[1]

14   Boxhall bumped into the carpenter, John Hutchinson, on his way down to A-deck.

15   "The captain wants you to sound the ship," Boxhall told him.

16   "The ship is making water," Hutchinson responded quickly. Boxhall then proceeded below while Hutchinson went to the bridge.

17   Boxhall soon found out that the mailing room was rapidly filling with water and he returned quickly to the bridge to tell the captain of the **grim** news.

18   Bruce Ismay, who had been asleep in his luxurious suite on B-deck, had also been awakened by the strange noise caused by the iceberg. Without bothering to change out of his nightclothes, he went to the bridge and asked Captain Smith what had happened.

19   "We have struck ice," came Smith's reply.

20   "Do you think the ship is seriously damaged?" Ismay asked, hoping that things weren't as bad as they might be.

21   "I am afraid she is."

22   The rest of the conversation between the two men has not survived, but it is very likely that Ismay must have been shocked by the news. His dream was turning into what would become a nightmare.

23   Thomas Andrews, managing director of Harland & Wolff, arrived on the bridge a few minutes later after Ismay departed. He told Captain Smith, in detail, of the full seriousness of the *Titanic's* current situation. It was clear, based on reports received from throughout the ship, that the *Titanic's* first six watertight compartments had been **ruptured.** The ship had never been designed to take this kind of damage. Over two hundred feet of the ship had been opened to the sea.

24   Andrews, who knew the ship better than anyone, estimated that the great ship had only

---

[1]**sound the ship:** measure the level of water in the ship

a little more than an hour of life left. He also was quite aware of the shortage of **lifeboats.**

25   Captain Smith now faced the worst situation any captain could face. His ship was sinking fast and the lives of more than 2,200 people were in **jeopardy.** He and his officers realized that the *Titanic* was doomed, but the passengers and the remainder of the crew were mostly unaware of the serious situation.

26   In the next few hours, a life and death struggle would begin that will forever remain in our history.

After You Read

A. Read "A Night to Remember" a second time. As you read the full text, practice the clustering technique. Read clusters of words rather than one word at a time.

B. Comprehension: Mark the following statements "True" or "False" to check your comprehension. Discuss your answers with classmates.

_____T_____ 1. The collision of the *Titanic* and an iceberg was unavoidable.

_____T_____ 2. The *Titanic* was seriously damaged when it hit an iceberg.

_____F_____ 3. Captain Smith was worried about the condition of the ship.

_____ 4. The ship had plenty of lifeboats.

_____T_____ 5. Most of the crew and passengers knew the ship was in danger.

Vocabulary Building

Good readers guess the meaning of unfamiliar words by examining them in the context of other more familiar vocabulary words. Read the passages below without a dictionary. Use surrounding words and the events in the story to guess the meaning of the words in italics. Write your definitions in the blanks that follow. Check your definitions by consulting your instructor or a dictionary.

1. The collision occurred at 11:40 P.M., a collision which could have, perhaps, been avoided. Murdoch had ordered the engines reversed which had, ironically, *sealed the Titanic's doom.* Like all ships, the Titanic turned more quickly the greater her forward motion. Had the Titanic proceeded ahead and turned, it is most likely that she would have avoided hitting the iceberg all together.

    "Sealed the Titanic's doom" probably means _____

    _____

2. Almost everyone in the first-class smoking room stood up from their seats when the *jarring* motion disturbed the room. Quartermaster George Rowe, located on the poop deck at the very stern

of the ship, felt the *jarring* motion and, seeing the iceberg, walked to the rail to watch it pass.

"Jarring" probably means _____

3. Boxhall bumped into the carpenter, John Hutchinson, on his way down to A-deck.

   "The captain wants you to sound the ship," Boxhall told him.

   "The ship is making water," Hutchinson responded quickly. Boxhall then proceeded below while Hutchinson went to the bridge.

   Boxhall soon found out that the mailing room was rapidly filling with water and he returned quickly to the bridge to tell the captain of the *grim* news.

   "Grim" probably means _____

Getting Ready to Read

A. Using your own knowledge of the *Titanic* and shipwrecks along with the information in Reading 2, answer the following questions:

1. What actions might be taken *before* a ship is abandoned?

2. Who gives the order to abandon a ship?

3. What actions does a crew take after the order is given?

4. How do the crew and passengers interact?

5. What are some different ways to abandon a ship?

6. What happens to people after they abandon a ship?

B. Read "Abandon Ship" in two sittings. Time your reading and record your rate on page 226. Do the activities after Part One before you continue reading.

Vocabulary Check

The following words appear in Part One of Reading 3. Are they familiar to you? Put a checkmark next to words you know. Write new words and their definitions in your Vocabulary Log. Discuss them with classmates.

distress   plight   assembled

capacity   mount   flickering

chuckling

Read

Reading 3: *The Story of the Titanic:* **"Abandon Ship"**

by Gary Arnold   Starting Time: 4:28 : _____

PART ONE
. . . .

1 As the *Titanic* sat motionless on the ocean, her forward compartments slowly filling with water, a drama was unfolding upon her decks that will be forever replayed in history. Fourth Officer Joseph Boxhall, who was still standing in the wheel house inside the bridge even though the ship no longer needed steering, realized that the *Titanic* was doomed.

2 Suddenly, the wheel house telephone rang and Boxhall, answering it, was greeted by the voice of Quartermaster George Rowe, who had been keeping watch on the **aft**[1] docking bridge. Rowe reported that he had just seen a lifeboat in the water just off the starboard side of the ship.

3 Boxhall was surprised by this information, as he had not ordered the launching of any lifeboats. He ordered Rowe to get some **distress** rockets and bring them to him on the bridge.

4 Meanwhile, **steerage**[2] passengers were beginning to gather on the aft well deck. Many had tried to go to the boat deck but had found it blocked by closed doors or crewmen who refused to allow them to enter the first-class or second-class areas.

5 On the boat deck, First Officer Murdoch found himself in charge of the odd-numbered starboard lifeboats, while Chief Officer Wilde was in charge of the even-numbered ones on the port side.

6 Third Officer Herbert Pitman, who was working under Murdoch, was preparing boat No.5 for lowering. Bruce Ismay, who was standing nearby, watched Pitman impatiently.

7 "There is not time to waste," Ismay suddenly announced, apparently suggesting that Pitman was working too slowly. Pitman did not recognize the managing director of the White Star Line and so ignored the comment.

8 After a few more comments from Ismay, Pitman suddenly realized that this gentleman talking to him matched a description he had been given of the White Star managing director and so walked forward to the bridge and informed the Captain. After acknowledgment from Captain Smith, he was ordered to carry on with his work.

9 Pitman returned to boat No.5 and jumped into it. He then called out to some ladies to get into the lifeboat. After a number of women, children, and men had gotten aboard, Ismay called out several times to see if there was anyone else before the boat was lowered. Finally a lady came running up.

10 "Come along, jump in," he ordered.

11 "I am only a stewardess," she replied.

12 "Never mind," Ismay told her. "You are a woman. Take your place."

13 Pitman allowed a few more men into the lifeboat until the boat held over forty occupants, its **capacity** being 65. He then jumped out of the boat to assist in lowering it and left Quartermaster Alfred Olliver in charge.

14 As the lifeboat was lowered, someone on deck yelled down, "Be sure and see the plug is in that boat," referring to the hole that allowed water to drain from the lifeboats when they were stored on deck. As the lifeboat was lowered into the water, Quartermaster Olliver began searching frantically for the plug and asked the passengers to move out of the way. He finally ended up pushing past them and forced the plug in only after water had started to enter the boat.

15 Back in the **wireless**[3] room, Jack Phillips continued sending out distress signals that

[1]**aft:** close to the stern (rear) of a ship

[2]**steerage:** the lower section of a passenger ship, usually the cheapest

[3]**wireless:** radio telegraph

the *Titanic* was sinking and in need of immediate assistance. A response was soon received from the German steamer *Frankfurt,* asking him to stand by, probably while the operator informed his captain. Phillips told Harold Bride to tell Captain Smith.

16   By the time the operator had returned, Phillips had received a response from the Cunarder *Carpathia,* who gave her position and said that she was **coming hard.**[4] Upon Bride's return, Phillips ordered him again to inform Captain Smith of the contact. Smith soon returned with Bride and asked Phillips what other ships he had contacted, the reply being the *Olympic,* the *Titanic's* sister ship. However, the *Olympic* was headed toward England and was five hundred miles away.

17   "What are you sending?" Smith asked.

18   "CQD," Phillips replied, which was the standard distress signal at that time. Bride suggested to Phillips that he send the new signal, SOS. He remarked that it was probably their last chance to send it and this caused some **chuckling** between the operators who were apparently still finding it difficult to take the ship's **plight** seriously. Smith left a few moments later without comment.

19   Only three ships, so far, had responded to the *Titanic's* distress signals. The *Frankfurt* signal seemed the strongest, but when she sent her position, it was discovered that she was 170 miles away. The *Olympic* wouldn't arrive until sometime the next night. Only the *Carpathia* was anywhere close. Would the *Titanic* survive long enough for the Cunarder ship to reach her and **mount** a rescue attempt?

20   On the port side of the ship, work continued to ready the lifeboats for lowering. Soon the ship's band came up from the lounge and **assembled** on the deck. They then began to play cheerful **ragtime**[5] numbers.

21   Fourth Officer Boxhall, who was still standing on the bridge, waited impatiently for Quartermaster Rowe to arrive with the rockets he had asked for. The reason for his impatience lay roughly ten miles away from the *Titanic* off her port side. Looking once again through a pair of binoculars, Boxhall tried to make out the light that kept **flickering** into view. There was no doubt in his mind that what he was seeing was a steamer, and she appeared to be approaching. He wanted to use the distress rockets to draw the unknown ship's attention.

22   When it appeared that the steamer was in signaling range, Boxhall began using the morse lamp from the port side of the bridge. Captain Smith, seeing what Boxhall was doing, ordered him to tell the ship to come at once.

23   Soon, Quartermaster Rowe arrived on the bridge with the rockets. Smith ordered him to fire a rocket every five or six minutes. The time was now 12:45 a.m. Just over an hour had passed since the *Titanic* had hit the iceberg.

Ending Time: 4:40 : _____

Total Number of Minutes: _____

Total Number of Words: 1045

_____ Words/Minute

Briefly describe the activities involving these elements of the story to check your comprehension of the main events in Part One. Discuss your ideas with classmates.

- rockets
- lifeboats
- ladies
- wireless operator

[4]**coming hard:** moving quickly

[5]**ragtime:** type of jazz music

Vocabulary Check

The following words appear in Part Two of "Abandon Ship." Are the words familiar to you? Discuss them with classmates. Add any new words to your vocabulary log.

(handwritten: very large) gigantic   *(handwritten: adj tight)* taut   buckle (verb)   *(handwritten: (v) appear large & dangerous.)* looming

(handwritten: tràn ngập, overwhelm) engulfed   *(handwritten: for nothing without success.)* in vain   *(handwritten: wonderful)* spectacular   collapsible (adj) *(handwritten: fall into ruin.)*

(handwritten: hallway) corridor *(handwritten: hành lang)*   frantically *(handwritten: very rush)*   propellers *(handwritten: cánh quạt)*

Time your speed in reading Part Two. Record your reading rate on page 226.

PART TWO   Starting Time: _____ : _____

24 On the port side forward boat deck, boat No. 8 was slowly being loaded with women. Ida Straus, wife of the founder of Macy's Department Store, was about to get on the lifeboat with her maid, Ellen Bird. Mrs. Straus handed a blanket to her and then returned to her husband, Isidor, and said: "We have been living together for many years, and where you go, I go."

25 She was urged by a friend to reconsider but she refused. "I will not be separated from my husband. As we have lived, so we will die together."

26 In all, only two dozen women entered the lifeboat. Seaman Thomas Jones, who was onboard the lifeboat, was ordered by Captain Smith to row straight for the ship lights that had been seen by Boxhall earlier.

27 At approximately 1:00 a.m., there were now five lifeboats in the water. However, many people still did not realize the seriousness of the situation. Word was still spreading that everyone was to put on their lifejackets and prepare to abandon ship. Many passengers continued to place hope that the nearby steamer, whose lights still remained visible, would come to their rescue. Other passengers assumed that many ships would be racing to

their assistance and arrive long before a ship such as the size of the *Titanic* could sink. Surely the *Olympic* would be there within an hour or so and wouldn't it be fantastic to see the two sisters side by side on the calm ocean?

28 Most passengers on the well deck waited quietly, watching the lifeboats pulling away from the side of the ship, and the rockets bursting overhead. At one point, an officer came and told the hundreds gathered there to be quiet because a ship was coming. Without saying anything else, the officer left.

29 Although everything appeared calm on the boat deck, deep within the **bowels**[1] of the Titanic, crewmen still labored hard to keep the lights burning and the pumps working, despite risking their own safety. In boiler room No.5, which was directly below the forward Grand Staircase, a **gigantic** wave of green foam suddenly came pouring from between the forward boiler, flooding the room.

30 **Stoker**[2] Fred Barrett was climbing up an escape ladder when he watched in horror as two engineers were **engulfed** by water. Unable to help, he continued climbing.

31 Steward F. Dent Ray had returned to his room to get his overcoat when he discovered

[1]**bowels:** the interior of a ship

[2]**stoker:** person who tends a furnace

that the water had reached E-deck in the forward part of the bow. The **corridor** was flooded almost as far as the main staircase. As the forward compartments filled with water and spilled over into those farther aft, the rate of sinking increased. The *Titanic* was now quickly dying.

32   Boat No.13, under Sixth Officer James Moody's charge, was soon filled to capacity. The boat then began a shaky descent to the sea, tilting down at the bow one moment and the stern the next. Ruth Becker, a young passenger aboard the lifeboat, looked up and saw that the decks above were crowded with faces. "How were all these people to be saved?" she wondered.

33   When the lifeboat finally hit the ocean's surface, the wash from the nearby exhaust water pushed it astern until the ropes still attached to it grew **taut**. Boat No.13 was suddenly directly below boat No.15 which was being lowered! The crew desperately sought **in vain** to release the ropes, but they were so tight that the mechanisms would not work. As No.15 continued to descend, those in boat No.13 called out **frantically** to stop lowering it, but they were either unheard or ignored.

34   Fred Barrett, who was aboard boat No.13, jumped to the aft with a knife while Seaman Robert Hopkins did the same at the bow. Both cut the ropes at the same time and No.13 drifted out from under just before boat No.15 landed.

35   As boat No.14 began to lower, Officer Lowe could see certain men who looked as if they were preparing to jump in. Scared that the sudden increase in weight might **buckle** the boat, he fired his revolver along the side of the ship. No one jumped.

36   It was now well past 1:30 a.m. The view of the *Titanic* from the fourteen lifeboats that had left the ship were presented with a **spectacular** sight. The **leviathan**[3] stood dead still in the wa-

ter, her bow deep into the water and her huge **propellers looming** out of the water. The decks, however, were still brightly lit, and the strains of music drifted across the ocean surface.

37   Aboard the *Titanic,* Thomas Andrews, who had spent much of the time opening staterooms searching for passengers, was shocked at how many women still remained aboard. "Ladies, you must get in at once," he cried as the last boats were being loaded. "There is not a minute to lose. You cannot pick and choose your boat. Don't hesitate. Get in. Get in!"

38   At around 2:00 a.m., all of the *Titanic's* rockets had been fired and all the lifeboats had been lowered save for **collapsible** boats C and D. Collapsibles A and B were still lashed upside down to the roof of the officers' quarters.

39   Collapsible C was soon filled with women and children and, as it was being lowered, two gentlemen stepped on board. One was William Carter, the other Bruce Ismay. With the *Titanic* close to sinking, Ismay had clearly decided to save himself.

40   Second Officer Lightoller was working on lowering collapsible D. When several men tried to rush the boat, he drew a gun from his pocket and ordered them to back off. The crew then formed a ring around the lifeboat and allowed only women to pass through. Once loaded, the collapsible was lowered to the ocean and with it, the last means of escape.

41   Time had run out for the Titanic and there was still over fifteen hundred people aboard her.

Ending Time: _____ : _____

Total Number of Minutes: _____

Total Number of Words: 998

_____ Words/Minute

 **After You Read**

Expressing the Main Idea: Write two or three sentences to express the main ideas of Part Two of "Abandon Ship." Share your sentences with classmates.

---

[3]**leviathan:** something unusually large of its kind

LANGUAGE LEARNING STRATEGY

Synthesize ideas from different sources in order to evaluate subjects and draw conclusions supported by different events and viewpoints. You do vast amounts of reading in college, and, consciously or not, you often synthesize ideas. As you read and gain information from different sources, you put the information together in your mind for a particular purpose. On an anthropology essay examination, you might compare and contrast marriage customs in different cultures. In a psychology report, you might provide evidence from different sources to support a thesis or argument. Synthesizing, or combining, ideas occurs naturally when you read a lot, so it is a skill required in many college assignments. A history instructor may ask you to synthesize information about different wars and draw a conclusion about wars in general on an examination. An English professor may ask you to put together information from a variety of sources and write a research paper.

Apply the Strategy

Think about the experiences described in "Survival at Sea" and *The Story of the Titanic* "A Night to Remember" and "Abandon Ship." What do these different experiences tell you about sea travel and about people's will to survive? With a group of classmates, read each of the conclusions below. Do you agree with the statements? Discuss how all or some of the readings in this chapter support or do not support each conclusion statement. Write one or two additional conclusions that you reached after synthesizing the ideas in the readings. Share your statements with your class.

1. Sea travel causes dangers that most people don't expect.

2. A ship or plane should have the necessary equipment in case of disaster.

3. Crises may bring out the worst behavior in people.

4. Loved ones often draw closer together in life-threatening situations.

5. When the going gets tough, the tough get going.

6. _____ (your group's conclusion)

7. _____ (your group's conclusion)

Write

Write an essay about one of the conclusions that you reached by synthesizing the information you gained from the chapter's readings. Use this outline as a guide for organizing your essay:

I. Introduction
   A. Introduce readings
   B. State conclusion
II. Body
   A. Details
   B. Supporting references
III. Conclusion

> In 1514, Portuguese ships discovered a route to China–22 years after Christopher Columbus had tried to find a route from Spain and failed.

PUTTING IT ALL TOGETHER

Vocabulary Building

Reread the chapter's readings. Select 20 unfamiliar vocabulary words that you want to remember. Write each word on one side of a three-by-five-inch index card. Write the definition on the back of the card. Also, write a sentence in which you use the word.

With a partner, test each other on the 20 words that each of you has chosen. Take turns asking each other the meanings of the words. Ask each other to try to use the word in a sentence. Work together until you are familiar with the words.

leviathan

something unusually large of its kind

Final Project

Conduct an Internet search on one of the following topics or another topic related to the chapter readings. Consult the guide, "Evaluating Web Sites" in Appendix B on page 227. Find one article. Read it and identify the main ideas.

1. effects of extended time in ocean water

2. another sea survival story

3. *Titanic* disaster or another ship disaster

4. *Titanic* recovery or recovery of another sunken ship

If Internet access is unavailable, conduct the same research using print resources from a library. Use your library's databases to search for titles of books or magazine or newspaper articles. Many libraries provide entire magazine or newspaper articles on computer databases. Consult your instructor for information about using your college library. Find one article. Read it and find the main ideas.

Test-Taking Tip

Learn to analyze the main idea of a reading on reading comprehension tests. On these kinds of tests, you will often be presented with a number of statements and asked to choose the statement which best conveys the main idea of a reading. When answering this type of question, it is a good idea to first eliminate any statements which you know to be false. Next, eliminate any statements that relate only to a specific portion of the reading, or to supporting or secondary ideas in the reading. Look for the choice that best expresses the overall idea of the reading.

CHECK YOUR PROGRESS

On a scale of 1 to 5, rate how well you have mastered the goals set at the beginning of the chapter:

1 2 3 4 5   build up your reading rate in order to handle a heavy academic reading load.

1 2 3 4 5   create a study schedule.

1 2 3 4 5   synthesize material from different sources.

If you've given yourself a 3 or lower on any of these goals:

- visit the *Tapestry* web site for additional practice.
- ask your instructor for extra help.
- review the sections of the chapter that you found difficult.
- work with a partner or study group to further your progress.

Look at the photo. Then discuss these questions with your classmates:

- Is the food served here clean or dirty? What makes you think so?
- Do you eat out a lot? Do you think the food is safe in the places where you eat?

IS YOUR FOOD SAFE?

Eating a quick lunch from a fast-food place, or even from your own kitchen, can be dangerous. Thousands of people die each year because of bacteria created by poor food handling or preparation. Food safety is a prominent topic in college nutrition, health, nursing, and biology textbooks and U.S. government materials, which are the sources for this chapter's readings.

Setting Goals

In this chapter you will learn how to:

◈ utilize visual features in readings.

◈ review the meanings of common word parts.

◈ use government online and print resources.

What other goals do you have for this chapter? Write one or two of them here.

_____

_____

Getting Started   The writers in this chapter present three topics about food safety. Look at the titles of the readings and answer the questions that follow.

Readings:

vi khuẩn

"Microbes and Food Safety"

"Can Your Kitchen Pass the Food Safety Test?" by Paula Kurtzweil

"In Street Vendors' Smorgasbord, Threat of Sickness Lurks" and

"Cooking Curbside: A Consumer's Guide" by Donna St. George

1. *Microbes* are tiny life forms. How do you think they affect food safety?

   They affect food safety is get away from microbes, it must be clean.

2. Is your kitchen as clean as it should be? Why or why not?

   Yes, it is. because it make you feel safer & clean. When your kitchen isn't clean it make your food has more bacteria.

3. Have you eaten food from a street vendor's cart? What kind(s) of food?

   Yes, I have. Corn dog

4. What are your health concerns when eating at a fast-food place?

   Fast-food is not a healthy food and they have a lot of oil,

5. Preview the photos and charts in the chapter. What do these tell you about the topics of the readings?

   Food safety

 **Getting Ready to Read**

A. Use the chart that follows to describe your eating habits. For each statement in the chart, check the word that best describes your habits.

My Eating Habits	always	sometimes	usually	never
I eat at fast-food restaurants.		✓		
I eat street vendor food.		✓		
I wash my hands before eating.	✓			
I am careful about keeping food I take from home at safe temperatures.	✓			
The restaurants where I eat look clean.	✓			
My kitchen is clean.	✓			
I buy groceries that are fresh.	✓			
I refrigerate ~~raw~~ uncooked foods after I buy them.	✓			
I clean out my refrigerator regularly.	✓			

Share your chart with one or more classmates. Compare your food safety habits. Are you less or more aware of food safety than your classmate(s)? When is it difficult to pay attention to food safety? Why?

B. Predict whether the following statements are *True* or *False* before reading "Microbes and Food Safety." As you read, check whether your predictions were accurate or inaccurate.

_F_ 1. At least one-half of all Americans suffer from food poisoning every year.

_T_ 2. About 9,000 people die every year from food poisoning.

_F_ 3. People know when they have food poisoning.

_F_ 4. Botulism is a harmless type of food poisoning.

_F_ 5. A person would have to eat at least a pound of food infected by botulism to get sick.

_T_ 6. Most food poisoning is caused by errors made by consumers after they buy food from a grocery store.

_F_ 7. Raw meat rarely contains disease-causing germs.

_F_ 8 You shouldn't buy canned food if the can is damaged.

_T_ 9. It's important that you store and prepare raw foods, such as eggs, carefully.

> **Mad cow disease, a fatal disease affecting a cow's nerves and brain, plagued cattle herds of Great Britain and caused the deaths of 10 humans there in 1996.**

Vocabulary Check

Check the words you know. Work with a partner to find the meanings of new words. Use a dictionary, if necessary. You can add any new words you learn to your Vocabulary Log.

- microbe
- food poisoning
- steadily
- diarrhea
- mistakenly
- intoxication
- microorganisms
- digestive tract
- contaminated
- symptoms
- bout
- malnourished
- fatal
- botulism

- constitute
- rendered
- consumption
- flaws
- tainted
- patrons
- stricken
- revelations
- overhaul
- stools
- detect
- decay
- batch
- incurred

LANGUAGE LEARNING STRATEGY

Utilize visual features in a reading as they identify, repeat, or summarize important information. Textbooks and magazine and newspaper articles employ visual features to draw your attention to important information. Here are some of the visual features you find in textbooks and other readings:

- photos or illustrations

- charts, graphs, or tables

- guiding questions at the beginning and end of chapters

- headings or titles of sections

- key points marked by check marks, "bullets," or numbers

- bold-faced vocabulary words (key terms), often with definitions

- glossaries in margins or before or after readings

- margin notes and important facts

- summaries of key points at the end of sections

Often, these features appear in different colors, in attention-grabbing shapes or positions on the page, or in bold-faced or larger print. The features attract your eyes for a reason. They are saying, "Look at me! I contain important ideas from the reading. Study me!" Indeed, if you pay attention to the visual features in readings, you will find that they often identify, repeat, or summarize important ideas. The features help you remember key points and give you clues about what to study.

Apply the Strategy

Reading 1, "Microbes and Food Safety," is taken from *Nutrition: Concepts and Controversies,* a college nutrition textbook. The reading is printed here along with the visual features that accompany it. Before you read it, preview the features that appear. With a partner, identify the following visual features. Be prepared to explain where and why the writer uses each feature.

1. glossary

2. margin facts

3. charts

4. tables

5. bold-faced vocabulary words

6. headings

7. summary of reading

8. photos

Read

Reading 1: Microbes **and Food Safety**

1 Episodes of **food poisoning** cause illness in at least one-third of the U.S. population each year, and their number is **steadily** increasing. Between 21 million and 81 million cases of **diarrhea** that are treated in the United States each year are from **food-borne**[1] illnesses. Some 9,000 people a year die of food poisoning. Nearly everyone else experiences illness from food poisoning every year, but may **mistakenly** pass it off as "flu."

The Threat from Microbial Contamination
....

2 Food-borne illness can be caused either by infection or by **intoxication. Microorganisms** such as *Salmonella* varieties that occur in foods commonly infect the human body themselves. Other microorganisms in foods produce **enterotoxins**[2] or **neurotoxins**[3] in foods or in the human **digestive tract.** Bacteria may multiply or act in food during improper preparation or storage, or within the digestive tract after a person eats **contaminated** food. If you experience digestive tract disturbances as the major or only **symp-**

[1]**food-borne:** carried by food

[2]**enterotoxins:** poisons that act upon mucous membranes, such as those of the digestive tract

[3]**neurotoxins:** poisons that act upon the cells of the nervous system

botulism an often-fatal food poisoning caused by botulinum toxin, a toxin produced by the *Clostridium botulinum* bacterium that grows without oxygen in nonacidic canned foods.

Warning Signs of Botulism:

✔ Double vision
✔ Weak muscles
✔ Difficulty swallowing
✔ Difficulty breathing

toms of your next **bout** of "flu," chances are excellent that what you really have is food poisoning. For people who are otherwise ill or **malnourished** or for the very old or young, even these relatively mild disturbances can be **fatal.**

3   The symptoms of one neurotoxin stand out as severe and commonly fatal—those of **botulism,** caused by the toxin of the Clostridium botulinum bacterium that grows inside improperly canned (and especially home-canned) foods, improperly prepared vacuum-packed foods, or in oils flavored with herbs, garlic, vegetables or other edible agents and stored at room temperature. The microbe grows only in the absence of oxygen, in low-acid conditions, and at temperatures that support growth of most bacteria −40° to 120° Fahrenheit.

4   Botulism danger signs **constitute** a true medical emergency. Even with medical assistance, survivors can suffer symptoms for months, years, or a lifetime. So potent is the botulinum toxin that an amount as tiny as a single grain of salt can kill several people within an hour. The botulinum toxin is destroyed by heat, so canned foods that contain the toxin can be **rendered** harmless by boiling them for ten minutes. Home-canned food can be prepared safely only if proper canning techniques are followed **to the letter.**[4]

✔ **KEY POINT**   **Each year in the United States, many millions of people suffer from mild to life-threatening symptoms caused by food poisoning.**

Safety in the Marketplace

5 Overwhelmingly, most food poisoning results from errors consumers make in handling foods after purchase. While commercially prepared food is usually safe, rare accidents do occur, however, and they can affect many people at once. This makes news reporters take notice. Milk producers, for example, rely on **pasteurization,**[5] a process of heating milk to kill many disease-causing organisms and make milk safe for **consumption.** When, on occasion, a major dairy develops **flaws** in its pasteurization system, tens of thousands of cases of food-borne illness may result.

6   In 1994, a fast-food restaurant chain in the Northwest served undercooked hamburgers **tainted** with a particularly dangerous

[4]**to the letter:** following rules precisely

[5]**pasteurization:** the treatment of milk with heat sufficient to kill certain pathogens (disease-causing microbes) commonly transmitted through milk; not a sterilization process. Pasteurized milk retains bacteria that cause milk spoilage. Raw milk, even if labeled "certified," transmits many food-borne diseases to people each year and should be avoided.

For other forms of food poisoning, get medical help when these symptoms occur:

✔ bloody **stools**
✔ headache accompanied by muscle stiffness and fever
✔ rapid heart rate, fainting, dizziness
✔ fever of longer than 24 hours' duration
✔ diarrhea of more than 3 days' duration
✔ numbness, muscle weakness, tingling sensations in the skin

strain of E. coli bacteria. As a result, three lives were lost and hundreds of other **patrons** were **stricken** with serious illness. This incident focused the national spotlight on two important food safety issues: that live, disease-causing organisms of many types are routinely found in raw meats, and that thorough cooking is necessary to make animal-derived foods safe. These **revelations** have led to a much-needed **overhaul** of the country's mechanisms for ensuring food safety.

7   One outcome of the concern about food-borne illness is a law requiring that producers of meat, poultry, and seafood employ an effective prevention method, the **Hazard Analysis Critical Control Point (HACCP)**[6] plan. The method requires identification of "critical control points" in food production where the risk of food contamination is high. A plan must then be developed and implemented to prevent loss of control at those critical points. For many years, meat and seafood inspectors relied on their senses of sight, smell, and touch to detect bad meat and seafood. Unfortunately, human senses cannot **detect** dangerous organisms until after the food has begun to **decay.** Newer, more accurate tests for microbial contamination must be used to verify that each HACCP plan for a food-producing company is effective. The Food and Drug Administration estimates that these safety regulations should prevent up to 60,000 to 80,000 cases of food-borne illness each year from seafood poisoning alone.

8   Luckily, large-scale commercial incidents, while dramatic, make up only a fraction of the nation's total food-poisoning cases each year. Most cases arise from one person's error in a small setting and affect just a few victims. Some people have come to accept a yearly bout or two or intestinal illness as inevitable, but in truth, these illnesses can and should be prevented. To prevent them, consumers need to learn how to select, prepare, and store food safely.

9   Canned and packaged foods sold in grocery stores are easily controlled, but rare accidents do happen. **Batch** numbering makes it possible to recall contaminated foods through public announcements via newspapers, television, and radio, and the FDA monitors large suppliers. You can help protect yourself, too. Carefully inspect the seals and wrappers of packages. Reject leaking or bulging cans. Many jars have safety "buttons," areas of the lid designed to pop up once opened; make sure that they are firmly sealed. If a package on the shelf looks ragged, soiled, or

[6]**Hazard Analysis Critical Control Point (HACCP):** a systematic plan to identify and correct potential microbial hazards in the manufacturing, distribution, and commercial use of food products.

punctured, do not buy the product; turn it in to the store manager. A badly dented can or a mangled package is useless in protecting food from microorganisms, insects, spoilage, or even vandals. Frozen foods should be solidly frozen.

10   Raw foods from the grocery store, especially meats, poultry, eggs, and seafood, contain microbes, as all things do. Whether or not the microbes from those sources will multiply and cause illness can be largely a matter of what you do in your own kitchen.

✔ KEY POINT   **Industry employs sound practices to safeguard the commercial food supply from microbial threats. Still, incidents of commercial food poisoning have** incurred **widespread harm to health.**

◀ **After You Read**

A. Expressing the Main Idea: Write one sentence that expresses the main idea of Reading 1. Compare your sentence with those of classmates.

B. Confirming Predictions: Did you accurately predict if the statements about Reading 1 were True or False? Read the statements from the prediction activity on page 67 and 68 again, and correct any errors you made in your predictions.

C. Utilizing Visual Features: With a group of classmates, look over the visual features in Reading 1. Answer these questions:

1. Are the visual features helpful? Why or why not?

2. Which of the features contain information that you might need to study for an exam? Make a list of key words that will help you remember this information.

3. Are any of the visual features distracting? In other words, do any of them get in the way of your reading? Explain.

D. Reactions: Discuss the following questions with classmates:

1. Was any of the information from the reading surprising to you? Why or why not?

2. What did you learn from Reading 1?

3. How do you feel about food safety after reading the textbook article?

4. Will you change your eating habits in any way? Why or why not?

In 1997, a U.S. Food and Drug Administration flyer warned that consumers should no longer drink fresh, unpasteurized apple cider because it could contain dangerous bacteria.

Reading Journal

Reread paragraph one of Reading 1. What are your reactions to the information in this paragraph? Did you know that food poisoning was such a serious problem? Did you or someone you know ever have food poisoning? If so, describe what happened.

LANGUAGE LEARNING STRATEGY

Review the meanings of common word parts such as prefixes, suffixes, and roots in order to increase your vocabulary. If you know the meanings of common word parts, you can understand the meanings of thousands of words in English. Recognizing word parts also helps you to identify a word as a noun, verb, adjective, or adverb. By doing this, you can use the appropriate word in writing and speaking.

Apply the Strategy

A. Study the list of common prefixes and their meanings in the following chart.

COMMON PREFIXES		
Common Words	Common Prefix	Meaning
improper	im	not
preparation	pre	before
detect	de	away, down, from
inspectors	in	into
commercial	com, con	together
overwhelmingly	over	above
mistakenly	mis	wrong
transmitted	trans	across, beyond, through
unfortunately	un	not

B. With a partner, use the list of common prefixes to help you guess the meanings of the following words. Next to each word, write your guess. Then, use a dictionary to confirm your answers, if necessary.

COMMON WORDS

Words	Guessed Meaning	Dictionary Meaning
improbable	not	
precondition	before	
degenerate		
incapable		
contaminated		
overshadow		
misinterpretation		
transplant		
unstable		

C. With a classmate, discuss the meanings of the following words from Reading 1. Use your knowledge of the meanings of prefixes to help you define the words.

improperly   decay   contamination

prevent   infect   overhaul

◆Getting Ready to Read   In the chart below, list steps a person can take to store and prepare food safely in a kitchen. Share your list with a classmate.

To store food safely, you should...	To prepare food safely, you should...
in the refrigerator	
in the clean place	

Vocabulary Check

Check the words you already know. Work with a partner to find the meanings of new words. Add any new words you learn to your Vocabulary Log.

_____ gleaming _____ particles

_____ spotless _____ bacterial

_____ sanitized _____ violating

_____ chlorine

Read

Reading 2: Can Your Kitchen Pass the Food Safety Test?

by Paula Kurtzweil

What comes to mind when you think of a clean kitchen? Shiny waxed floors? **Gleaming** stainless steel sinks? **Spotless** counters and neatly arranged cupboards?

They can help, but a truly "clean" kitchen—that is, one that ensures safe food—relies on more than just looks: It also depends on safe food practices.

In the home, food safety concerns revolve around three main functions: food storage, food handling, and cooking. To see how well you're doing in each, take this quiz, and then read on to learn how you can make the meals and snacks from your kitchen the safest possible.

Quiz
......

Choose the answer that best describes the practice in your household, whether or not you are the primary food handler.

1. **The temperature of the refrigerator in my home is:**
   a. 50 degrees Fahrenheit (10 degrees Celsius)
   b. 41° F (5° C)
   c. I don't know; I've never measured it.

2. **The last time we had leftover cooked stew or other food with meat, chicken, or fish, the food was:**
   a. cooled to room temperature, then put in the refrigerator
   b. put in the refrigerator immediately after the food was served
   c. left at room temperature overnight or longer

3. **The last time the kitchen sink drain, disposal, and connecting pipe in my home were** sanitized **was:**
   a. last night
   b. several weeks ago
   c. I can't remember.

4. **If a cutting board is used in my home to cut raw meat, poultry, or fish and it is going to be used to chop another food, the board is:**
   a. reused as is
   b. wiped with a damp cloth
   c. washed with soap and hot water and sanitized with a mild **chlorine** bleach solution

5. **The last time we had hamburgers in my home, I ate mine:**
   a. rare   b. medium   c. well-done

6. **The last time there was cookie dough in my home, the dough was:**
   a. made with raw eggs, and I sampled some of it
   b. store-bought, and I sampled some of it
   c. not sampled until baked

7. **I clean my kitchen counters and other surfaces that come in contact with food with:**
   a. water
   b. hot water and soap
   c. hot water and soap, then bleach solution
   d. hot water and soap, then commercial sanitizing agent

8. **When dishes are washed in my home, they are:**
   a. cleaned by an automatic dishwasher and then air-dried
   b. left to soak in the sink for several hours and then washed with soap in the same water
   c. washed right away with hot water and soap in the sink and then air-dried
   d. washed right away with hot water and soap in the sink and immediately towel-dried

9. **The last time I handled raw meat, poultry, or fish, I cleaned my hands afterwards by:**
   a. wiping them on a towel
   b. rinsing them under hot, cold, or warm tap water
   c. washing with soap and warm water

10. **Meat, poultry, and fish products are defrosted in my home by:**
    a. setting them on the counter
    b. placing them in the refrigerator
    c. microwaving

Answers
··········

1. Refrigerators should stay at 41° F (5° C) or less, so if you chose answer B, give yourself two points. If you didn't, you're not alone. According to Joseph Madden, Ph.D., strategic manager for microbiology in the Food and Drug Administration's Center for Food Safety and Applied Nutrition, many people overlook the importance of maintaining an appropriate refrigerator temperature. "According to surveys, in many households, the refrigerator temperature is above 50 degrees (10° C)," he said. His advice: Measure the temperature with a thermometer, and, if needed, adjust the refrigerator's temperature control dial. A temperature of 41° F (5° C) or less is important because it slows the growth of most bacteria. The temperature won't kill the bacteria, but it will keep them from multiplying, and the fewer there are, the less likely you are to get sick from them. Freezing at zero F (minus 18° C) or less stops bacterial growth (although it won't kill all bacteria already present).

2. Answer B is the best practice; give yourself two points if you picked it. Hot foods should be refrigerated as soon as possible within two hours after cooking. But don't keep the food if it's been standing out for more than two hours. Don't taste test it, either. Even a small amount of contaminated food can cause illness. Date leftovers so they can be used within a safe time. Generally, they remain safe when refrigerated for three to five days. If in doubt, throw it out, says former FDA microbiologist Jeffery Rhodehamel, now with W.R. Grace and Co.: "It's not worth a food-borne illness for the small amount of food usually involved."

3. If answer A best describes your household's practice, give yourself two points. Give yourself one point if you chose B. According to FDA's Madden, the kitchen sink drain, disposal, and connecting pipe are often overlooked, but they should be sanitized periodically by pouring down the sink a solution of 1 teaspoon (5 milliliters) of chlorine bleach in 1 quart (about 1 liter) of water or a solution of commercial kitchen cleaning agent made according to product directions. Food **particles** get trapped in the drain and disposal and, along with the moistness, create an ideal environment for **bacterial** growth.

4. If answer C best describes your household's practice, give yourself two points. Washing with soap and hot water and then sanitizing

with a mild bleach solution is the safest practice, said Dhirendra Shah, Ph.D., director of the division of microbiological studies in FDA's Center for Food Safety and Applied Nutrition. If you picked A, you're **violating** an important food safety rule: Never allow raw meat, poultry, and fish to come in contact with other foods. Answer B isn't good, either. Improper washing, such as with a damp cloth, will not remove bacteria.

5. Give yourself two points if you picked answer C. The safest way to eat hamburgers is to cook them until they are no longer red in the middle and the juices run clear. That doesn't happen with rare-cooked meats, and it may not happen with medium-cooked ones. Cooking food, including ground meat patties, to an internal temperature of at least 160° F (71° C) usually protects against food-borne illness. Well-done meats reach that temperature. To be on the safe side, check cooked meat, fish, and poultry with a meat thermometer to ensure that they have reached a safe internal temperature. For microwaved food, follow directions, including the standing time, either in or out of the microwave, after cooking. Microwave cooking creates pockets of heat in the food, but allowing the food to stand before eating allows the heat to spread to the rest of the food.

6. If you answered A, you may be putting yourself at risk for infection with *Salmonella enteritidis,* a bacterium that can be in shell eggs. Cooking the egg or egg-containing food product to at least 140° F (60° C) kills the bacteria. So answer C—eating the baked product—will earn you two points. You'll get two points for answer B, also. Foods containing raw eggs, such as homemade ice cream, cake batter, mayonnaise, and eggnog, carry a salmonella risk, but their commercial counterparts don't. Commercial products are made with pasteurized eggs; that is, eggs that have been heated sufficiently to kill bacteria, and also may contain an acidifying agent that kills the bacteria. Commercial preparations of cookie dough are not a food hazard. If you want to sample home-made dough or batter or eat other foods with raw-egg-containing products, consider substituting pasteurized eggs for raw eggs. Pasteurized eggs are usually sold in the grocer's refrigerated dairy case.

7. Answers C or D will earn you two points each; answer B, one point. According to FDA's Madden, bleach and commercial kitchen cleaning agents are the best sanitizers—provided they're diluted

according to product directions. They're the most effective at getting rid of bacteria. Hot water and soap does a good job, too, but may not kill all strains of bacteria. Water may get rid of visible dirt, but not bacteria. Also, be sure to keep dishcloths and sponges clean because, when wet, these materials harbor bacteria and may promote their growth.

8. Answers A and C are worth two points each. There are potential problems with B and D. When you let dishes sit in water for a long time, it "creates a soup," FDA's Madden said. "The food left on the dish contributes nutrients for bacteria, so the bacteria will multiply." When washing dishes by hand, he said, it's best to wash them all within two hours. Also, it's best to air-dry them so you don't handle them while they're wet.

9. The only correct practice is answer C. Give yourself two points if you picked it. Wash hands with warm water and soap for at least 20 seconds before and after handling food, especially raw meat, poultry, and fish. If you have an infection or cut on your hands, wear rubber or plastic gloves. Wash gloved hands just as often as bare hands because the gloves can pick up bacteria. (However, when washing gloved hands, you don't need to take off your gloves and wash your bare hands, too.)

10. Give yourself two points if you picked B or C. Food safety experts recommend thawing foods in the refrigerator or the microwave oven or putting the package in a water-tight plastic bag submerged in cold water and changing the water every 30 minutes. Changing the water ensures that the food is kept cold, an important factor for slowing bacterial growth that may occur on the outer thawed portions while the inner areas are still thawing. When microwaving, follow package directions. Leave about 2 inches (about 5 centimeters) between the food and the inside surface of the microwave to allow heat to circulate. Smaller items will defrost more evenly than larger pieces of food. Foods defrosted in the microwave oven should be cooked immediately after thawing. Do not thaw meat, poultry, and fish products on the counter or in the sink without cold water; bacteria can multiply rapidly at room temperature.

Rating Your Home's Food Practices

| 20 points: | Feel confident about the safety of foods served in your home. |

Two favorite places for microbes to grow in a kitchen: sponges and wooden cutting boards.

12 to 19 points: Reexamine food safety practices in your home. Some key rules are being violated.

11 points or below: Take steps immediately to correct food handling, storage, and cooking techniques used in your home. Current practices are putting you and other members of your household in danger of food-borne illness.

After You Read

A. Discuss these questions with classmates:

1. What did you learn from the article?

2. What surprised you about the article? Why?

3. What parts of the reading did you not understand? Why?

B. Reviewing Common Word Parts: Study the chart of common suffixes, their meanings, and the parts of speech that they indicate. Test your knowledge of suffixes by completing the sentences in part C.

COMMON SUFFIXES			
Word from Reading 2	Suffix	Meaning	Part of Speech
sanitize	ize	to make	verb
sanitizing	ize + ing	to make + continuous tense verb, gerund, or participle adjective	verb
sanitized	ize + ed	to make + past tense verb or participle adjective	verb
sanitizer	ize + er	to make + person or thing that performs a task	noun
bacteria	a	condition, state	noun
bacterial	al	of, relating to	adjective
microbiology	ology	the study of	noun
microbiologist	ist	person who does/studies	noun

C. Use the words listed to complete the following sentences.

sanitize   sanitizer   sanitizing

1. The best way to _____sanitize_____ your kitchen counter is to wash it with warm soapy water and bleach.

2. Commercial food companies are careful about _____sanitizing_____ food, but sometimes accidents occur.

3. Chlorine bleach is a good _____sanitizer_____.

bacteria   bacterial

4. _____Bacterial_____ growth occurs when food is stored at temperatures of 40 to 80 degrees Fahrenheit.

5. The E. coli _____bacteria_____ found in raw meat resulted in many illnesses.

microbiology   microbiological   microbiologist

nhà vi khuẩn học

6. A _____microbiology_____ examines tiny organisms.

7. In the field of _____microbiology_____ scientists study the origin and growth of bacteria.

8. The _____microbiological_____ division of the FDA studies the presence of microorganisms in food.

TUNING IN: "Anatomy of a Breakout"

A. Discuss these questions with classmates before you view "Anatomy of a Breakout," a CNN video clip.

1. What does the title of the video clip suggest about the video content?

2. List what you think are some causes and effects of food poisoning.

B. After you view, discuss these questions with classmates.

1. Check off the effects of food poisoning that are mentioned in this video clip:

bad for body   *nôn mửa*

- [ ] death
- [ ] dehydration
- [x] vomitting

- [x] fever, high temperature
- [x] cramps   *đau bụng*
- [ ] fatigue

- [x] diarrhea   *đi ỉa*
- [x] nausea   *not good feeling*

© CNN

hydrate : water

2. What was the cause of the food poisoning described in the video? *The bad food*

3. What effect do you think the incident had on this small town? *it happen* *scary*

4. What effect did the information and pictures in the video have on you?

◇ Getting Ready to Read

Think about these questions before reading "In Street Vendors' Smorgasbord, Threat of Sickness Lurks" and the accompanying illustration, "Cooking Curbside: A Consumer's Guide." Share your thoughts with classmates.

1. What food items do street vendors sell?

2. In what kind of areas are street vendors' trucks or carts located?

3. Do you think these vendors' food poses a "threat of sickness"? Why or why not?

4. Do you eat food from street vendors? What type? Have you ever gotten sick from these foods?

Vocabulary Check

Check the words that you already know. Work with a partner to find the meanings of new words. You can add any new words you learn to your Vocabulary Log.

all kinds of food ___ smorgasbord   *serious* ___ chronic   *adj a chemical that stop the effect* ___ buffeted *by an acid*

food & drink ___ fare   *explain* ___ elaborate   *harmless* ___ benign *vô hại*

dangerous ___ hazardous   *equip* *trang bị* ___ geared   *thorough: hoàn toàn* ___ conscientious

ngẫu nhiên ___ random   ___ implicated   ___ perishables *(n)*

careless ___ lax   *find st.*   *thing is go bad.*

◇ Read

Reading 3: In Street Vendors' Smorgasbord, Threat of Sickness Lurks

by Donna St. George

1   They are a colorful part of New York's cityscape—street corner food vendors, with their tilting umbrellas and curbside cookeries. These days, they deliver a sidewalk smorgasbord as varied as the city itself—the traditional hot dogs and pretzels, along with hamburgers, chicken, pork, lamb, duck, even fish and tripe.

Lurk : to wait in hiding.

2   But with their diverse **fare,** many vendors are serving up a heightened risk of sickness, according to safety experts, city health records, and tests of sidewalk food.

3   The familiar stainless-steel carts are small and lack basic kitchen equipment, yet roughly 40 percent of New York's vendors handle foods that can be **hazardous,** according to city figures. Many show up in the morning with tubs of raw meat and poultry, which can carry disease-carrying bacteria. Food is often left un-chilled and unheated, ideal for the growth of E. coli, salmonella, and other germs. And some vendors wash their hands so seldom that they use their sinks for storage space.

4   Tests arranged by *The New York Times* on a **random** sampling of chicken, burgers, and kebabs from vendors' carts showed sig-nificant undercooking in 39 of 51 cases—meaning that bacteria would not be eliminated. Experts say it is a potentially dangerous combination: risky fare, poor facilities, and unsafe handling.

5   And even though New York has more food carts than any-where else in America, many of its regulations are far more **lax** than in other big cities. Most other cities, for example, have strict limits on what vendors can sell; New York allows anything but shellfish.

6   Inspections of the 4,100 licensed pushcarts in New York are spotty. Vendors without permits, safety training, or water—all required by city rules—are allowed to stay on the street.

7   Even **chronic** health violators continue to sell food, according to *The Times*'s review of 2,700 city inspection reports from 1996 and 1997. Moreover, weeks and months have often passed before inspectors have investigated pushcarts blamed for illness, those reports show.

8   And while the city requires vendors with more **elaborate** menus to take a food-safety course, it is broadly **geared** for all food-service workers, and vendors get no specific advice about how to manage the peculiar hazards of cooking and serving food in the street.

9   City health officials defend their efforts to police the trade, and they and vendors themselves insist that the food is generally safe. "We hold the carts to very high standards, and our inspec-tions are tough to pass," said Maryann Lienhard, an assistant health commissioner in charge of inspections.

10   There are no precise statistics on how many pushcart cus-tomers suffer food poisoning—which most often results in a day or two of vomiting or diarrhea—and the city says no cases of se-vere illness have been linked to sidewalk vendors. But doctors and other experts say the risks are clear.

11   Dr. Michael P. Lucchesi, chief of the city's busiest emergency room, at Kings County Hospital Center, said tainted food was

implicated in many of 2,715 cases of **gastroenteritis**[1] there in 1997. In some of those cases, food from street carts was suspected, though doctors almost never do the tests to confirm the origin of such an illness.

12   A 1995 City Council survey of 401 New York pedestrians found that 1 out of 10 said they had become ill after eating from a cart.

13   "When you look at the conditions on these carts and you have patients coming in, complaining about them," Dr. Lucchesi said, "it strongly suggests there is a problem."

14   Of 610 food-cart operators whose inspection records were reviewed, half had at least one critical violation in 1996 and 1997. Some lacked permits or could not show they had undergone required safety training; some had no provisions for hand washing or touched ready-to-eat food with bare hands; some left foods out at temperatures ideal for the growth of hazardous bacteria.

15   Safety questions about street vendors come as consumers across the country are **buffeted** by warnings about a widening array of hazards in food—including such seemingly **benign** sources as fresh apple juice, imported raspberries, and lettuce.

16   Experts note that the potential risks of sidewalk fare are far fewer among those vendors who sell bagels, packaged goods, produce, and precooked hot dogs—in all, about 60 percent. And no doubt many of New York's street vendors are **conscientious.**

17   Andrew Ramrattan, who cooks chicken, vegetables, whiting, and falafel for as many as 500 people a day at the northeast corner of 43rd Street and Avenue of the Americas, said that if some vendors created problems, they did not represent the whole industry.

18   Eating a steaming plate of his own curried chicken, Mr. Ramrattan, 21, poked his fork at the tiny bits of food. "We chop it up like this," he said "so all the chicken cooks real good." The only complaints he ever gets, he said, are about long lines at his cart.

19   But Ryan Halpner, 22, had a different view of the food-cart industry one day when he decided to pick up a lamb shish kebab for lunch from another cart, near Rockefeller Center. Later, his stomach churned, his face flushed, and he rushed to the restroom, deeply regretting his choice.

20   "Either it wasn't cooked fully or something was wrong with it," he said. "My guess is the meat wasn't fresh. It was right when I ate it, but it wasn't right afterward."

angry

[1]**gastroenteritis:** inflammation of the stomach and intestine

by street

Cooking Curbside: A Consumer's Guide

Some things to keep in mind when buying food from a street vendor.

Handling
Ready-to-eat food should not be touched by hand. (Note that gloves are not a **cure-all**; if worn, they should be clean and changed as often as hands would be washed.)

Selection
Precooked hot dogs and prepared food like pretzels carry less risk than foods that are cooked on the cart.

Sinks
Vendor should wash hands between handling raw and cooked food.
Sink should be in use, with running water and soap.

Hygiene
Check for cleanliness of vendor's clothes, hands and cart as an indicator of hygiene.

Temperature
No meat or **perishables** should be sitting out unheated or unchilled (between 45 and 140 degrees).
Food should be piping hot when served.

Unheated storage

Steam table *for heated storage*

Cold storage

License
Vendor should display a **permit decal**, and vendors who cook on the cart should have a certificate from the city's food-safety course. (Location of decal may vary depending on the cart model.)

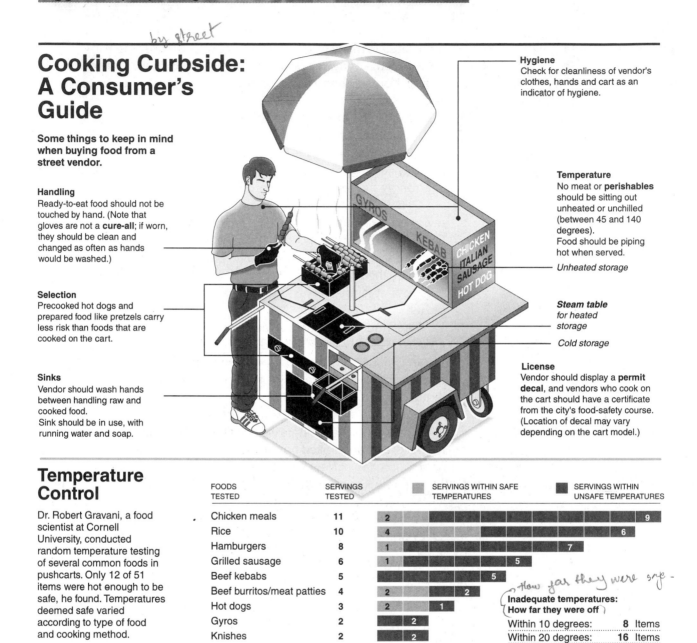

GYROS KEBAB CHICKEN ITALIAN SAUSAGE HOT DOG

Temperature Control

Dr. Robert Gravani, a food scientist at Cornell University, conducted random temperature testing of several common foods in pushcarts. Only 12 of 51 items were hot enough to be safe, he found. Temperatures deemed safe varied according to type of food and cooking method.

Sources: Dr. Robert Gravani, Push-Cart International Inc.

FOODS TESTED	SERVINGS TESTED	SERVINGS WITHIN SAFE TEMPERATURES	SERVINGS WITHIN UNSAFE TEMPERATURES
Chicken meals	11	2	9
Rice	10	4	6
Hamburgers	8	1	7
Grilled sausage	6	1	5
Beef kebabs	5		5
Beef burritos/meat patties	4	2	2
Hot dogs	3	2	1
Gyros	2		2
Knishes	2		2

How far they were safe —

Inadequate temperatures: How far they were off

Within 10 degrees:	**8** Items
Within 20 degrees:	**16** Items
More than 20 degrees:	**15** Items

N.Y. Times News Service

cure-all: solution

steam table: table in which containers of food are kept warm by heated water

permit decal: sticker showing the required government permit for a business operation

 **After You Read**

A. Expressing the Main Idea: Write one or two sentences that express the main ideas of Reading 3. Compare your sentence(s) with classmates. *They was talking about food in the street is something is not safety.*

B. Reactions: Discuss these questions with classmates:

1. What is your reaction to the information in the reading? *Be careful when you eat food in the street.*

2. Will it change your eating habits? If so, how? *Yes, I it. Less eat food in the street and very careful.*

3. What should be done about poor food safety practices on food trucks or carts? *I think they should pay more attention when they cook & more safety to use secable*

C. Utilizing Visual Features: Discuss these questions with classmates.

well-know & respected.

1. What is the most prominent item in the illustration? *photography*

2. Are the illustration and text easy to read? Why or why not?

3. Look at the "Temperature Control" section under the illustration. What information did the Cornell University scientist want to find? What did he discover?

4. Is the temperature graph easy to read? Explain.

ACADEMIC POWER STRATEGY

Use government online and print resources as an easy, free source of information for college research and personal use. The Canadian, U.S., United Kingdom, and other governments publish English-language information on almost every topic that you can imagine—food and nutrition, cars, children, education, employment, health, housing, money, small business, travel and hobbies, and government services. The publications can provide up-to-date information for a college research report or your personal use. You can access this material in several ways: in a library, by phone, by mail, through government bookstores, or on the Internet. Major Canadian, UK, and U.S. cities have government bookstores where brochures, booklets, articles, and books are offered free or sold at low prices. Look for the "government listings" section in the telephone directory. Government publications are also shelved in the reference section of most libraries. However, the fastest and easiest way to get government publications is to visit government web sites to order publications online, save them onto disk, or print them out. Here are a few names of government departments and their Web site addresses:

Agriculture and Agri-Food Canada   http://aceis.agr.ca/

Canada Department of Finance   www.finb.gc.ca/

Government of Canada—Overview   http://canada.gc.ca/howgoc/

United Kingdom House of Parliament
    www.parliament.uk/hophome.htm

United Kingdom Department of Trade and Industry
    http://dtinfo1.dti.gov.uk/

United Kingdom Foreign & Commonwealth Office   www.fco.gov.uk

U.S. Food and Drug Administration (FDA)   www.fda.gov

U.S. Department of Agriculture (USDA)   www.usda.gov

The U.S. White House   www.whitehouse.gov

Apply the Strategy

On your own or with a group of classmates, think of an unanswered question that you have about food safety, or choose a subject that

1 look at the context words
chunks : a group.

was mentioned in any of the readings in this chapter which you would like to know more about. Narrow your research to one topic within the broad area of food safety.

Use a government resource to find one reading about this subject. Search the appropriate government Web site, or go to your campus or local public library to find a government article that tells more about the subject. Your instructor and library staff will help you to utilize printed materials in a library.

Here are some subjects that you might like to research:

1. botulism
2. pasteurization
3. government laws on food preparation
4. E. coli bacteria
5. raw meat
6. microwave
7. food safety in industry or one company

Bring your article to class and discuss it with classmates. Be prepared to answer the following questions:

1. Briefly, what did you learn from the reading?
2. What surprised you about the reading?
3. How did you find the reading?
4. Which web sites were the most useful? Why?
5. Which web sites were the least useful? Why?
6. Which web site would you go to again? Why?

PUTTING IT ALL TOGETHER
• •

Vocabulary Building

Work with a group of classmates to complete the following sentences with words taken from the chapter's vocabulary check activities. Do not look back at the vocabulary lists. Do not use a dictionary or your Vocabulary Log.

First, answer the one that you are certain you know. Then let another group try to correctly complete another sentence. Try to be the first group to correctly complete at least three sentences in a vertical, horizontal, or diagonal line, like tic-tac-toe.

microorganism		
1. A __✓__ is a tiny life form. (two possible answers)	2. Frozen food should be _____ in a microwave or a refrigerator.	3. A sickess caused from eating contaminated food is called _____ .
4. You can _spotless_ your kitchen sink by washing it with warm soapy water and bleach.	5. Another word for *customers* of a restaurant is _____ .	6. Food sellers who repeatedly violate health regulations can be called _____ violators.
7. Eating food from street vendors' carts may be _____ to your health.	8. Some people have a yearly _____ of intestinal illness.	9. A buffet meal featuring a variety of dishes is called a _____ .

Final Project

Write a research report or essay about three major problem areas in food safety. Use information from the chapter readings, your government resource research, and your personal experience. Organize your composition with an introduction (to introduce the subject of food safety and your main idea: the three problem areas), a body (which supports the main idea with information from readings and experience), and a conclusion which summarizes your main idea.

When you write sentences about information you have taken from readings, be sure to include the title and author (if known) of the article. Here are some ways to do this:

EXAMPLES: The reading "Cooking Curbside: A Consumer's Guide" reports some of the problems of food handling. The reading says that a street vendor should wear clean gloves.

In "Can Your Kitchen Pass the Food Safety Test?" author Paula Kurtzweil says that food preparation is important.

Reading Journal

Answer these questions in your reading journal: What is the most important information that you have learned about food safety? Will this information cause you to change any of your habits? Explain.

Test-Taking Tip

Make a study schedule for your test. Make a list of the tasks you must complete to prepare for the test. Try to determine what topics will be most important on the test, then set priorities among your study tasks and plan to do the most important tasks first.

CHECK YOUR PROGRESS

On a scale of 1 to 5, rate how well you have mastered the goals set at the beginning of the chapter:

1 2 3 4 5   utilize visual features in readings.

1 2 3 4 5   review the meanings of common word parts.

1 2 3 4 5   use government online and print resources.

If you've given yourself a 3 or lower on any of these goals:

- visit the *Tapestry* web site for additional practice.

- ask your instructor for extra help.

- review the sections of the chapter that you found difficult.

- work with a partner or study group to further your progress.

Look at the photo. Then discuss these questions with your classmates:

- Is this an appropriate place for a woman? Why or why not?
- What should a woman's role be in a family? Explain.
- Have women's roles changed in your native culture? Explain.
- Have men's roles changed? Explain.

5

THE GENDER-ROLE REVOLUTION

The topics of women's and men's roles in society, family, and work appear across the college curriculum. History courses present changes in women's roles over time. Anthropology and sociology courses compare the status of men and women across cultures. Business classes explore the changing position of both genders in the workplace. In this chapter, you will read about and discuss key gender-role issues.

Setting Goals

In this chapter, you will learn how to:

◈ identify causes and effects in readings.

◈ create graphic organizers.

◈ recognize and use bibliographic citations.

What other goals do you have for this chapter? Write one or two of them here.

_____

_____

 **Getting Started**

The writers in this chapter explore four aspects of women's and men's roles in society. Look at the titles of the readings and answer the questions that follow.

Readings:

"Traditional Sex-Role Expectations"

"The Sex-Role Revolution"

"Median Weekly Earnings of Full-Time Workers"

"The New Majority"

1. What does the term *sex role* mean? What are the traditional *sex roles* of men and women in a family?

    _____

    _____

    _____

2. What might a *sex-role revolution* mean? Do you think a *sex-role revolution* has occurred? Why?

    _____

    _____

    _____

3. Do you think men and women earn the same salaries for the same jobs? Why or why not?

    _____

    _____

    _____

4. Are women the majority or the minority in the workplace in the U.S.? In college?

    _____

    _____

    _____

5. Preview the photos and charts in the chapter. What do these tell you about the topics of the readings?

    _____

    _____

    _____

 **Getting Ready to Read**

A. Read paragraph 1 of Reading 1. Discuss these questions with classmates.

1. What are the traditional gender roles in families in your native culture? Do you think these differ from the gender roles in U.S. families?

2. Does stereotyping of women occur in your native culture? Does it occur in the United States? Explain.

3. Does stereotyping of men occur in your native culture? Does it occur in the United States? Explain.

B. Predicting Ideas: In Reading 1, the writer also explains that men and women in the United States are traditionally expected to show certain personality traits. For example, a woman is expected to be *affectionate* and a man is expected to be *strong*. In the chart, write other adjectives that describe qualities that societies expect males and females to have:

TRADITIONAL GENDER-ROLE EXPECTATIONS	
Men Should Be . . .	Women Should Be . . .
strong	affectionate

Vocabulary Check

Which of these words do you already know? Check them. Work with a partner to find the meanings of new words. Use a dictionary, if necessary. Write an original sentence using each new word. Try to make the sentences relate to the topic of women and men. Add new words you learn to your Vocabulary Log.

_____ stereotypes	_____ intuitive	_____ self-reliant
~~to credit~~ attributing	_____ nurturing	_____ sturdy
_____ passive	_____ self-sacrificing	_____ vulnerable
_____ conforming	~~unwieldly~~ aggressive wanting to do s.t.	anxious

_____ daring   _____ fare   _____ whereas

_____ inadequacy   _____ homosexual

C. Handling a Heavy Reading Load: Manage your reading load by reading the following text with your class in three minutes. If you do so, you will be reading at an ideal rate—about 150 words per minute. Begin reading on your instructor's signal. At the end of the first minute, jump to the large number "1" in the right margin if you are not there yet. If you are ahead of the "1," keep going. Try to read to the "2" by the time your instructor calls two minutes, and try to finish the reading by the time the instructor tells you to stop. Record your reading speed in the chart in Appendix A on page 226. Practice again in a second reading at home.

 Read

Reading 1: Traditional Sex-Role Expectations

1   *Sex roles* are learned patterns of behavior that are expected of the sexes in a given society. Sex-role expectations, which define how men and women are to behave and how they are to be treated by others, are based largely on **stereotypes.** *Stereotyping* involves the **attributing** of fixed and usually inaccurate and unfavorable qualities to a category of people. Stereotyping makes it easier for discrimination (unequal treatment) to occur.

2   American women traditionally are expected to be affectionate, **passive, conforming,** sensitive, **intuitive,** and dependent— **"sugar and spice and everything nice."**[1] They are supposed to be concerned primarily with domestic life, to be **nurturing,** to love to care for babies and young children, to fuss over their personal appearance, and to be **self-sacrificing** for their family. They should not appear to be ambitious, **aggressive,** competitive, or more intelligent than men. They should be ignorant about and uninterested in sports, economics, and politics. Also, they are not supposed to initiate relationships with men but are expected to be tender, feminine, emotional, and appreciative when in those relationships.

3   There are also a number of traditional sex-role expectations for males in our society: A male is expected to be tough, fearless, logical, **self-reliant,** independent, and aggressive. He should have definite opinions on the major issues of the day and make authoritative decisions at work and at home. He is expected to be strong—a **sturdy** oak—and never to be depressed, **vulnerable,** or **anxious.** He is not supposed to be a "**sissy**"[2]— to cry or openly display emotions that suggest vulnerability. He is expected to be the provider, the **breadwinner.**[3] He should be competent in all situations, physically strong, athletic,

---

[1]**"sugar and spice and everything nice":** part of a nursery rhyme describing sex-role expectations of girls

[2]**"sissy":** a feminine-acting boy (slang)

[3]**breadwinner:** one who supports a family with his or her earnings

confident, **daring**, brave, and forceful. He should be in a position to dominate any situation—to be a **"Rambo"**[4] or a **"Clint Eastwood."**[5] He is supposed to initiate relationships with women and to be dominant in these relationships. Men who are supported by their wives, or who earn less than their wives, are likely to experience feelings of shame and **inadequacy.**

4   Even very young boys are expected to be masculine. Parents and relatives are far more concerned when a boy is a "sissy" than when a girl is a **"tomboy."**[6] A tomboy is expected to outgrow her "masculine" tendencies, but it is feared that a sissy will never **fare** well in our competitive society and may even become **homosexual.** (The right of a boy to wear his hair long had to be won in many court battles in this country, **whereas** hardly anyone is concerned when a girl wears her hair short.)

After You Read

In 1968, American women's liberation activists protested the Miss America beauty contest by burning their bras in public.

A. Expressing the Main Idea: Tell a classmate briefly the main idea of Reading 1. Remember not to include simply the topic (*sex roles*), but also tell what the reading says *about the topic*. Compare your main idea statement with other classmates.

B. Reactions: Discuss these questions with classmates:

1. What is your reaction to the stereotypes of women described in Reading 1? Do you agree that these stereotypes exist? Explain.

2. What is your reaction to the stereotypes of men described in Reading 1? Do you agree that these stereotypes exist? Explain.

3. Do *you* fit the traditional, stereotypical description of a man or a woman? In what ways?

Reading Journal

Write about these topics in your reading journal: Is it difficult to read fast? Why or why not? Does increasing your reading speed interfere with your understanding of the reading? What strategies do you have to use to keep up the 150 word-per-minute rate? Were you able to do it?

---

[4]**"Rambo"**: tough male character in a U.S. film

[5]**"Clint Eastwood"**: U.S. actor who commonly portrays strong men

[6]**"tomboy"**: a girl who behaves like a boy (slang)

LANGUAGE LEARNING STRATEGY

Learn to identify causes and effects in readings to better understand the relationships between main ideas. One of the most common patterns of academic writing is the cause-effect organization. In history writing, for instance, writers may explain the causes of a war. Chemistry textbooks often describe the effects of combining chemical elements. Sociology and anthropology texts may relate the causes and effects of certain behavior in a culture. Reading 1 explains how stereotypes affect the way society in the United States expects men and women to behave.

To identify cause-effect organization, consider the content. If the reading tells "why" something happens, then it presents *causes*, or reasons, for occurrences. If the reading tells "what happens after" something happens, then it presents *effects*. Successful students pay attention to the main organization of academic texts to isolate main ideas. By identifying the main idea of a reading as the causes of an action, you can restate that information into a simple list of causes and effects so that it is easy to study.

Apply the Strategy

Reading 1 describes how U.S. stereotypes of women and men (the causes) produce certain expectations about how men and women should act (the effects). In paragraphs 2 and 3 of the reading, find the effects. Fill in the following chart. Discuss your answers with classmates.

EFFECTS OF STEREOTYPES OF WOMEN AND MEN	
Causes	**Effects**
CAUSE—Stereotype 1 Women in the U.S. traditionally are expected to be affectionate, passive, conforming, sensitive, intuitive, and dependent—"sugar and spice and everything nice." (paragraph 2)	
CAUSE—Stereotype 2 A male is expected to be tough, fearless, logical, self-reliant, independent, and aggressive. (paragraph 3)	

Getting Ready to Read

Reading 2 is entitled "The Sex-Role Revolution." What do you predict this reading will be about? Discuss your ideas with a classmate.

Vocabulary Check

Check the words that you already know. Work with a partner to find the meanings of new words. Use a dictionary, if necessary. Add the new words to your Vocabulary Log.

_____ distinctions	_____ disorderly	_____ irrational
_____ vocational	_____ egalitarian	_____ inferiority
_____ proportion	_____ extent	_____ destiny
_____ confined	_____ potentially	_____ entail
_____ pursuing	_____ province	_____ linger
_____ obstacles	_____ expenditure	_____ speculate
_____ subdue	_____ substantial	_____ barriers
_____ handcuff	_____ child rearing	_____ feminists
_____ offender	_____ perceived	_____ socialized

Reading 2: The Sex-Role Revolution

1   There is currently a sex-role revolution occurring in our society. Men as well as women are becoming aware of the negative effects of sex-role **distinctions.** Increasingly we see courses on this topic in high schools, **vocational** schools, and colleges. More and more women are entering the labor force. The **proportion** of employed females to employed males is about 45 to 55.[72]

2   Women are becoming more involved in athletics than they were in the past, and they are entering certain types of competition previously **confined** to males. Women are now playing basketball, football, baseball, and volleyball. There are increasing numbers of women in track and field events, swimming, boxing, wrestling, weight lifting, golf, tennis, and stock-car racing.

3   In 1983, Sandra Day O'Connor became the first woman justice on the United States Supreme Court. In 1984, Geraldine Ferraro was the first woman selected to be a vice-presidential candidate for a major political party.

4   Women are also **pursuing** a number of professions and careers that previously were nearly all male: the military, engineers, lawyers, judges, firefighters, physicians, dentists, accountants, administrators, police officers, managers. Entering these new professions often has presented **obstacles.** Carl Glassman, for example, reports that women police officers receive stares from other citizens and are often viewed with suspicion by male partners.[73] (Male police partners fear that women may break under pressure, may not be able to **subdue** and **handcuff** a resisting **offender,** and may not be able to control **disorderly** males and several other types of violent situations.)

5   Human interactions are also changing, with more women being assertive and seeking out **egalitarian** relationships with males. To some **extent,** men are also (more slowly) beginning to realize that sex-role stereotypes limit the opportunities open to them in terms of emotional expression, interpersonal relationships, occupations, and domestic activities. Jack Sawyer notes:

6   If men cannot play freely, neither can they freely cry, be gentle, nor show weakness—because these are "feminine," not "masculine." But a fuller concept of humanity recognizes that all men and women are **potentially** both strong and weak, both active and passive, and that these and other human characteristics are not the **province** of one sex.

7   The acceptance of sex-role stereotypes not only limits the individual, but also has bad effects on society generally.[74]

8   Sex-role stereotypes have been costly to society. They have prevented a number of people from assuming more productive roles and have resulted in the **expenditure** of **substantial** re-

sources on emotional and physical problems generated by these stereotypes.

9   Men also are taking on new roles and entering new careers. It is becoming increasingly common for men to accept equal responsibility for domestic tasks and for **child rearing.** In addition, we are now seeing more male nurses, secretaries, child-care workers, and nursery school teachers, telephone operators, and flight attendants.[75]

10   In the past two decades, millions of Americans have begun to change their ideas about the "naturalness" of sex roles. Traditional discriminations are coming to be **perceived** as an **irrational** system that threatens women with lifelong **inferiority** and wasted potential and restricts men to the role of always being competitive, aggressive, and emotionally insensitive.

11   What will the future be like? Predicting the precise direction that sex-role stereotypes will take is difficult. As Thomas Sullivan et al. note:

12   It seems likely that any meaningful change in our sex-role structure will involve some degree of redefinition of both masculinity and femininity. In the years to come, it is likely that we will see significant shifts in the way children are socialized and revisions of our legal system that affect both men and women. The extent of the change that will occur is something that cannot yet be determined. . . . We are in the midst of a very exciting era of experimentation. We have an opportunity to shape our **destiny** in this area. If people decide that sexual differences are important, this need not **entail** a return to the inequality, discrimination, and oppression that were common in the past and still **linger** today.[76]

13   If men and women achieve sexual equality in our society, what will be the effects? Kornblum and Julian **speculate:**

14   One obvious answer is that society's supply of talent in every segment of the work force would increase. More men would participate in traditionally female fields. . . . Breaking down the occupational **barriers** that separate women and men would also help them relate to each other as equals. Also, because fewer men would be the sole support for their families, there would be more flexibility in working life: Men and women would be freer to leave their jobs if they were unhappy with them, and in general there would be greater sharing of economic and homemaking responsibilities. This would reduce the pressures that exist for men to "succeed" and for women to remain dependent. The most important result of true sexual equality, then, may be simply that people would be free to be themselves.[77]

15   Some **feminists** and social scientists have urged that men and women be **socialized** to be flexible in their role playing and to express themselves as human beings rather than in traditional feminine or masculine ways.[78] This idea is called "androgyny," from *andro* (male) and *gyne* (female). The notion is to have people explore a broad range of role-playing possibilities and to choose to express emotions and behaviors without regard to sex-role stereotypes. People thus are encouraged to pursue tasks and careers at which they are most competent and with which they are most comfortable and to express the attitudes and emotions they really feel. If a male wants to be a cook or an elementary school teacher and a female wants to be a soldier or an athlete—and they're good at it—then it is functional for society if both develop their talents and are allowed to achieve everything they're capable of.

Notes:
72. U.S. Bureau of the Census, *Statistical Abstract of the United States, 1992.*
73. Carl Glassman, "How Lady Cops Are Doing," *Parade*, July 27, 1980, pp. 4-5.
74. Jack Sawyer, "On Male Liberation," in *Men and Masculinity*, Joseph H. Pleck and Jack Sawyer, eds. (Englewood Cliffs, NJ: Prentice-Hall, 1974), p. 172.
75. *Statistical Abstract of the United States, 1992.*
76. Thomas Sullivan, Kenrick Thompson, Richard Wright, George Gross, and Dale Spady, *Social Problems* (New York: Wiley, 1980), p. 474.
77. William Kornblum and Joseph Julian, *Social Problems*, 7th ed. (Englewood Cliffs, NJ: Prentice-Hall, 1992), p. 316.
78. Janet S. Hyde, *Understanding Human Sexuality,* 4th ed. (New York: McGraw-Hill, 1990), pp. 383-385.

◆ After You Read

Empress Wu Zhao ruled China with her son in the 7th century, and is still recognized as one of China's strongest leaders.

A. Expressing the Main Idea: Reread paragraph 1 of Reading 2. Find a sentence that expresses the main idea. Share the sentence with a classmate.

B. Confirming Predictions: Were your predictions about the subject of the reading correct? Why or why not?

C. Identifying Causes and Effects: Reading 2 begins with the statement: "There is currently a sex-role revolution in our society." Find sentences in the reading that explain the effects of this "revolution." Compare your answers with classmates.

LANGUAGE LEARNING STRATEGY

Create a graphic organizer to help you visualize and remember important ideas and how they relate to each other in a reading. A graphic organizer is a chart or drawing of important ideas in a reading. It's called *graphic* because it lets you visualize the most important ideas in a text. It's an *organizer* because it shows the relationship between those ideas. Look at these graphic organizers, which show ideas about traditional sex roles from Reading 1:

linear : line ⊥

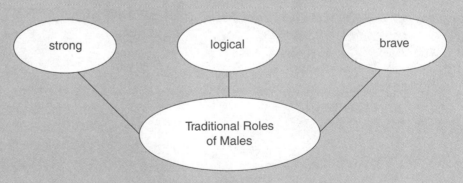

Traditional Sex-Role Expectations of Men

(continued on next page)

A graphic organizer may organize information in a "cluster," as the first example does, or like a "flow chart" of boxes and arrows, like the second example. To create a good graphic organizer, first think about the main ideas in a reading. Then visualize the best graphic way to show how these ideas connect to each other. You can use your graphic organizer to study and remember the information that you read.

Apply the Strategy

A. Choose a title and description from these three choices that best describes the sample graphic organizers below:

- Cycle Organizer—shows how a series of events produce effects over and over again.

- Central Idea Organizer—shows a main idea and supporting details.

- Cluster—shows qualities or characteristics of a main idea.

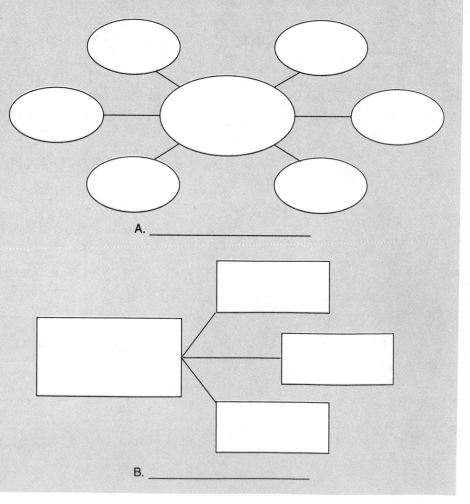

A. _____

B. _____

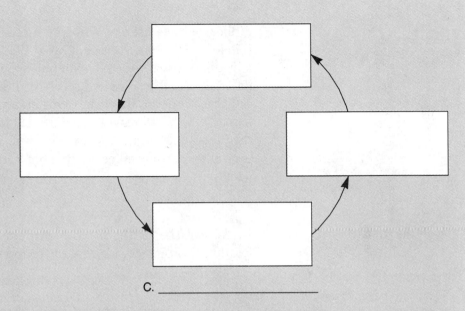

C. _____

Discuss what types of information you might put in each graphic organizer. Share your ideas with your classmates.

B. With a partner, choose and discuss one paragraph in Reading 2. Then use one of the graphic organizers shown here as a model to create your own graphic organizer. You do not need to include all the ideas in the paragraph. Select some ideas that you and your partner think are important. Discuss which graphic organizer would best represent these ideas and the way the ideas relate to each other. Draw the graphic organizer that appeals to you the most in your notebook.

ACADEMIC POWER STRATEGY

Recognize and use bibliographic citations in order to find and cite information. A bibliographic citation identifies the title, author, and source of a reading. Bibliographic citations are used within a reading when a writer wants to identify information that comes from other sources. The writer gives credit to the original source with a

(continued on next page)

bibliography (a list of a writer's sources of information) or footnotes (bibliographic entries that appear at the "foot" or bottom of a page in a reading). Usually the bibliography appears at the end of a reading, as in Reading 2. There are several styles of bibliographic entries, but typically each contains the name of the author, the name of the reading, the name of the book, magazine, or journal in which the reading appeared, the place, date and company which published it, and the page numbers. If the reading comes from a book, the book may have an editor's name.

Apply the Strategy

A. Reread the first two bibliographic citations on page 102 after Reading 2. For each, identify the following items:

Author or Editor: _____

Title of the Source (name of book, magazine, or journal, or article

    plus book or magazine): _____

Place of Publication (city): _____

Publisher (company): _____

Year of Publication: _____

B. Reread the entire bibliography that follows Reading 2 on page 102. Identify the special type styles and punctuation used for each piece of information in the citations (such as italic type, parentheses, commas, and periods).

◇ Getting Ready to Read

Before you look at Reading 3, discuss the following questions with a group of classmates:

1. What do you think is the median (middle) weekly salary of women in the town or city where you live? Men?

2. Do you think salaries are different for different ethnic groups? Explain.

3. Are salaries different in your native country for women and men? For different ethnic groups? Explain.

Read

During World War II, a character called "Rosie the Riveter" appeared on posters throughout the U.S. to symbolize the millions of women doing "men's work" in production plants while men were at war.

Reading 3: Median Weekly Earnings of Full-Time Workers

Median Usual Weekly Earnings of Full-Time Wage and Salary Workers by Selected Characteristics, 1998

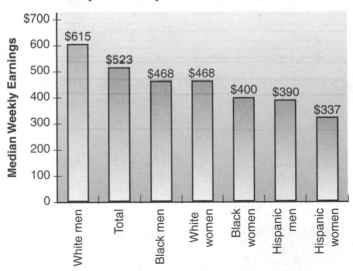

Characteristic	Median Weekly Earnings
White men	$615
Total	$523
Black men	$468
White women	$468
Black women	$400
Hispanic men	$390
Hispanic women	$337

Source: Monthly Labor Review, U.S. Department of Labor, February 1999.

After You Read

A. Confirming Predictions: Discuss the following questions:

1. Were your predictions about salaries accurate?

2. Were you surprised by the information in the table? Explain.

B. Expressing the Main Idea: Which of the following statements best expresses the main idea of Reading 3? Discuss your answer with classmates.

Statement 1:   Median weekly earnings for white men are $615, compared to $468 for white women, in the U.S.

Statement 2:   Median earnings for Hispanics are lower than those for blacks or for whites in the U.S.

C. Utilizing Visual Features: Discuss the following questions and complete the activity with classmates:

1. Was the Reading 3 chart difficult to understand? Did you choose the correct main idea sentence from the previous activity? If not, what made the reading problematic?

2. Would the information have been as clear if it had been printed in paragraph form, rather than a chart? Why or why not?

3. Use the information in the chart to write two or more sentences about the median weekly salaries in the United States.

Reading Journal

Answer the following questions in your journal: Are certain jobs in your native country commonly held by women? What are they? Do women earn less money than men do?

TUNING IN: "Working Women"

© CNN

Pre-Viewing

Discuss these questions with classmates before you view the CNN video clip "Working Women," about working women across the globe.

1. In which of these countries and regions do you think women and men have equality in salaries? Rate the countries from "1" to "5," where "1" indicates the place where men's and women's salaries for the same work are most equal, and "5" where they are most different.

———— Tanzania   ———— Europe

———— South Korea   ———— Japan

———— United States

Discussion

Read these questions before you view the video clip. Then, listen and write down the answers while you view. Discuss your answers with classmates after viewing.

1. In a world work force of 5.7 billion people,

   ———— % are women, and ———— % are men.

2. Check your predictions about the pay ratio (comparison between men's and women's salaries for the same work) in the five countries listed. Write the percentage that shows how much women are paid in comparison with men.

   ————% Tanzania   ————% Europe

   ————% South Korea   ————% Japan

   ————% United States

   Were your predictions accurate?

3. The video clip says that working women of the 1990s want to "have it all"? What does this mean?

> **In 1951, Eva Peron tried to become the vice president of her husband (Argentine president Juan Peron), but the country's leaders would not agree.**

Getting Ready to Read

Predicting Ideas: The final reading in Chapter 5 is a short excerpt from a textbook. "The New Majority" presents facts about women at colleges and universities. Before you read, make predictions about this topic. Mark the following statements as *True* or *False*.

———— 1. American women have always been allowed to attend universities.

———— 2. African-Americans were once prohibited from attending colleges.

———— 3. Most U.S. men's colleges have become schools for men and women in the past 25 years.

———— 4. Some women's colleges now also admit male students.

———— 5. The majority of today's college students are women.

Vocabulary Check

Which of these words do you already know? Check them. Find the meanings of new words. Use a dictionary, if necessary. Discuss the words with your instructor. Add the new words to your Vocabulary Log.

_____ barred   _____ integrated

_____ higher education   _____ curricula

_____ coeducation

 Read

Reading 4: The New Majority

American women were at one time **barred** from **higher education**. In 1833 **Oberlin College**[1] became the first to admit women, as well as African Americans. It was only when publicly funded, **land grant universities**[2] were founded under the Morrill Act of 1862 that **"coeducation"** became at all common. And only in the last twenty-five years have most men's colleges become schools for men and women, with fully **integrated** degree programs, residences, and **curricula.** Facing social and financial pressures, many formerly all-women's colleges have also opened up their admissions to men. Women now make up the majority of college students—about 54 percent.

 **After You Read**

A. Confirming Predictions: Were your predictions about "The New Majority" accurate? In what areas were your ideas different from the facts in the reading? Correct the statements from the Predicting Ideas activity, and discuss them with classmates.

B. Reactions: Discuss these questions with classmates:

1. Should all-women's and all-men's colleges exist? Explain.

2. Are colleges and universities in your native country open to both men and women? Are they coeducational? If not, explain why.

3. Should college residences be coeducational? Why or why not?

---

[1]**Oberlin College:** a private university in Ohio

[2]**land grant universities:** government-supported universities

PUTTING IT ALL TOGETHER

> **From 1975 to 1996, the percentage of women in the full-time work force rose from 46% to 59% in the United States.**
>
> SOURCE: *U.S. BUREAU OF LABOR STATISTICS*

Final Project

Research one of the following topics with a group of classmates to expand your knowledge of gender issues:

A. Conduct an Internet search on one of the following topics or another topic of your group's choice related to the chapter readings. Consult the guide, "Using the Internet as a Reading Source" in Appendix B on page 227. Find two to three articles. Read them and identify the main ideas.

1. women's status in _____ (one society)
2. women's roles in family
3. men's roles in family
4. women in _____ (one profession)
5. men in _____ (one profession)
6. women's colleges
7. men's colleges

B. If Internet access is unavailable, conduct the same research using print resources from a library. Use your library's databases to search for titles of magazine or journal articles or books. Many library databases provide full-text (entire) magazine and journal articles. Consult your instructor for information about using your college library. Find one article. Read it and find the main ideas.

Using Bibliographic Citations

Write a bibliography of the two to three readings that you found with your classmates. Refer to the examples from Reading 2 on page 102 in this chapter. To cite sources from the Internet, consult Appendix B on page 227, "Using the Internet as a Reading Source." Consult your instructor, if necessary.

Oral Presentation

Use this suggested outline as a guide for delivering a group presentation on the articles you researched on the Internet or in your college library. Divide up the speaking tasks equally among group members. Photocopy your bibliography, and pass the copies out to your classmates before giving your presentation.

I. Introduction
   Name of reading, author, source. Main ideas of readings.

II. Body
   Explain the most important supporting points in the readings.

III. Conclusion

Explain one or more of the following: how the information in these readings compared with information in a chapter reading; your evaluation of the readings in terms of interest level, content, and accuracy; or your opinion about the subject matter presented in the readings.

Ask for and answer questions. Thank the audience.

Test-Taking Tip

Learn all you can about the test beforehand. Ask the instructor how long the test will be, what kind of questions will be on it, what concepts are likely to be covered, which chapters to focus on, and what the format of the test will be (essay, multiple choice, matching, etc.). Also, ask your instructor if you can see some sample test questions or a copy of a similar test given in the past.

CHECK YOUR PROGRESS

On a scale of 1 to 5, rate how well you have mastered the goals set at the beginning of the chapter:

1 2 3 4 5   identify causes and effects in readings.

1 2 3 4 5   create graphic organizers.

1 2 3 4 5   recognize and use bibliographic citations.

If you've given yourself a 3 or lower on any of these goals:

- visit the *Tapestry* web site for additional practice.
- ask your instructor for extra help.
- review the sections of the chapter that you found difficult.
- work with a partner or study group to further your progress.

L ook at the photo. Then discuss these questions with your classmates:

- Do you feel that there is too much sex and violence in movies and on TV today? Why?
- Should movies and TV be censored? If so, what should be censored?
- Are movies and TV censored or regulated in your native country? How?

MEDIA AND CULTURE

The mass media has so much influence on the world today that debate over the suitability of its content is widespread. Parents are concerned about the influences of movies and TV on children. Some governments censor films because of their political or sexual themes. Meanwhile, artists argue for freedom of expression in the media.

Setting Goals

In this chapter, you will learn how to:

◈ decide in advance how you want to participate in class discussions of readings.

◈ distinguish fact from opinion in readings.

◈ group words into similar domains (groups) to remember new vocabulary.

What other goals do you have for this chapter? Write one or two of them here.

_____

_____

**Getting Started**

The writers in this chapter discuss topics related to film, television, and other media. Look at the titles of the readings and answer the questions that follow.

Readings:

"The Culture War"

"The Entertainment Media and the Social Construction of Crime and Justice"

"Motion Picture Association of America and TV Parental Guidelines Monitoring Board Ratings"

"Cannes Loves to Hate Censorship"

1. Considering the titles of the other readings, what might "the culture war" refer to?

   _____

   _____

2. Reading 2 has a complex title. What is "the entertainment media"? How do you think it is related to "crime and justice"?

   _____

   _____

3. Should the U.S. movie rating system be voluntary?

   _____

   _____

4. What are the different television ratings used in the U.S.?

   _____

   _____

5. What is film censorship? Do you know of any films that have been censored in your home country?

   _____

   _____

6. Preview the photos and charts in the chapter. What do these tell you about the topics of the readings?

   _____

   _____

 **Getting Ready to Read**

Reading 1, "The Culture War," describes the current conflict in the U.S. over the content of television shows, films, and publications. What do you think could be the main issues in the "culture war"? The reading explains that *conservatives* and *liberals* disagree over the content of TV and movies. In politics, what do the terms *conservative* and *liberal* mean? What elements of television and movies do you think they disagree about? Under each political group, briefly write their possible concerns regarding TV and movies.

	Possible Issues in "The Culture War"
Conservatives	
Liberals	

Vocabulary Check

Check the words you already know. Work with a partner to find the meanings of new words. If you need to, use a dictionary. You can add any new words you learn to your Vocabulary Log.

_____ mass media   _____ pornography

_____ conservatives   _____ interstellar

_____ biased   _____ malevolently

_____ censor, censorship _____ liberals

_____ ridiculing   _____ obscenity

_____ grassroots   _____ stark

_____ accountable   _____ depicted

_____ evangelicals   _____ parental

_____ boycotts   _____ self-restraint

_____ drenched   _____ attuned

_____ gore

Read

Reading 1: The Culture War

1 By the 1990s, conflict over the content of television programs, the visual arts, school curriculum, books and magazines, films, and even computer networks, could be seen, in the words of James Davison Hunter, as a culture war. For Hunter, the culture war is a struggle over national identity, defining what America has been, what it is today, and what it will be in the future. The conflict is about values. Such cultural conflict often occurs when a society is experiencing rapid changes in uncertain times.

2 Because America's population is so diverse, its people possess quite different ideas concerning authority, the meaning of truth, the limits of free expression, and the nature of community. The culture war affects the lives of all Americans. It involves nearly every part of American life, especially the **mass media.**

3 In selecting what stories to cover, what music to play, what films to produce and distribute, what art to sponsor and display, and what books to publish, the mass media define what is important and what issues are worthy of public consideration. The persons and groups who make these decisions have enormous cultural and political power. Controlling and influencing the mass media is therefore a central feature of the culture war.

4 **Conservatives** generally believe that the media are unfairly **biased** against traditional values. They claim that the mass media often **censor** their books, films, and other forms of expressions, by ignoring or **ridiculing** them. For example, they claim that subjects such as religion are often portrayed in the worst possible light.

5 Conservatives have developed many strategies to influence the mass media. First, **grassroots** organizations that hold the media **accountable** for the content of programs and products have sprung up across the nation. These include Parents' Music Resource Center and the American Family Association, among many others. Second, by the early 1990s, religious **evangelicals** were operating 1,300 radio stations, 200 television stations, three television networks, 80 publishing houses, over 6,000 independent bookstores, and a number of independent movie studios. Third, conservatives have threatened consumer **boycotts** of offending local theaters and bookstores and of sponsors of television programs.

6 On the other side of the culture war, liberals and media decision-makers have argued that all forms of entertainment are driven by market forces. They claim it is the consumers who determine the content of popular culture. As writer Katha Pollitt argued,

People like pop culture—that's what makes it popular. Movies **drenched** in sex and **gore, gangsta rap,**[1] even outright **pornography** are not some sort of alien **interstellar** dust **malevolently** drifting down on us, but products actively sought out and beloved by millions.

7 **Liberals** have defended the content of the mass media. Author John Edgar Wideman asked, "Which is more threatening to America— the violence, **obscenity,** sexism, and racism of movies and records, or the **stark** reality these movies and music reflect?" Moreover, Wideman relied on the value of freedom of expression—"We can't have the best art unless we are willing to risk living with the rest, the second rate and 15th rate, the stuff that eventually [disappears] because its worthlessness teaches us not to buy or listen."

8 A recent opinion poll discovered that many people were very concerned about the amount of sex and violence **depicted** in movies, television shows, and popular music. This poll also discovered, however, that most people thought that individuals should take responsibility to correct the problems. The vast majority favored such solutions as tighter **parental** supervision, warning labels on records, and voluntary **self-restraint** by entertainment companies. Only

[1]**gangsta rap:** type of music in which rhyming lyrics are spoken to a beat

27 percent favored government **censorship.** At the same time, there was growing concern about the impact of television on children. Research has shown that by the time Americans reach age 18, they have spent more time watching television than in school. The prob-lem, according to Newton Minnow, was that "Our television system is a business **attuned** to the marketplace. Children are treated as a market to be sold to advertisers at so many dollars per thousand eyeballs."

 **After You Read**

Write a sentence or sentences that express the main idea of Reading 1. Share your sentence(s) with a classmate. Use the following strategy in discussing the main idea with your entire class.

ACADEMIC POWER STRATEGY

Decide in advance how you want to participate in class discussions. When you plan in advance, you can focus your thinking and sharpen your vocabulary. This will help you feel more confident about what you want to say.

Before you go to class, plan how you want to participate in the class discussion. You could decide to make comments about any of the following:

- the main idea
- something you would like to understand better
- your reaction
- an interesting point
- an example

Here are a few suggestions about how to begin your comments:

- To me, "X" means . . .
- I would like to make a point about . . .
- I understood the main idea, but some parts confused me. I need some help with . . .
- This was interesting to me because . . .
- This made me think about . . .

(continued on next page)

- Here are some examples that might be relevant to this discussion. . . .

- I was talking about "X" with my roommate (or family), and we thought . . .

- "X" is a new idea for me. Can you tell me more about . . .

Apply the Strategy

Think about the topic you are studying right now in your favorite class. Then plan to make relevant comments about the topic the next time your class meets. Below write at last three comments that would be relevant to the topic you are now studying:

Comment 1:

_____

_____

Comment 2:

_____

_____

Comment 3:

_____

_____

The next time your class meets, make at least one of these comments. Then write below your own reactions to the experience of participating well in the class discussion. Write any other comments you want to make about the discussion, as well.

_____

_____

_____

_____

_____

_____

© CNN

TUNING IN: "Violent Teens"

A. Pre-Viewing

Discuss these questions with classmates before you view "Violent Teens," a CNN video clip: Which of these factors do you think is the greater cause of teen violence? Which factor do you think teenagers identify as the greater cause?

The media (TV, movies)   Parents' behavior

B. Discussion

As you view "Violent Teens," look for the answers to the following questions. Discuss them with classmates.

1. Which factor is the greater cause of teen violence, according to American teenagers? What percentage of teens believe that teen violence is caused by each factor?

    _____ % TV   _____ % Parents

2. Observe the activities of teenagers at the teen center. What do they do there? Is this a good place for teenagers to spend time? Explain.

3. Do you agree with the teenagers' opinions about the causes of teen violence? Explain.

LANGUAGE LEARNING STRATEGY

Distinguish fact from opinion in readings and speech in order to make clearer judgments about the information you receive. Your ability to distinguish fact from opinion in readings and spoken language is a critical language learning skill. When you read academic texts or listen to lectures, always consider whether the writer or speaker is telling you a *fact*, or whether he or she is trying to persuade you with an *opinion*. If you can do this, you can make clearer judgments about the information you receive. Ask yourself: Has the writer proven this idea? Is it really true? Or is it just the writer's opinion? Don't always believe something just because it is printed or spoken.

For instance, examine this passage from Reading 1:

Conservatives generally believe that the media are unfairly biased against traditional values. They claim that the mass media often censor their books, films, and other forms of expressions, by ignoring or ridiculing them. . . . Conservatives have developed many strategies to influence the mass media. First, grassroots organizations that hold the media accountable for the content of programs and products have sprung up across the nation.

Do these sentences tell about *facts* or *opinions*? The first two sentences relate the *opinions* of conservatives. The last two sentences relate *facts*; they tell about actions that have taken place.

Apply the Strategy

Examine these sentences taken from Reading 1. Mark the statements as F (fact) or O (opinion). Compare your answers with classmates.

_____ 1. The culture war affects the lives of all Americans. (paragraph 2)

_____ 2. "We can't have the best art unless we are willing to risk living with the rest, the second rate and 15th rate . . . ." (paragraph 7)

_____ 3. A recent opinion poll discovered that many people were very concerned about the amount of sex and violence depicted in movies, television shows, and popular music. (paragraph 8)

_____ 4. "Children are treated as a market to be sold to advertisers at so many dollars per thousand eyeballs." (paragraph 8)

LANGUAGE LEARNING STRATEGY

Group words into similar domains, or fields, in order to effectively remember new vocabulary. One way to study unfamiliar words is to put several words together into one domain, or area. For example, you can place the words *political, grassroots,* and *authority* into a group entitled "political words." In addition, in Chapter 4, you could make a group called "types of food poisoning words." Grouping words in such a way organizes them in your mind, and helps you remember their meanings. This is especially useful when you have many groups of academic- or work-related words to remember.

Apply the Strategy

Reread "The Culture War" and find words or phrases from the reading that belong in each of the groups listed below. Compare your lists with classmates. Add your classmates' words to your list.

Types of Media

_____

_____

_____

_____

Controversial Things in TV and Movies

_____

_____

_____

_____

Methods for Controlling Media

_____

_____

_____

_____

Getting Ready to Read

The Bible and The Qur'an were both removed from numerous libraries and banned from import in the Soviet Union from 1926 to 1956.

[handwritten: opinionated (adj)]
[handwritten: tone :]

Reading 2, "The Entertainment Media and the Social Construction of Crime and Justice" is an excerpt from a criminal justice textbook. In the book, the author explains how the media portrays or *constructs* a picture of crime and justice in our society. Before you read, consider this question: Do you think the writer will argue that the media portray crime as it actually occurs in society? Or will he argue that the media portray crime inaccurately? Why do you think so? Discuss these questions with classmates.

Vocabulary Check

Check the words you already know. Work with a partner to find the meanings of new words. Use a dictionary, if necessary. You can add any new words you learn to your Vocabulary Log.

_____ underrepresented _____ portrayals _____ constructions

_____ overrepresented —to attack assault *[handwritten: holding of a person.]* arrestee

[handwritten: objective (adj) without opinion.]
[handwritten: n goal.]

Read

Reading 2: The Entertainment Media and the Social Construction of Crime and Justice

1   What are viewers likely to see in the media? Are they exposed to situations and behaviors they might not experience in reality? In terms of crimes, the offenses that are most likely to be emphasized on television are those that are least likely to occur in real life, with property crime **underrepresented** and violent crime **overrepresented**.[75] And while there are recent reports of declines in television violence and fewer **portrayals** of violence as graphic or heroic,[76] media portraits of crime greatly overemphasize individual acts of violence.[77] If one looks at combined criminal and noncriminal violence on television, the levels are even higher.[78] Murder and robbery dominate, with murder accounting for nearly one-fourth of all television crimes. In a representative content study by Lichter and Lichter, murder, robbery, kidnapping, and aggravated **assault** made up 87 percent of all television crimes.[79] In contrast, murders account for only one-sixth of 1 percent of the FBI Crime Index. At the other extreme, thefts account for nearly two-thirds of the FBI Crime Index, but only 6 percent of television crime.

2   Thus a large difference exists between what viewers are likely to experience in reality and what they are likely to see in the media.[80] This perhaps would not be a concern if the portrayals of crime and justice in the media were balanced in other aspects and presented various competing **constructions** of the world. That, however, is not the case.

3   For example, there is also almost no correspondence between media portraits of criminals and official statistics of persons arrested for crimes.[81] The typical criminal as portrayed in the entertainment media is mature, white, and of high social status, whereas statistic-

ally the typical **arrestee** is young, black, and poor—all they have in common is that both are male.[82]

Notes

[75] Carlson 1985; Dominick 1978; Estep and MacDonald 1984; and Gerbner 1976.

[76] Cole 1996.

[77] See Antunes and Hurley 1977; Borner 1984; Graber 1980; Jones 1976; Pandiani 1978; and Sherizen 1978.

[78] The 1969 National Commission on the Causes and Prevention of Violence found vi-

olent episodes in more than 80 percent of shows (National Commission on the Causes and Prevention of Violence 1969; see also Newman 1990)

[79] See Estep and MacDonald 1984, p. 115; Lichter and Lichter 1983, p. 10; Maguire 1988, p. 175.

[80] Lewis 1984; Lichter and Lichter 1983.

[81] Garofalo 1981a; Maguire 1988.

[82] See Dominick 1973; Estep and MacDonald 1983; Graber 1980; Hauge 1965; and Roshier 1981.

 **After You Read**

A. Confirming Predictions: What does the writer argue—that the media accurately portray crime as it occurs in society, or that the media construct crime in an inaccurate way from reality? Were you correct in your prediction, or incorrect? Discuss the writer's idea with classmates.

B. Distinguishing Fact from Opinion: Reading 2 describes the media's portrayal of crime and justice in society. Reread all the sentences in the reading that are marked with a small number that refers to a footnote. Are these sentences fact or opinion statements? Does the bibliographic citation change your evaluation of the sentences as fact or opinion? Discuss your answers with classmates.

C. Recognizing a Writer's Tone: The writer of Reading 2 expresses his tone, or attitude, toward the subject of the media and its portrayal of crime through *word choice* (the words he uses) and *content* (the ideas he includes). Read the following passage from Reading 2. Underline the words that show the writer's tone. Discuss your answers with classmates.

In a representative content study by Lichter and Lichter, murder, robbery, kidnapping, and aggravated assault made up 87 percent of all television crimes. In contrast, murders account for only one-sixth of 1 percent of the FBI Crime Index. At the other extreme, thefts account for nearly two-thirds of the FBI Crime Index, but only 6 percent of television crime.

Thus a large difference exists between what viewers are likely to experience in reality and what they are likely to see in the media.[80] This perhaps would not be a concern if the portrayals of crime and justice in the media were balanced in other aspects and presented various competing constructions of the world. That, however, is not the case.

D. Synthesizing Material from Different Sources: Readings 1 and 2 describe different aspects of the media. By *synthesizing*, or putting together, the information from both readings, you can understand the subject more completely. Skim the two readings. Then, discuss these questions in a small group of classmates. Share your answers with your class.

1. In "The Culture War," the writer describes the battle between conservatives and liberals over the content of films and TV. Do you think the author of Reading 2, "The Entertainment Media and the Social Construction of Crime and Justice" would agree with the conservative or the liberal view? Why?

2. Does the information in Reading 2 support government censorship of the media? Why or why not?

Reading Journal

Based on your viewing experience and the information in Readings 1 and 2, answer these questions in your reading journal: How do you feel about the freedom of the mass media in the U.S.? Should television and films be censored? Should they be controlled in any way? Should they be required to portray society in a more realistic way? Explain.

Getting Ready to Read

Reading 3 shows the ratings lists for movies and TV in the United States. Before you read, discuss the following questions with classmates:

1. What are the different movie ratings used in the United States? Make a list of the ratings and a brief explanation of each.

2. What are the different U.S. television ratings? What does each rating mean?

3. Does the presence of these ratings effectively control the audience of movies and TV? Why or why not?

4. Should the ratings systems be voluntary or mandatory? Explain.

Vocabulary Check

Which of these words do you already know? Check them. Work with a partner to find the meanings of new words. You can add any new words you learn to your Vocabulary Log.

_____ voluntary _____ suitability _____ monitoring

_____ cautioned _____ combative _____ graphic

_____ guardian _____ signify _____ explicit

_____ animated _____ infrequent _____ crude

_____ themes _____ coarse _____ indecent

_____ developmental _____ suggestive

[handwritten annotations:]
work without paid — voluntary
to observe the actions of other (v) — monitoring
to warn s.o. about s.t. — cautioned
eager to fight or argue — combative
describe in a very clear & detailed way — graphic
a person legally responsible for another — guardian
to show; indicate — signify
clear — explicit
make s.t or so. full of life e.g. fun / to enliven — animated
not often — infrequent
unfinished — crude
central ideas — themes
of poor quality / bad — coarse
not good — indecent
growth — developmental
interesting (adj) — suggestive

Read

Reading 3: Motion Picture Association of America and TV Parental Guidelines Monitoring Board Ratings

Voluntary Movie Rating System	
G	GENERAL AUDIENCES All ages admitted.
PG	PARENTAL GUIDANCE SUGGESTED Some material may not be suitable for children.
PG-13	PARENTS STRONGLY **CAUTIONED** Some material may be inappropriate for children under 13.
R	RESTRICTED Under 17 requires accompanying parent or adult **guardian.**
NC-17	NO ONE 17 AND UNDER ADMITTED

Parental Guide Television Ratings

TVY   All Children

This program is designed to be appropriate for all children. Whether **animated** or live-action, the **themes** and elements in this program are specifically designed for a very young audience, including children from ages 2–6. This program is not expected to frighten younger children.

TVY7   Directed to Older Children

This program is designed for children age 7 and above. It may be more appropriate for children who have acquired the **developmental** skills needed to distinguish between make-believe and reality. Themes and elements in this program may include mild fantasy violence or comedic violence, or may frighten children under the age of 7. Therefore, parents may wish to consider the **suitability** of this program for their very young children. Note: For those programs where fantasy violence may be more intense or more **combative** than other programs in this category, such programs will be designated TV-Y7-FV.

TVG   General Audience

Most parents would find this program suitable for all ages. Although this rating does not **signify** a program designed specifically for children, most parents may let younger children watch this program unattended. It contains little or no violence, no strong language and little or no sexual dialogue or situations.

TVPG   Parental Guidance Suggested

This program contains material that parents may find unsuitable for younger children. Many parents may want to watch it with their younger children. The theme itself may call for parental guidance and/or the program contains one or more of the following: moderate violence (V), some sexual situations (S), **infrequent coarse** language (L), or some **suggestive** dialogue (D).

TV14   Parents Strongly Cautioned

This program contains some material that many parents would find unsuitable for children under 14 years of age. Parents are strongly urged to exercise greater care in **monitoring** this program and are cautioned against letting children under the age of 14 watch unattended. This program contains one or more of the following: intense violence (V), intense sexual situations (S), strong coarse language (L), or intensely suggestive dialogue (D).

TVMA   Mature Audience Only

This program is specifically designed to be viewed by adults and therefore may be unsuitable for children under 17. This program contains one or more of the following: **graphic** violence (V), **explicit** sexual activity (S), or **crude** and **indecent** language (L).

◀After You Read

A. Confirming Predictions: How accurate were your lists of TV and movie ratings? Which ratings were you less familiar with—TV or movie ratings?

B. Synthesizing Material from Different Sources: Answer these questions about the two ratings systems with classmates:

1. Which ratings system do you prefer? Why?

2. Which ratings system do you think is more effective in controlling the age at which viewers watch certain shows—the movie ratings or TV ratings? Why?

3. The two ratings systems are both *voluntary*. Do you think they should be *mandatory*? Why or why not?

4. If the systems were mandatory, how could they be enforced? By whom?

C. Write: Rewrite one of the two ratings lists so that it reflects your ideas about the appropriate viewing ages for each category of movies or TV shows. Add or remove levels of ratings, if you like. Revise the description of each level to suit your ideas.

D. Reactions: Do the following activities with classmates:

1. Share your revised ratings lists with a small group of classmates. Compare your ideas for movie or TV ratings.

2. Explain to your class how movies are rated or otherwise regulated in your native country. Who regulates the cinema? What do they regulate? How do movies in your native country compare with U.S. movies?

3. Discuss television ratings or regulations in your native country. How do the TV programs compare with those in the U.S.?

◆ Getting Ready to Read

In June 1998, the Motion Picture Association of America announced that it would regulate the content of Internet advertisements of movies with the same standards it uses to regulate print, TV, and radio ads.

SOURCE: *E!* **ENTERTAINMENT MAGAZINE**

Reading 4, "Cannes Loves to Hate Censorship," is a newspaper report about international films that were recently shown at the Cannes Film Festival in France. Before you read, discuss the following questions with a group of classmates:

1. Think about one of your favorite movies. What type of movie is it? Why do you like it?

2. What types of content might governments censor in movies?

3. Does the government of your native country censor movies?

Vocabulary Check

Which of these words do you already know? Check them. Work with a partner to find the meanings of new words. You can add any new words you learn to your Vocabulary Log.

_____ wielded   _____ implied   _____ barred

_____ pines (verb)   _____ commentary   _____ massacring

———— metaphor ———— grudgingly ———— deprive

———— cinematography ———— bleak ———— taboo

———— acclaim ———— outskirts ———— hardline

———— entwined ———— shallow

Read

Reading 4: Cannes Loves to Hate Censorship

ASSOCIATED PRESS

1 CANNES, MAY 20, 1998: Ahead of **Hong Kong's handover**[1] to China, the Cannes film festival named Wong Kar-Wai Best Director for a kind of cinema he fears he may not be able to make in a few months.

2 Iranian Abbas Kiarostami's film about suicide almost didn't make it to Cannes and ended up winning the **Golden Palm**[2] on Sunday night. But China blocked one film and a director from a festival that **wielded** its palms to fight the shadow of censorship.

3 "Our role is always to defend freedom of expression," said Pierre Viot, festival president. "By presenting films that are not always welcome in their country, we contribute to freedom."

4 Even for Cannes, the conflict over censorship played an especially large role this year. China pulled the film *Keep Cool* from the festival competition. Directed by Zhang Yimou, it's the story of a bookseller who **pines** for a liberated, sexy young woman going out with a **nouveau riche**,[3] an **implied** critical **commentary** of China's **go-go**[4] '90s. Beijing also **barred** Zhang Yuan from attending the festival, where his film *East Palace, West Palace* showed in the festival after being secretly shot in China. The film's title refers to two Beijing restrooms that are gay meeting sites.

5 "The authorities are **massacring** their own cinema," said Christopher Jung, who co-produced the film. "It'll get worse with Hong Kong. What's going to happen with Wong Kar-Wai?"

6 Wong said uncertainty after the July 1 handover of Hong Kong to China prompted him to hurry up and make *Happy Together,* the story of two homosexual men and their love-hate relationship as a **metaphor** for Hong Kong and China. "It's one of the reasons. I'm not sure if it's OK or not OK after the first of July," he said as he took a break from intense **roundtable**[5] interviews to walk on Cannes beach.

7 The 38-year-old director's French **new wave**[6]-inspired **cinematography** (*Chungking Express* and *Fallen Angels*) has drawn critical **acclaim** and become the **rage**[7] among many young Asian filmmakers.

[1]**Hong Kong's handover:** July 1, 1999 takeover of Hong Kong by the People's Republic of China

[2]**Golden Palm:** film award at Cannes Film Festival in France

[3]**nouveau riche:** French phrase meaning "newly-rich"

[4]**go-go:** energetic, lively

[5]**roundtable:** discussion with several participants

[6]**new wave:** experimental, unconventional style of filmmaking

[7]**rage:** fad, craze, very popular thing

8   That his film is a metaphor for China's re-unification? "You can apply it to that context also, but I won't say it," he said. Ironically, the poster used at the festival, of the two male characters horizontally **entwined a-la-swept away**,[8] was banned by the British-led government in Hong Kong, Wong said. Kiarostami exhibited great care in talking to the western media about his film, after Tehran **grudgingly** allowed his film to come to Cannes at the last minute.

9   Despite his film that portrays desperate living and appears to **poke fun at**[9] the Iranian military, "my intention was not to talk about Iranian society," he told a beach club luncheon. Filming the **bleak outskirts** of Tehran, Kiarostami tells the story of Badii, who is so tired of life that he drives around looking to hire someone to bury him alive as he lays in a **shallow** grave.

10   He finds a museum employee who is willing to help him, but insists on knowing why commit suicide in a world full of small pleasures. "You want to **deprive** yourself of the taste of the cherry? Then do it," he defies Badii.

11   In the end, one never knows if Badii ever went through with it. Kiarostami denied he was challenging the Muslim **taboo**—and thus Iran's **hardline** religious leadership—of discussing suicide. "I don't want to think politically. It's something international, universal," he said.

12   "All religions condemn suicide." But he added: "We as artists are to develop an idea, not to condemn it."

After You Read

U.S. astronaut Neil Armstrong's 1969 moon walk was not reported to the Chinese public, due to governmental censorship.

SOURCE: *ASIA MEDIA ONLINE GUIDE*

A. **Expressing the Main Idea:** What is the main idea of Reading 4? Write one sentence to tell the main idea, or find one sentence from the reading that expresses the main idea. Share your sentence with classmates.

B. **Analysis:** Discuss these questions with classmates:

1. The reading mentions China and Hong Kong. What do you know about the political relationship between these two places?

2. The reading describes a Chinese filmmaker whose movies have been censored by the Chinese government. Why do you think China has censored these films?

3. A film censored by the Iranian government is also mentioned here. The writer says the Iranian film was censored because it portrayed suicide, which is taboo in the Muslim religion. What other features in movies do you think the Muslim government might censor?

4. After reading this article, what do you see as some of the key reasons that a film might be censored?

---

[8]**a-la-swept away:** in the style of *Swept Away,* a French film about lovers

[9]**poke fun at:** make fun of

In 1997, 44% of all American homes were connected to the Internet.

SOURCE: *MOTION PICTURE ASSOCIATION OF AMERICA*

Reading Journal

Do you agree with the censorship that was described in Reading 4? Did the Chinese government have good reasons for censoring the films? Did the Iranian government have equally good reasons? Should governments or other groups censor movies? If so, what should be censored? Respond to these questions in your journal.

PUTTING IT ALL TOGETHER

 **Vocabulary Building**

Take this self-test to evaluate your knowledge of vocabulary words that you encountered in the chapter readings. Choose the word from the list that most appropriately completes each sentence.

portrayals	commentary	censor
graphic	wield	liberals
themes	biased	parental
conservatives	suitable	cautioned
coarse	signify	monitoring

1. Governments may _censor_ films that contain sexual situations, violence, or political criticism.

2. Some TV programs and films suggest that _parental_ guidance be used in determining whether children should view the shows.

3. In the U.S., the Motion Picture Association of America is a _monitoring_ organization for the movie industry.

4. _Graphic_ violence in the media refers to scenes that depict violent activities in realistic detail.

5. Conservatives believe that the media are _____ against their traditional values.

6. _Conservative_ claim that the media portray religion in a negative way.

7. Parents are _cautioned_ against allowing children to watch certain TV shows by the ratings on the screen.

8. _Coarse_ language is also called *obscenity*.

9. The "TVY" and "TVG" ratings _signify_ television programs that are designed for all ages.

10. Movies with "R" ratings are not considered _suitable_ for young children.

11. The media _portrayals_ of crime do not reflect real life, according to the author of Reading 2.

12. The film *Keep Cool* was considered to be a critical _commentary_ of Chinese social problems.

13. Governments _wield_ a great deal of power when they censor the media.

14. _Liberals_ are opposed to government censorship of the media.

15. _themes_ in television programs with the "TVY7" rating may include mild violence.

Final Project

Complete one of the projects listed below on your own, with a partner, or with a group of classmates.

A. Censorship of the Internet
Find at least *two* readings that describe efforts in the U.S. and worldwide to control the content of the Internet. Write a brief report that tells the main ideas of your readings and answers the following questions: What types of controls do governments or organizations seek to place on the Internet? Why are these controls sought? Who is seeking them? What is the status of their efforts?

B. Freedom of the Internet
Find at least *two* readings that describe efforts in the U.S. and worldwide to fight efforts to regulate the Internet. Write a brief report that tells the main ideas of your readings and answers the following questions: What types of controls do organizations or governments seek to place on the Internet? Why do some groups oppose regulation of the Internet? Who are the anti-Internet regulation groups? What are their arguments for keeping the Internet free? What is the status of their efforts?

C. Government Controls of a Medium
Find at least *two* readings that describe the controls that your native country or another country outside the U.S. places on one medium (i.e. movies, television, books, music, or textbooks). Write a brief report that tells the main ideas of your readings and answers the following questions: What types of regulations does the government of this country place on the medium? Explain the reasons given for the regulations, if they are provided in your readings.

D. Your "Rating" of a Movie or TV Show

Find at least *two* readings that describe a recent movie or current television program. The readings may be critical reviews of a movie or TV show, or a story that describes an upcoming show. After you read the texts, if possible, view all or part of the movie or show it describes. Write a brief report in which you tell the main idea of the readings and your opinion about whether the show they describe should be censored or not.

Share the information that you gained from your research in a brief presentation to classmates. Answer the following questions about your classmates' reports:

1. What is your reaction to the information from the readings?

2. Do you agree with the opinions of your classmate(s)? Why?

3. What did you learn from this presentation?

Test-Taking Tip

Use memory aids, such as acronyms, to remember information for tests. An acronym is a series of letters that make a word or phrase. Each letter in the word stands for the first letter of a word you are trying to remember. For example, many students in the United States, when learning about the Great Lakes, remember the word "HOMES": H (for Huron), O (For Ontario), M (for Michigan), E (for Erie), and S (for Superior). You can make up your own acronyms to help you remember information for tests.

CHECK YOUR PROGRESS

On a scale of 1 to 5, rate how well you have mastered the goals set at the beginning of the chapter:

1 2 3 4 5   decide in advance how you want to participate in class discussions of readings.

1 2 3 4 5   distinguish fact from opinion in readings.

1 2 3 4 5   group words into similar domains (groups) to remember new vocabulary.

If you've given yourself a 3 or lower on any of these goals:

- visit the *Tapestry* web site for additional practice.

- ask your instructor for extra help.

- review the sections of the chapter that you found difficult.

- work with a partner or study group to further your progress.

L ook at the photo. Then discuss these questions with your classmates:

- Does this person look like a typical shopper? Why or why not?
- Are American consumers different from consumers in other cultures that you know? If so, in what ways?
- What do you like to shop for the most? Why?

AFFLUENZA

Not everyone dreams of owning a mansion and a brand-new car. In recent years, there has been a worldwide trend toward simpler living and fewer material goods. Some people believe that we suffer from *affluenza*, "an epidemic of stress, overwork, waste, and indebtedness."

Setting Goals

In this chapter, you will learn how to:

◈ draw inferences from reading.

◈ communicate with your professors regularly.

◈ evaluate different viewpoints on a common subject.

What other goals do you have for this chapter? Write one or two of them here.

_____

_____

◆ **Getting Started**

The writers in this chapter present three topics related to consumers and material goods. Look at the titles of the readings and answer the questions that follow.

Readings:

"Affluenza"

"Does Economic Growth Improve Human Morale?" by David G. Myers, Ph.D.

"Keeping the American Dream" by Nha Dominic Cao Bui

1. Now that you have read the definition of *affluenza,* do you think such a problem exists? Why?

   _____

   _____

   _____

2. What does *economic growth* mean? What does *morale* mean? How might these two terms be connected?

   _____

   _____

   _____

3. What is the American Dream? Is it a positive or negative "dream"? Why?

   _____

   _____

   _____

4. Preview the photographs and charts in the chapter. What do these tell you about the topics of the readings?

   _____

   _____

   _____

◆ **Getting Ready to Read**

Mark each statement True (T) or False (F) to determine your views on consumption and spending. Compare your answers with classmates.

1. _____ Most of the things I do in my free time cost little or no money.

2. _____ I'm willing to pay more for clothing that has a designer label on it.

3. _____ Shopping cheers me up if I'm feeling sad or bored.

4. _____ The number of material goods a person owns shows how successful he or she is.

5. _____ I walk, ride public transportation, bicycle, or carpool to school.

6. _____ I spend a lot of time thinking about all the things that I want to buy.

7. _____ The most important consideration in choosing a career is how much money I'll make.

8. _____ One of my favorite pastimes is shopping.

9. _____ I'll be happier if I'm richer.

10. _____ I'm rarely influenced to make purchases because of advertisements I see on TV or in print.

11. _____ I stay in fashion by replacing my clothes often with new styles.

Vocabulary Check

Are you familiar with the vocabulary words below? Put a checkmark next to words you already know. Look up the meanings of new words in a dictionary, and add them to your Vocabulary Log. In your log, also write the sentence from Reading 1 in which each new word appears. Discuss the words with classmates.

_____ exceed	_____ indebtedness	_____ consumerism
_____ anti-consumer	_____ dogged	_____ chronically
_____ overconsumption	_____ unsustainable	_____ durability
_____ materialism	_____ addiction	_____ insatiable
_____ coined	_____ affluence	_____ quest
_____ bloated	_____ influenza	_____ discarding
_____ sluggish	_____ consumption	_____ consignment
_____ unfulfilled	_____ depleting	_____ harried
_____ epidemic	_____ induced	_____ exemption

Read

Reading 1: Affluenza

1   Modern-day families are buying more than ever before. The typical American family owns more goods than families fifty years ago—second cars and televisions, VCRs, CD players, and kitchen appliances and clothing that far **exceed** their living space. As the income of today's family has increased, so have the number and frequency of purchases.

2   For many people, economic growth and an increase in possessions are signs of progress, but for **anti-consumer** groups **overconsumption** and **materialism** are sicknesses. A recent Public Broadcasting Service documentary **coined** the term *affluenza,* which describes consumption of material goods in a strongly negative way:

> Af-flu-en-za *n.* 1. The **bloated, sluggish** and **unfulfilled** feeling that results from efforts to **keep up with the Joneses.**[1] 2. An **epidemic** of stress, overwork, waste and **indebtedness** caused by **dogged** pursuit of the American Dream. 3. An **unsustainable addiction** to economic growth.

3   The term *affluenza* combines two words: *affluence* and *influenza.* According to anti-consumer and environmental rights organizations, the high **consumption** lifestyles of affluence cause people to be less happy even though they are acquiring more "things." The major negative effect on the environment is that overconsumption is **depleting** the world's natural resources, anti-consumer groups argue.

4   Anti-consumer activist Noam Chomsky, a Massachusetts Institute of Technology professor, points out that the United States has five per cent of the world's population, yet consumes forty per cent of the world's resources. Chomsky believes that "a lot of that consumption is artificially **induced**—it doesn't have to do with people's real wants and needs. People would probably be better off and happier if they didn't have a lot of those things." Indeed, anti-consumer groups assert that without advertisements by corporations, people would be less likely to overconsume goods.

5   An activist group called Overcoming Consumption warns that **consumerism** causes people to **chronically** purchase "new goods and services, with little attention to their true need, **durability,** product origin or the environmental consequences of manufacture." Furthermore, the group observes that "an artificial, ongoing and **insatiable quest** for things and the money to buy them" has replaced "the normal desire for an adequate supply of life's necessities, community life, a stable family, and healthy relationships."

---

[1]**keep up with the Joneses:** match one's neighbors or friends in success or lifestyle

6   Today's families are replacing items much more frequently than in the past. For example, many Americans now treat clothing as "disposable," **discarding** clothes when fashion changes, and creating a boom in thrift stores, **consignment** shops, and yard sales. New Threads, a nonprofit clothing recycler, reports that the U.S.A.'s eighth largest export is now used clothes. About 2.5 million tons of unfashionable old clothes and rags are sold to Third World countries every year.

7   The anti-consumer movement has even produced a new holiday: Buy Nothing Day. The holiday began on Sept. 24, 1992, and has been observed every year since in the U.S. and 15 other countries on the day after Thanksgiving. It has evolved into a forum for consumer issues.

8   Organizations and publications have also attacked the advertising industry. Adbusters is a group that critically analyzes the content of advertising. Street Cents, a Canadian Broadcasting Corporation children's consumer program, awards "bouquets" to smart consumers. The show recently awarded a bouquet to the Lakehead School Board in Ontario for refusing to accept $200,000 from McDonald's, Coca-Cola, and Minute Maid to put ads on **computer screensavers**[2] in schools in their district. Books such as *Marketing Madness*, *Kids As Customers* and *Giving Kids the Business* negatively report that corporate advertisers and marketers are invading American life.

9   Books with anti-consumer messages are also filling bookstore shelves, with titles such as *How Much Is Enough*, *The **Harried** Leisure Class*, *The Poverty of Affluence*, *The Simple Living Guide*, and *Your Money or Your Life*.

10   In the U.S., the pre-Christmas season is the most active purchasing time. Recently, San Francisco area-environmental groups sponsored a meeting in Palo Alto, California, to discuss alternative holiday gift giving. Speakers encouraged participants to give "gift-**exemption** certificates" to friends and family members that say:

To _____:

Because . . . I already have plenty of great "stuff" in my home, because . . . the planet's resources are precious, because . . . you don't need to buy me something to show me that you care about me—I know that you do and I care about you, too—please don't buy me a gift this holiday season. Instead . . . take care of yourself, your loved ones, and celebrate the beauty of our planet's natural environment.

From _____.

Use it up, wear it out, make it do, or do without.

—NEW ENGLAND PROVERB

[2]**computer screensavers:** a program which keeps a computer screen active to avoid damage

After You Read

A. Reactions: Discuss these questions with classmates:

1. Do you believe that modern people suffer from *affluenza*? Why?

2. Do you or does someone you know have *affluenza*? Explain.

3. Is it wrong to want to have more things? Why or why not?

4. Do things make you happier? Why or why not?

B. Identifying Causes and Effects: Reading 1 discusses many causes and effects of *affluenza*. Match each of the following phrases to form a complete cause-and-effect sentence. Write the letter next to the appropriate number. Check your answers with one or more classmates.

Causes	Effects
_____ 1. As the income of today's family has increased,	a. cause people to be less happy.
_____ 2. High consumption lifestyles of affluence	b. so have the number and frequency of purchases.
_____ 3. Without advertisements by corporations,	c. An epidemic of stress, overwork, waste and indebtedness
_____ 4. Overconsumption	d. people would be less likely to overconsume goods.
_____ 5. is caused by the dogged pursuit of the American Dream.	e. is depleting the world's natural resources.

Reading Journal

Write about this topic in your journal: Do you or someone you know spend money unwisely? In what ways? What can be done to change unwise spending habits?

 Getting Ready to Read

Preview Reading 2 to find the headings. Discuss any unfamiliar vocabulary in the headings. Some of the headings are written as questions. Discuss these questions with classmates. For the headings written as statements, write questions about the ideas in the headings. Discuss those questions.

Vocabulary Check

Which of these words do you already know? Check them. Use a dictionary to find the meanings of new words. Discuss any "problem" words with your classmates. Add new words to your Vocabulary Log.

_____ sabbatical	_____ diminishing	_____ influx
_____ disconnection	_____ affliction	_____ recalibrating
_____ well-being	_____ devastation	_____ relics
_____ Spartan	_____ imposed	_____ morale
_____ well off	_____ able-bodied	_____ scrutinized
_____ caste	_____ underlie	_____ euphoria
_____ correlation	_____ deject	_____ pale (verb)
_____ negligible	_____ subtler	_____ utter

Read

As you read, try to find answers to the questions from the headings. This will help to focus your reading.

Reading 2: Does Economic Growth Improve Human Morale?

by David G. Myers, Ph.D.

1   During the mid-1980s, my family and I spent a **sabbatical** year in the historic town of St. Andrews, Scotland. Comparing life there with life in America, we were impressed by a seeming **disconnection** between national wealth and **well-being**. To most Americans, Scottish life would have seemed **Spartan**. Incomes were

about half that in the U.S. Among families in the Kingdom of Fife surrounding St. Andrews, 44 percent did not own a car, and we never met a family that owned two. Central heating in this place not far south of Iceland was, at that time, still a luxury.

2   In hundreds of conversations during our year there and during three half-summer stays since, we repeatedly noticed that, despite their simpler living, the Scots appeared no less joyful than Americans. We heard complaints about **Margaret Thatcher,**[1] but never about being underpaid or unable to afford wants. With less money, there was no less satisfaction with living, no less warmth of spirit, no less pleasure in one another's company.

Are Rich Americans Happier?

3 Within any country, such as our own, are rich people happier? In poor countries, such as Bangladesh and India, being relatively **well off** does make for somewhat greater well-being. Psychologically as well as materially, it is much better to be **high caste**[2] than low caste. We humans need food, rest, warmth, and social contact.

4   But in affluent countries, where nearly everyone can afford life's necessities, increasing affluence matters surprisingly little. In the U.S., Canada, and Europe, the **correlation** between income and happiness is, as University of Michigan researcher Ronald Inglehart noted in a 1980s 16-nation study, "surprisingly weak (indeed, virtually **negligible**)." Happiness is lower among the very poor. But once comfortable, more money provides **diminishing** returns. The second piece of pie, or the second $50,000, never tastes as good as the first. So far as happiness is concerned, it hardly matters whether one drives a BMW or, like so many of the Scots, walks or rides a bus.

5   Even very rich people—the **Forbes'**[3] 100 wealthiest Americans surveyed by University of Illinois psychologist Ed Diener—are only slightly happier than average. With net worths all exceeding $100 million, providing ample money to buy things they don't need and hardly care about, 4 in 5 of the 49 people responding to the survey agreed that "Money can increase OR decrease happiness, depending on how it is used." And some were indeed unhappy. One fabulously wealthy man said he could never remember being happy. One woman reported that money could not undo misery caused by her children's problems.

[1]**Margaret Thatcher:** former prime minister of Great Britain

[2]**high caste:** high social class

[3]**Forbes:** business magazine

Adapting to Fame, Fortune, and Affliction
••

6 At the other end of life's circumstances are most victims of disabling tragedies. With exceptions—vicious child abuse or rape, for example—most people who suffer negative life events do not exhibit long-term emotional **devastation.** People who become blind or paralyzed, perhaps after a car accident, thereafter suffer the frustrations **imposed** by their limitations. Daily, they must cope with the challenges imposed by their disabilities. Yet, remarkably, most eventually recover a near-normal level of day-to-day happiness. Thus, university students who must cope with disabilities are as likely as **able-bodied** students to report themselves happy, and their friends agree with their self-perceptions. "Weeping may linger for the night," observed the **Psalmist,**[4] "but joy comes with the morning."

7   These findings **underlie** an astonishing conclusion from the new scientific pursuit of happiness. As the late New Zealand researcher Richard Kammann put it, "Objective life circumstances have a negligible role to play in the theory of happiness." In a society where everyone lived in 4,000-square-foot houses, people would likely be no happier than in a society in which everyone lived in 2,000-square-foot houses. Good events—a pay hike, winning a big game, an A on an important exam—make us happy, until we adapt. And bad events—an argument with one's mate, a work failure, a social rejection—**deject** us, but seldom for more than a few days.

8   Feeling the short-run influence of events, people use such events to explain their happiness, all the while missing **subtler** but bigger influences on their long-run well-being. Noticing that an **influx** of cash feels good, they may accept the Hollywood, **Robin Leach**[5] image of who is happy—the rich and famous. In reality, we humans have an enormous capacity to adapt to fame, fortune, and affliction.

9   We adapt by **recalibrating** our "adaptation levels"—the neutral points at which sounds seem neither loud nor soft, lights neither bright nor dim, experiences neither pleasant nor unpleasant. Here in Michigan on a winter's day, 60 degrees would feel warm, but not when we are adapted to summer's heat. So it is with things. Our first desktop computer, with information loaded from a cassette tape, seemed remarkable, until we got that speedier hard-drive machine, which itself became **pokey**[6] once we got a faster, more powerful machine. So it happens that yesterday's luxuries become today's necessities and tomorrow's **relics.**

[4]**Psalmist:** taken from Psalm 30 in the Christian *Bible*

[5]**Robin Leach:** host of television program about lifestyles of the rich

[6]**pokey:** slow (slang)

Does Economic Growth Improve Human Morale?

10 We have **scrutinized** the American dream of achieved wealth and well-being by comparing rich and unrich countries, and rich and unrich people. That leaves the final question: Over time, does happiness rise with affluence?

11 Typically not. Lottery winners appear to gain but a temporary jolt of joy from their winnings. Looking back, they feel delighted to have won. Yet the **euphoria** doesn't last. In fact, previously enjoyed activities such as reading may become less pleasurable. Compared to the high of winning a million dollars, ordinary pleasures **pale.**

12 On a smaller scale, a jump in our income can boost our morale, for a while. "But in the long run," notes Inglehart, "neither an ice cream cone nor a new car nor becoming rich and famous produces the same feelings of delight that it initially did . . . Happiness is not the result of being rich, but a temporary consequence of having recently become richer." Ed Diener's research confirms that those whose incomes have increased over a 10-year period are not happier than those whose income has not increased. Wealth, it therefore seems, is like health: Although its **utter** absence can breed misery, having it does not guarantee happiness. Happiness is less a matter of getting what we want than of wanting what we have.

◄After You Read

A. Expressing the Main Idea: The title of Reading 2 is "Does Economic Growth Improve Human Morale?" What answer does the writer give in his reading? State the writer's main idea in one sentence. Briefly tell a classmate the writer's main point about what economic growth has done to human morale.

B. Analysis: Discuss the following questions with classmates:

1. Based on your understanding of Reading 2, do you agree with the author's description of how modern-day people spend money and live?

2. Do you think his assertion that people are less happier now, despite their possessions, is true? Why?

3. Briefly, how do *you* characterize the affluence and morale of the society in which you now live?

LANGUAGE LEARNING STRATEGY

Draw inferences, or conclusions, from your reading to fully understand a writer's meaning. Drawing inferences is often called "reading between the lines." This means that a successful reader can draw inferences, or conclusions, about a topic even when the conclusions are not directly stated in the reading. Reading 2 contains strong messages about economic growth. Although the writer has ideas, he does not always state his ideas directly because he wants the ideas presented to seem reasonable, and thus, persuasive. Understanding ideas that are stated indirectly helps you to grasp a writer's main idea as well as his or her purpose for writing.

Apply the Strategy

Read the following sentences from Reading 2. What does the writer mean to say about the subject? What is his main point? Discuss your ideas with a classmate. One sentence is done as an example.

> **EXAMPLE:** *Comparing life there with life in America, we were impressed by a seeming disconnection between national wealth and well-being.* (paragraph 1)
>
> The writer means that *Americans connect happiness with wealth.*

1. One fabulously wealthy man said he could never remember being happy. One woman reported that money could not undo misery caused by her children's problems. (par. 5)

2. In a society where everyone lived in 4,000-square-foot houses, people would likely be no happier than in a society in which everyone lived in 2,000-square-foot houses. (par. 7)

3. Noticing than an influx of cash feels good, they may accept the Hollywood, Robin Leach image of who is happy—the rich and famous. (par. 8)

4. Our first desktop computer, with information loaded from a cassette tape, seemed remarkable, until we got that speedier hard-drive machine, which itself became pokey once we got a faster, more powerful machine. (par. 9)

© CNN

TUNING IN: "Consumer Credit"

A. Pre-Viewing

1. Before you view the CNN video "Consumer Credit," take this test about personal debt which appears in the video. Answer each question with Yes or No as it applies to you or your household (the people that you live with, such as your parents or spouse). Leave blank any items that do not apply to you. Discuss your answers with your classmates.

_____ Are you using credit to pay for items for which you used to pay cash?

_____ Are your credit cards charged to the limit?

_____ Are you unsure how much you owe?

_____ Are you only able to make the minimum payment on your credit cards?

_____ If you lost your job, would you be in immediate financial trouble?

2. How do you think the average American would answer the above questions? Discuss your ideas with your classmates.

B. Discussion

As you view "Consumer Credit," find the answers to these questions. Discuss your answers with classmates after you view.

1. In 1996, how many Americans filed for bankruptcy?

2. How did the couple in the video clip manage their debt?

3. What do you call organizations or programs that help people with their credit or debt problems? Listen for several names in the video clip.

4. Is consumer credit rising or dropping in the U.S.? By what percentage?

Reading Journal

In your journal, write about these questions: How does the affluence of the society you are living in now compare with other societies you know well? In general, are people richer or poorer? Do they have more material possessions? Do they rely on credit cards more than in other societies? Explain.

ACADEMIC POWER STRATEGY

Communicate with your professors regularly in order to discuss your academic progress and obtain extra help. College and university professors commonly complain that students distance themselves from teachers. One professor said, "I expect students to go halfway with me if they need extra help." "Going halfway" means communicating with your professor regularly. To do this, familiarize yourself with your professors' offices and office hours. Make appointments to discuss your progress and to get extra assistance with problem assignments or difficult topics. In time, a professor may also become a mentor to guide you through the college environment, or provide you with job and college transfer recommendation letters.

Apply the Strategy

Find out the office hours of one of your professors. Make an appointment with him or her to discuss your academic progress or a difficult topic in your course. Here are some areas that you may wish to discuss with your instructor:

1. your current grade

2. any missing assignments

3. your overall progress in learning

4. suggestions for building skills

5. recommendations for the next course

6. questions about a topic that you find difficult

Getting Ready to Read

Reading 3, "Keeping the American Dream," was written by a Vietnamese-American. Before you read, discuss these questions with classmates:

1. What is the American dream? Do you think the American Dream is a good dream? Why?

> Poverty often deprives a man of all spirit and virtue; it is hard for an empty bag to stand upright.
>
> —BENJAMIN FRANKLIN

2. Do you think people in your native country believe that most Americans are rich, middle-class, or poor? Where do they get their ideas?

3. Do people in your native country believe that you can become rich by emigrating to other countries?

4. What kind of job, house, and life does the typical person in your country dream of having?

Vocabulary Check

Check the words you already know. Work with a partner to find the meanings of new words. If you need to, use a dictionary. You can add any new words you learn to your Vocabulary Log.

_____ myth	_____ magnificent	_____ anticipation
_____ perpetuate	_____ skyscraper	_____ instilled

 Read

Reading 3: Keeping the American Dream

by Nha Dominic Cao Bui

1   I spent the first seven years of my life in a small Vietnamese town named Vung Tao, in a community of closely bonded people who shared beliefs and ideas. We based our view of America mainly on letters and pictures from our relatives. To our community, America was a land of freedom and opportunity and also a land of great wealth. It seemed that there was paradise on Earth, after all. America was a country where no one goes hungry, everyone has wealth, and people live in harmony with each other. I know that this is a **myth,** yet I continue to **perpetuate** it.

2   In our small town, whenever a family got a letter from a relative in America, the letter was shared with everyone. In these letters, our relatives told us only about how good life was for them. They would mention their successes and not their problems, so that we would not worry. By revealing only the good aspects of their lives, they protected us, but as a result, our view of America was shaped falsely.

3   Pictures from our relatives served as physical evidence of the words written in their letters. They strengthened our false ideas of America because we could see with our own eyes what we had read. In one picture, our relatives wore beautiful clothes as they stood smiling with a **magnificent skyscraper** in the background. In another, they posed in front of a new car with snow covering the ground and trees. When the holidays arrived, we received

pictures of flashing Christmas trees with presents stacked high. America was clearly a land of riches, with plenty of material goods and easy access to them.

4   From time to time, my family would receive packages from our relatives in America. One day, our neighbors gathered at my house because a package had arrived. Everyone was filled with **anticipation.** This particular box contained beautiful clothes for my family and a set of colorful toy cars for me. These cars were just pieces of red, blue and yellow metal on wheels that rolled with a gentle push; they were not motorized or able to be transformed into robots. But I treasured them like a person who has found a rock from outer space. They were from America and they belonged only to me.

5   We believed deeply in the stories and myths of America, and our beliefs were revealed whenever we acquired an object related to America. One afternoon, a boy had bought an apple. Apples, which are rare in my town, were known to us as an American fruit. All of the neighborhood children, including me, gathered around him. He held the red and shining fruit in his hand. It was as if it had come straight from the **Garden of Eden.**[1] Each of us wanted a bite of that apple. If we could just have a small bite of that apple, then we could taste America.

6   Since arriving in America, I have come to understand that what was **instilled** in me as a child was a myth. I see that America is not only a country of wealth and riches but also a country of homelessness and poverty. Yet when I write back to Vietnam, it is of the successes in America. When I send a picture, there is still a tall skyscraper or a car in the background. I know that I am helping to create for my people the same false ideas of America that I had as a child, but I think they are necessary. My people have a need for dreams. I want them to live each day knowing that there could be something better for them. I do what I can to make sure that they do not lose their dreams.

> We grew up founding our dreams on the infinite promise of American advertising.
>
> —ZELDA FITZGERALD

 **After You Read**

Reactions: Discuss these questions with classmates:

1. Was the author right to describe America as a land of riches? Why?

2. The author also describes America as a "country of homelessness and poverty." Is this characterization also accurate? Why?

3. Do you or someone you know do the same thing as the author—describe life in the country you are living in now as better than

[1]**Garden of Eden:** the "paradise" of Christianity, Judaism, and Islam

life in your native country in order to perpetuate the dreams of the people in your native country? If so, what do you (or someone you know) tell people in your native country about the country you are living in?

LANGUAGE LEARNING STRATEGY

Evaluate different viewpoints and ideas on a common subject to become a critical reader. This will help you think carefully and reach *your own* conclusion.

When you read extensively on one subject, you are likely to encounter different views about the same topics. Readings 2 and 3 both discuss material goods; however, they take different views about the value of possessions. The author of Reading 2 shows that more material wealth does not make people happier. In contrast, the author of Reading 3 shows how material possessions represent hope and happiness. Critical readers recognize that different sources often present very different views on the same subject. Knowing this, they can identify the different ideas, think carefully, and evaluate them.

Apply the Strategy

Read the following sets of sentences taken from Readings 2 and 3. Think about the main points of the sentences from each reading. Fill in the statements following the chart to describe each author's view of material goods. Then, decide which of the two views you prefer. Complete the statement to explain your evaluation. Be prepared to present and discuss your statements with classmates.

DIFFERENT VIEWS FROM TWO SOURCES	
Reading 2	**Reading 3**
So far as happiness is concerned, it hardly matters whether one drives a BMW or, like so many of the Scots, walks or rides a bus.	*In one picture, our relatives wore beautiful clothes as they stood smiling with a magnificent skyscraper in the background.*
Wealth, it therefore seems, is like health: Although its utter absence can breed misery, having it does not guarantee happiness.	*When I send a picture, there is still a tall skyscraper or a car in the background. I know that I am helping to create for my people the same false ideas of America that I had as a child, but I think they are necessary.*
Happiness is less a matter of getting what we want than of wanting what we have.	*I want them to live each day knowing that there could be something better for them.*

The author of Reading 2 believes that _____

_____

_____

_____

The author of Reading 3 believes that _____

_____

_____

_____

I agree with the views in Reading _____ because _____

_____

_____

_____

PUTTING IT ALL TOGETHER

Vocabulary Building

1. As you learned in Chapter 6, studying vocabulary by domain (or group) can help you remember new words. Study the following lists of groups of words, taken from the chapter readings. Review the definitions of the words in your Vocabulary Log.

   With one or more classmates, group the words into the six domains listed below. Discuss your groupings with your entire class. Then, put the words in your log again, putting them in the appropriate groups. Do the activities that follow.

   Words about Having Too Many Things

   Words about Happiness

   Words about Unhappiness

   Words about Sickness

   Words that mean "Not Enough"

   Words about Poverty

overconsumption	indebtedness	affliction
despondent	elation	unsustainable
keep up with the Joneses (slang)	unfulfilled	depleting
well-being	materialism	addiction
diminishing	anguish	privation
euphoria	epidemic	impoverishment

2. Use the following words to complete the paragraph. Use each word only once.

unsustainable	indebtedness	unfulfilled
well-being	epidemic	overconsumption

Affluenza is an _____ that is afflicting
many people today, according to the writers in Chapter 7. Nowa-
days, people have an insatiable desire to buy more things. This
_____ does not increase people's sense of
elation or _____; instead, it makes people
feel _____ and despondent. When people
try to keep up with the Joneses by acquiring more and more possessions, they spend too much money. Their _____
can cause them stress. Some people today don't like materialism
because they say that producing more things may deplete the
world's _____ resources.

3. Discuss the completed paragraph above with classmates. With a
partner, look again at the lists of vocabulary by domain. Are
there other words from the lists that could be used to complete
the sentences in the paragraph? Write those words above the appropriate blanks. Discuss your word choices with classmates.

Reading Journal

Write a journal entry that describes your views about materialism.
Do you consider yourself materialistic? How do you feel about material possessions? What level of affluence would you like in your lifetime? What material "things" will make you happy? After reading

the articles in Chapter 7, have you changed your ideas about materialism? Why or why not? Which of the ideas in the readings affected the way you think about material goods?

Final Project

Complete one of the projects listed below.

A. Simple Living Sites on the Internet

On your own, find at least *two* of the following Web sites (or any other appropriate sites that you find) that deal with simplifying your life. Each of these sites contains a vast amount of information, so from each site, select three to five ideas that interest you. Write a brief report that explains the main points that you found on each Web site. Use the article "Evaluating Web Sites" of Appendix B as a resource.

Suggested Web sites:

The Simple Living Network	http://www.slnet.com
Seeds of Simplicity	http://www.seedsofsim@aol.com
Overcoming Consumerism	http://www.hooked.net/users/ verdant/index.htm
Voluntary Simplicity and Financial Independence	http://www.scn.org/earth/lightly/
Tightwad Gazette Fan Club	http://users.aol.com/maryfou/ tightwad.html
PBS Online: *Affluenza*	http://www.pbs.org/kcts/affluenza/ treat/resources.html
Center for the New American Dream	http://www.cnad.org

B. Comparing Affluence in Two Countries

With a partner, find at least *two* readings that describe the levels of wealth of two countries. Do not select very short readings from encyclopedias that quantify the average income of persons in a country. Instead, find a book or periodical article in your library that describes the country's wealth in more detail. Try to answer the following questions about each country: How much money does the average person earn in the country? How has this amount changed in recent years? How does this salary relate to how much people typically pay for housing? Food? Write a brief report that describes the level of affluence of people in the two countries. Your report may contain other main ideas from the readings that you think are important and/or interesting.

C. Living on a Budget

With a group of classmates, make a budget for living in your local area. To prepare your budget, research living costs in your area through the classified ads and newspaper advertisements. Use these sources to calculate monthly expenses in the following categories: housing, utilities, food, clothing, transportation, miscellaneous (haircuts, cosmetics, etc.), and entertainment.

Group members should share the tasks of researching and presenting information. Write your budget on the blackboard and explain the details of your living costs to your entire class. Be prepared to share your sources of information.

As you listen to the Final Project presentations, answer the following questions about your classmates' reports:

1. What is your reaction to the information from your classmates' research?

2. Do you agree with the opinions of your classmate(s)? Why or why not?

3. What did you learn from this presentation?

Test-Taking Tip

Recite information out loud when studying for a test. Verbalize the information you have studied in as complete and detailed a manner as you can. By actually speaking out loud the information you have studied, you can see how well you have retained and understood what you have studied.

CHECK YOUR PROGRESS

On a scale of 1 to 5, rate how well you have mastered the goals set at the beginning of the chapter:

1 2 3 4 5   draw inferences from reading.

1 2 3 4 5   communicate with your professors regularly.

1 2 3 4 5   evaluate different viewpoints on a common subject.

If you've given yourself a 3 or lower on any of these goals:

- visit the *Tapestry* web site for additional practice.
- ask your instructor for extra help.
- review the sections of the chapter that you found difficult.
- work with a partner or study group to further your progress.

L ook at the photo. Then discuss these questions with your
classmates:

• What does this photo tell you about life in this ancient Indian
culture?

• How do you think this culture may have influenced modern
cultures?

ANCIENT AMERICANS

T he date when the first people came to North America remains a mystery. Many scientists believe that a land bridge between Siberia and Alaska allowed early humans to travel to the North American continent. However, the date, the number of crossings, and the interaction among different groups all remain uncertain.

Setting Goals

In this chapter, you will learn how to:

◈ create time lines to help you recall dates and events in readings.

◈ distinguish main ideas from supporting ideas in readings.

◈ practice peer testing to prepare for examinations.

What other goals do you have for this chapter? Write one or two of them here.

_____

_____

 **Getting Started**

The writers in this chapter present four topics related to ancient Americans. Look at the titles of the readings and answer the questions that follow.

Readings:

"The First Americans"

"Ways of Life Change"

"Trading Networks"

"Ancient Mound Builders"

1. According to the chapter introduction, where may the first Americans have come from? What ethnic group would they have resembled?

   _____

   _____

2. What difficulties do you think ancient Americans faced? How could they change their lives to overcome the difficulties?

   _____

   _____

3. Different native American groups traded goods in ancient times. What types of things might they have traded?

   _____

   _____

4. Large earthen *burial mounds* were once used in ancient cultures. Why might the first Americans have buried their dead in this way?

   _____

   _____

5. Preview the photos and charts in the chapter. What do these tell you about the topics of the readings?

   _____

   _____

 **Getting Ready to Read**

A. Read this excerpt from a textbook. Discuss the different work of these three types of scientists with classmates.

Archeologists are scientists who study the material things of past human life and activities. They seek to reconstruct, or describe, the cultures of people who no longer exist. **Anthropologists** study the physical, cultural, and social factors of human behavior. **Geologists** examine the history and physical structure of the earth.

B. Read the groups of words in the following chart. Are they familiar? Look up any new words in your dictionary, and record the words and definitions in your Vocabulary Log. Match the scientists and their work by drawing a line to connect one word or words in each column of the chart to form a logical sentence. The sentences may be completed in more than one way. Discuss possible answers with classmates and your instructor.

Archeologists	discover	people to research their social structure.
		houses and other historic sites.
	excavate	rocks to determine their age.
Anthropologists		skeletal remains of ancient people.
	examine	tools and pottery of lost civilizations.
Geologists	live with	the evidence of ancient glaciers on the Earth's surface.

 Read

Reading 1: The First Americans

1 Geologists tell us that for thousands of years, great glaciers covered the northern regions of the world. Sheets of ice extended as far south as present-day Pennsylvania and Kansas in North America and present-day London, Kiev, and Krakow in Europe. Asia had fewer glaciers, but ice did cover most of Siberia. Because so much of the earth's moisture was locked up in great glacial sheets, part of the floor of the Bering Strait was exposed from time to time, forming a land bridge between northeastern Asia and Alaska.

Early Migrations

2 Many geologists believe this land bridge was open twice, first from about 40,000 to 32,000 years ago and again from about 20,000 to 10,000 years ago. This suggests that there were periods of several thousand years when human beings could simply have walked the fifty miles or so that separated Siberia from Alaska.

Possible Route of the First Americans, 40,000–10,000 B.C.

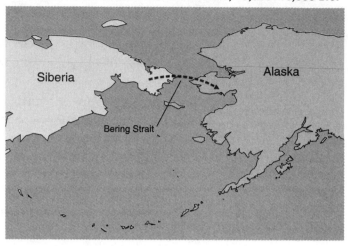

But, as some archeologists believe, it is also possible that people walked across the ice, or crossed in boats during the summer. It is known that boats or rafts carried the first people to Australia some 40,000 to 30,000 years ago, so a short voyage from Asia to America was certainly possible. The question of whether the Asian immigrants crossed the Bering Strait by walking across dry land, by walking across ice, or by crossing the open water in boats is important. The answer might help scholars to determine both when migrations occurred and how many migrations there were.

3   Because traces of human life have been found in many regions of the American continents, archeologists once believed that many separate, small groups moved into the Americas over thousands of years. They thought that each of these groups had different sets of ancestors. More recent theories about the migrations of Paleo-Indians (*paleo* means "old") to America come from considering such evidence as comparisons of the languages spoken by Indians and Asians of today, and of the tooth shapes of both populations. Neither basic language structures nor tooth shape changes much over time. Through study of these two traits in both American and Asian populations, many archeologists now believe that there were only three separate migrations of unrelated peoples who came to America at widely-spaced time periods.

4   A recent theory based on genetics holds that the first migrants came across the land bridge 40,000 to 20,000 years ago. The second migration probably came by sea some 12,000 to 6,000 years ago and blended with the existing Paleo-Indian groups. The third migration, 10,000 to 5,000 years ago, included Inuits, who stayed in Alaska and Western Canada, and the Navajo and Apache, who slowly moved to the Southwest about a thousand years ago.

English Names for the First Americans:

U.S.
   "Native Americans"

Canada and Alaska
   "American Indians"

5   Archeological and anthropological studies continue. Every
year brings more data, and scholars still seek to solve the myster-
ies surrounding the origins of the first Americans.

 **After You Read**

Write one sentence that expresses the main idea of the textbook passage, "The First Americans." Remember that the main idea sentence
should state the main *topic* of the reading as well as *what the reading says about* the topic. Compare your sentence with classmates'
sentences.

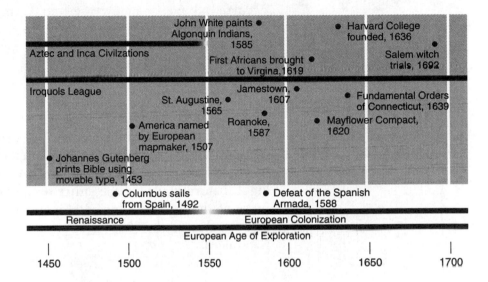

Aztec and Inca Civilzations

John White paints
Algonquin Indians,
1585

First Africans brought
to Virgina,1619

Harvard College
founded, 1636

Salem witch
trials, 1692

Iroquols League

Jamestown,
1607

St. Augustine,
1565

America named
by European
mapmaker, 1507

Roanoke,
1587

Johannes Gutenberg
prints Bible using
movable type, 1453

Fundamental Orders
of Connecticut, 1639

Mayflower Compact,
1620

Columbus sails
from Spain, 1492

Defeat of the Spanish
Armada, 1588

Renaissance   European Colonization

European Age of Exploration

1450   1500   1550   1600   1650   1700

LANGUAGE LEARNING STRATEGY

Create time lines to help you to recall important dates and events
after you read an historical text. "The time line is a visual tool
that is used to show the flow of history," according to historians
Matthew Downey, James Giese, and Fay Metcalf. As the sample
above illustrates, a time line is a horizontal line on which a person
can record dates and events. The information is recorded in left-to-
right order above or below the line. A time line shows the reader a
chronology of events. "Having a sense of chronology can help us
understand how events relate to each other," Downey, Giese and

(continued on next page)

Metcalf write. The time line is also a powerful study tool; it allows you to isolate important dates and events from your reading, restate them in a simple, visual form, and study them.

Apply the Strategy

With a partner or small group of classmates, read over "The First Americans" and circle the most important dates and events. Create a time line similar to the example on page 163 in which you place important dates on the line and brief descriptions of the events that occurred above or below the line. Compare your time line with classmates. Did your groups put the same information on the time line? Discuss which ideas are the most important.

◆ **Getting Ready to Read**

Reading 2, "Ways of Life Change," is a continuation of the history presented in Reading 1. The topics listed in the box below represent areas of change in the lives of ancient Americans presented in Reading 2. Before you read the entire text, scan the reading to find the types of changes that ancient Americans experienced at this time. List the changes by the topics in the box. Compare your list with classmates.

Ways that Ancient Americans' Lives Changed	
Weapons	
Animals	
Weather	
Crops	
Division of Work	

Vocabulary Check

Check the words you already know. Find the new words in your dictionary. Write the new words and definitions in your Vocabulary Log.

_____ wild game   _____ domesticated

_____ subsisting   _____ surplus

_____ spear   _____ fashioning (verb)

_____ flint   _____ artisans

_____ slay   _____ handiwork

_____ extinct   _____ tribute

_____ derived   _____ hereditary

_____ fertile   _____ nobility

_____ agricultural revolution   _____ irrigation

Read Reading 2: Ways of Life Change

1 There is some clear-cut evidence about the ways of life of the early Americans. Archeological digs provide data indicating that Paleo-Indians followed **wild game,** killing animals when they could and **subsisting** on wild plants when a hunt was not successful. Sites from 12,000 to about 10,000 years ago show that big-game hunters used well-crafted **spear** points made from **flint** and flint-like rocks. These large points could penetrate such huge game animals as the woolly mammoth, the mastodon, and the giant bison. Hunters set up kill sites by water holes and springs where the animals would come to drink. There the hunters could **slay** them **at will.**[1] With an abundance of food, the people could stay in one place for long periods of time.

2   About 9,000 to 7,000 years ago, the Archaic Era began. The climate slowly changed, and glacial ice melted. The warmer period turned grasslands into near deserts. Huge game animals became **extinct.** Archaic Indians learned to hunt for other animals, such as deer, elk, and a smaller species of bison, and they became more dependent on fishing and gathering edible plants. As Archaic Indians turned to new sources of food **derived** from plants, some people realized that wild seeds could be planted and would grow in moist, **fertile** soil. This discovery, a great technological breakthrough called the **agricultural revolution,** occurred independently in widely separated parts of the world.

3   In the Americas, several crops were **domesticated,** but the most important was maize, or Indian corn. It was grown in Mesoamerica, which included parts of what are now Mexico and Central America. Indian corn became a dependable food crop, and knowledge of its

[1]**at will:** whenever they wanted

cultivation spread to both North and South America. Other plants first domesticated in the Americas include squash, pumpkins, tomatoes, sweet potatoes, beans, bell and chili peppers, and tobacco.

Division of Labor

4   People who depended on **domesticated** crops needed to stay near their fields to care for their crops and to set up storage facilities for **surplus** food. As their need to gather wild plants and chase game diminished, many groups settled in permanent villages. Because only some of the people were needed to grow crops, labor became specialized. The needs and wants of the community were divided up, and different tasks were done by different people with special skills. In most farming areas, men cleared the fields and continued to hunt while women planted, cultivated, and harvested the crops. Some people became so expert at **fashioning** weapons, pottery, or cloth that they no longer participated in farming. Others in a village would provide these **artisans** with food in exchange for their **handiwork.**

5   Religious or political leaders became the rulers in some societies because of their supposed ability to communicate with the gods or because of their military strength. They organized work groups and demanded goods and surplus crops as **tribute** (a payment made for protection). These leaders and their relatives became a **hereditary nobility** that ruled over the rest of the people. As their power grew, the nobility forced the ordinary people to build large temples to glorify the gods, **irrigation** ditches to water their crops, and roads to help them extend their power over more and more people.

After You Read

Expressing the Main Idea: Write a sentence to express the main idea of Reading 2. Compare your sentence with classmates and refine your sentence to make it more accurate, if necessary.

LANGUAGE LEARNING STRATEGY

Distinguish main ideas from supporting ideas to recognize what's most important in what you read. In academic texts, one paragraph may contain more than one important idea supported by details or facts. Being able to read a text and separate the most important, main ideas from less important, supporting ideas is a useful academic skill. Successful students mentally distinguish main from supporting ideas. In writing a research paper, a student may summarize the main idea of a text. Responding to an essay examination question may require the student to state main ideas followed by supporting ideas. A multiple-choice (A, B, C, or D choice) examination may test a student's knowledge of supporting ideas. Supporting ideas may be descriptive or narrative details, facts, statistics, or examples.

Apply the Strategy

Underline the main ideas in the following paragraphs from Readings 1 and 2. The main ideas in the first paragraph have been underlined as an example. Compare your answers with classmates.

1. <u>Geologists tell us that for thousands of years great glaciers covered the northern regions of the world</u>. Sheets of ice extended as far south as present-day Pennsylvania and Kansas in North America and present-day London, Kiev, and Krakow in Europe. Asia had fewer glaciers, but ice did cover most of Siberia. <u>Because so much of the earth's moisture was locked up in great glacial sheets, part of the floor of the Bering Strait was exposed from time to time, forming a land bridge between northeastern Asia and Alaska</u>. (Reading 1, par. 1)

2. About 9,000 to 7,000 years ago, the Archaic Era began. The climate slowly changed, and glacial ice melted. The warmer period turned grasslands into near deserts. Huge game animals became extinct. Archaic Indians learned to hunt for other animals, such as deer, elk, and a smaller species of bison, and they became more dependent on fishing and gathering edible plants. As Archaic Indians turned to new sources of food derived from plants, some people realized that wild seeds could be planted and would grow in moist, fertile soil. This discovery, a great technological breakthrough called the agricultural revolution, occurred independently in widely separated parts of the world. (Reading 2, par. 2)

3. Religious or political leaders became the rulers in some societies because of their supposed ability to communicate with the gods or because of their military strength. They organized work groups and demanded goods and surplus crops as tribute (a payment made for protection). These leaders and their relatives became a hereditary nobility that ruled over the rest of the people. As their power grew, the nobility forced the ordinary people to build large temples to glorify the gods, irrigation ditches to water their crops, and roads to help them extend their power over more and more people. (Reading 2, par. 5)

Getting Ready to Read

Reading 3 tells you more about the development of native American cultures. Before you read, discuss these questions with a group of classmates:

1. What is a "trading network"?

2. Why do you think native Americans would want to create such networks?

3. Which goods do you think would have been the most valuable items to trade in ancient times?

4. Besides goods, what other things might native Americans have traded?

Vocabulary Check

Check the words that you already know. Look up unfamiliar words in the dictionary. Write the words, their definitions, and a sentence using each word in your Vocabulary Log. Check your sentences with your instructor.

_____ vast   _____ projectile   _____ profoundly

_____ obsidian   _____ waging   _____ sacrifice

Read

Reading 3: Trading Networks

1   Domesticated crops led to surplus food; specialized labor led to the development of goods that could be traded. Both foods and goods served as items of exchange in the trading networks that quickly spread across **vast** regions of the Americas. Salt for seasoning and preserving food, **obsidian** and flint for the **projectile** points of spears and arrows, bird feathers for clothing and decoration, and seashells and copper for jewelry became valued exchange goods. They also brought fresh ideas and new technologies for farming, hunting, fishing, or **waging** war. While not all American Indians adopted the practice of agriculture, most were **profoundly** influenced by the trading networks.

2   The Olmecs, who lived on the Gulf shore of present-day Mexico, were particularly influential. Called a mother culture because so much of their way of life was adopted by other people, the Olmecs lived in a society that had many classes of people. Religious leaders and merchants were the most powerful and formed the highest classes. Farmers and laborers formed the lowest class. The Olmecs built great temples on large mounds of earth. They developed a form of writing that used images

Ancient Chinese writing found on native American pottery has led a few scholars to suggest that native Americans originated in China.

SOURCE: *OMNI* MAGAZINE

and symbols to stand for ideas and words. Their calendar became the basis for a later Mayan calendar that was more accurate than any in Europe at the time. They played a game much like soccer on ball fields as large as today's football fields. Like other cultures of the time, the Olmecs may have practiced human **sacrifice.**

3   Because the Olmecs conducted trade both by land and along coastal waters, covering a vast network, their way of life spread. They had a direct influence on many societies in Mesoamerica. Through the many trading networks, the Olmecs also seem to have had an indirect influence on the peoples of the Southwest. However, the greater the distance between the cultures, the more difficult it is to trace Olmec influences.

 **After You Read**

A. Identifying Causes and Effects: Reread paragraph 1 of Reading 3. Does this paragraph focus on the *causes* or the *effects* of an action? Does it describe many *causes*? Does it present many *effects*? Share your ideas with a partner.

B. Creating a Graphic Organizer: Make a graphic similar to the one below to visually show the main *causes* or *effects* explained in this paragraph. Note that the number of causes or effects presented in the paragraph may not exactly match the sample graphic.

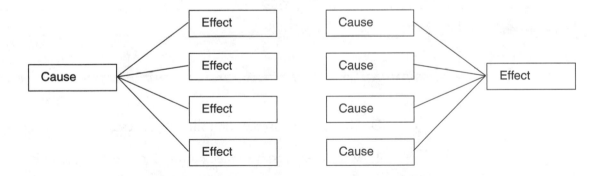

C. Distinguishing Main Ideas from Support: Reread paragraphs 2 and 3 of Reading 3. They each contain a main idea sentence and supporting ideas. The support consists of main supporting points supported by descriptive details and facts. Complete the chart on the following page to identify the main ideas and supporting ideas in paragraph 2. Some of the information has been supplied. Draw another chart to represent the main ideas and supporting ideas in paragraph 3. Review the ideas in both charts with a small group of classmates.

MAIN IDEAS AND SUPPORTING IDEAS IN READING 3	
Paragraph 2	
Main Idea Sentence:	
Main Supporting Point 1: Supporting Details:	Had classes
Main Supporting Point 2: Supporting Details:	
Main Supporting Point 3: Supporting Details:	Used writing
Main Supporting Point 4: Supporting Details:	
Main Supporting Point 5: Supporting Details:	Similar to soccer
Main Supporting Point 6:	

D. Reactions: Discuss the following questions in your group:

1. Which aspects of Olmec culture have influenced cultures today?

2. Which parts of their culture do you find the most interesting? Why?

◆Getting Ready to Read

Reading 4, "Ancient Mound Builders," describes the ways in which several native American cultures buried their dead. Before you read, discuss the following questions with classmates:

1. What is a "mound"? What do you imagine an earthen burial mound might look like?

2. What items do you think archeologists have uncovered in burial mounds?

3. What information might an anthropologist learn about life in an ancient culture by excavating a burial mound?

Vocabulary Check

Put check marks next to words you already know, and find new words in the dictionary. Discuss their meanings with classmates. Work with a partner to write original sentences in which you use each new word. Write new words in your Vocabulary Log.

_____ ironies	_____ creek
_____ tract	_____ bluff
_____ complexity	_____ earthen
_____ collectively	_____ exquisite
_____ flourished	_____ afterlife
_____ conical	_____ artifacts
_____ corpses	_____ drought
_____ tombs	

Reading 4: Ancient Mound Builders

1 One of the small **ironies** of history occurred in 1787, when the planners of Marietta, Ohio, discovered some ancient remains at the center of their new city. One feature was a carefully formed mound, 30 feet high and surrounded by a nearly circular wall. The planners did not know what the mound was for, but they preserved it in a **tract** set aside for the city cemetery. It was later discovered that the mound was one of those used for centuries as burial grounds by ancient people of the Hopewell culture. Without knowing what they were doing, the people of Marietta simply enclosed one cemetery within another. But they can hardly be blamed for not realizing what lay within the mound they fortunately preserved. Clues to the **complexity** and diversity of early American Indian societies are still being discovered.

2   The mound of earth that the people of Marietta found is only one of thousands that once spread across the lands along the Ohio and Mississippi valleys. They were built by groups of people **collectively** known to us as Mound Builders. While it is certainly possible that these different cultures decided on their own to

build mounds, it is also possible that they learned of the idea from migrants from Mesoamerica or from their trading partners. These trading partners included people of Mexico and people living as far north as the Great Lakes.

3   The Adena people, who are generally held to be responsible for the Great Serpent Mound in Ohio, may have **flourished** between 1000 B.C. and A.D. 200. Members of this culture grew some plants—pumpkins, gourds, and sunflowers—but they were primarily hunters and gatherers. Their burial mounds were **conical** and dome-shaped with the **corpses** placed in log-lined **tombs.** Other distinctive mounds were sometimes shaped like animals, such as the Great Serpent Mound itself, which stretches a quarter mile from tail to jaw along a **creek bluff** near Cincinnati.

4   **Earthen** mounds from the Hopewell culture dating between 300 B.C. and A.D. 700 were larger than those of the Adena. Many of their huge mounds were shaped like birds, snakes, or humans. The people of the Hopewell culture were particularly artistic. Found buried along with human bodies were **exquisite** carvings of birds and animals, as well as jewelry made of pearls, worked copper, and grizzly bear teeth. These valuable items suggest the people believed they would have some use in an **afterlife.** They practiced more extensive agriculture than the Adena, and they had a stricter class system.

5   A third great mound-building society, known as the Mississippian, reached its peak about A.D. 1100. Across the Mississippi River from present-day St. Louis, the city of Cahokia had a population of 20,000 to 30,000 people and over 1,000 mounds. It was the largest city in North America before the arrival of the Europeans. Monk's Mound, the largest of the mounds, spanning 15 acres, is a temple once inhabited by the Great Sun, Cahokia's god-like leader. Both the size of the structures of this Mississippean people and the superior workmanship of their **artifacts** indicate a highly sophisticated culture.

6   The region of mound cities stretched from present-day Oklahoma to the western edge of West Virginia, and from present-day Louisiana to Indiana and Ohio. Long before European explorers first entered this region most of the cities had been deserted. No one can be certain of why the people moved from these mound cities. They may have suffered a **drought,** they may have worn out their farm land, or they may have simply decided that they wanted to explore new territory. At any rate, some of the largest tribes of the Southeast such as the Creek, Cherokee, and Catawba seem to have been influenced by the Mississippian people, and the Choctaw and Chickasaw may even be descended from Mississippian groups. Natchez, a temple mound site in modern-day

Mississippi, was still inhabited when it was visited by the French in the 1720s. It provided important evidence about the complexity of the Mound Builders' culture.

After You Read

Creating a Time Line: Continue the time line that you produced on page 164 to represent the main dates and events in Reading 1. Extend your time line to include the main dates/events described in Readings 2, 3, and 4. Include the most important dates and brief descriptions of events presented in the readings. Compare your time line with a partner's. Discuss your time lines with your entire class.

Reading Journal

What do you think about the ancient native American ways of burial? Do they seem reasonable? Do they remind you of the burial practices of other cultures? Explain your ideas in a reading journal entry.

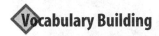
Vocabulary Building

Use the following words to complete the paragraph below about Reading 4. Use all the words once only.

earthen	artifacts
irony	corpses
exquisite	tombs
mound	conical
complexity	

In 1787, officials in Marietta, Ohio, discovered a 30-foot-high _____ in the city center. They didn't know what it was used for, but later learned it was an ancient burial place. This was an _____ because it had been set aside as a cemetery. Several mound-building Indian groups lived in America. The Adena people built mounds in animal or _____ shapes, with the _____ placed in _____ made of logs. The Hopewell Indians made larger, _____ mounds. They decorated the bodies with _____ carvings and jewelry. The superior _____ left in the mounds of the Mississippian Indians showed that this culture was even more sophisticated. Their mounds were still inhabited in the 1720s and served as evidence of the _____ of the Mound Builders' culture.

Several native American tribes sued the U.S. in the 1970s, claiming legal ownership to most of Maine. The tribes received land and money as a settlement.

© CNN

TUNING IN: "Thanksgiving"

A. Pre-Viewing

Before you view the CNN video clip "Thanksgiving," discuss the following questions with a small group of classmates:

1. Are these words familiar? Look up unfamiliar words in a dictionary. Discuss the meanings with your classmates:

   displaced   indigenous

   genocide   confrontation

2. What do you know about the first Thanksgiving celebration between early European settlers and the native Americans?

3. What do you think was the impact of European invasion on the native American population?

B. Discussion
Discuss these questions after you view the clip:

1. Where does this film clip take place?

2. How do the Wampanoag Indians in the video clip feel about their treatment by European settlers in the 17th century?

3. How do these native Americans feel about Thanksgiving?

4. What actions have the native Americans taken as a result?

ACADEMIC POWER STRATEGY

Practice peer testing to prepare yourself and a study partner for examinations. Tests are the most frequent way to measure what you have learned in a class. To be a good test taker, one of the keys is preparation, and one tried-and-true strategy is to write your own test. When a test is based on reading, you can reread the texts and write a set of likely test questions. Let the chapter headings guide you in finding the major sections of a textbook reading. Or go through any reading and find the main ideas and important supporting ideas in each paragraph or section. Write questions about these ideas. Then trade "test questions" with a study partner, and see how each of you do. A handy way to do this is to write the question on one side of an index card and the answer on the back. Peer testing not only helps you prepare for a test, but it also lets you know if you're "on track" in selecting the most important ideas in your reading—and the most likely test questions.

Apply the Strategy

Join a study group of at least four classmates. Each of you should reread one different chapter reading. For each reading, write one or more questions about the most important ideas in each paragraph. Ask yourself, "Which ideas would most likely appear on an exam based on this reading? Which ideas should a student in this class remember?" Test each other, using the practice questions. Afterwards, discuss your questions with other groups.

PUTTING IT ALL TOGETHER

• •

Review Test

Test your comprehension of main ideas and supporting ideas in the chapter readings by taking the following test. Do not look at the readings as you take the test. After you are finished, discuss your answers with your study group. Confirm your answers by looking back at the chapter readings. Discuss the test with your entire class. Determine your grade on the test.

Comprehension Test, Chapter 8

Part 1: True/False   Mark the following statements T (True) or F (False) based on information presented in Readings 1 and 2.

_____ 1. Ancient Americans probably came to America from northeastern Asia.

_____ 2. It was impossible for the first Americans to travel to America by boat.

_____ 3. Archeologists now believe there were only three migrations to America during ancient times.

_____ 4. Early Americans ate plants when there were no animals available to kill.

_____ 5. In the Archaic Era, Indians discovered seeds and planting.

_____ 6. The most dependable food crop of early Americans was rice.

_____ 7. In early farming communities, men planted and harvested the crops.

Part 2: Multiple Choice   Choose the best answer to complete the following sentences, using information from Readings 3 and 4.

_____ 8. Trading networks across the Americas were the result of

a. domesticated crops

b. surplus food

c. specialized labor

d. all of the above

_____ 9. The Olmecs were called a mother culture because

    a. they built temples to honor female gods

    b. they had powerful religious leaders

    c. their way of life was adopted by many others

    d. they practiced human sacrifice

_____ 10. According to Reading 3, the Olmec society influenced others by

    a. trading by land and along coastal waters

    b. attacking other Indian groups

    c. sending religious leaders to spread their beliefs

_____ 11. Each of the ancient mound building societies probably _____, according to Reading 4.

    a. decided on their own to build mounds

    b. learned to build mounds from other societies

_____ 12. The artifacts discovered in ancient burial mounds inform us about

    a. the food ancient Americans ate

    b the art of ancient Americans

    c. the religion of ancient Americans

    d. all of the above

Grade: _____ questions correct × 8.3 points each = _____ %

Final Project

Complete one of the projects listed below on your own, with a partner, or with a group of classmates.

A. Research on a Native American Group: Find at least *two* readings that describe one native American group, such as the Olmecs, the Hopewell, the Adena, or others. You may consult encyclopedias that provide details about the group's history, lifestyle, etc. The Internet is also a useful source. Try to find the same basic information about each group. When did they live? Where? What did they eat? What type of housing did they use? Write a brief report that describes each of the native American groups.

B. Research on an Ancient Group in Another Country: Find at least *two* readings that describe an ancient group of people in another country. Use the same guidelines as in topic A to write your report.

C. Research on Archeologists' Work: Find at least *two* readings that tell about the work of archeologists. An encyclopedia will be a good starting point, but may have very limited information.

You may want to check books in your library, or search the Internet. Write a brief report that defines the term "archeologist" and explains what types of work archeologists do, what education they have, where they work, what tasks they do, and typical salaries.

D. Research on the Job of Geologist: Find at least *two* readings that inform you about the profession of geology. Use the guidelines in topic C to prepare a written report.

Share the information that you gained from your research in a brief presentation to classmates. Answer the following questions about your classmates' reports:

1. What is your reaction to the information from the readings?

2. Do you want to know more about this subject? If so, what?

3. What other sources could have been used to find out more about the subject?

Reading Journal

In your reading journal, write about *one* of the questions below:

1. What are the most interesting things that you learned from this chapter? Why were they interesting?

2. What was the least interesting part of this chapter? Why?

Test-Taking Tip

Study with other students for upcoming tests and attend any review sessions available. Use these as opportunities to ask questions about material you do not completely understand. Do not expect review sessions to repeat any lectures. The purpose of these sessions is to give you the opportunity to further your understanding of the material that will be covered on the test.

CHECK YOUR PROGRESS

• •

On a scale of 1 to 5, rate how well you have mastered the goals set at the beginning of the chapter:

1 2 3 4 5   create time lines to help you recall dates and events in readings.

1 2 3 4 5   distinguish main ideas from supporting ideas in readings.

1 2 3 4 5   practice peer testing to prepare for examinations.

If you've given yourself a 3 or lower on any of these goals:

- visit the *Tapestry* web site for additional practice.
- ask your instructor for extra help.
- review the sections of the chapter that you found difficult.
- work with a partner or study group to further your progress.

nomadic people who move from place to place. They don't have benefit limit about life style.

L ook at the photo. Then discuss these questions with your
  classmates:

- What are the advantages of living like the people in this culture live?
- What are the disadvantages?
- How is their lifestyle different from or similar to the culture that you live in?

9

race

ETHNIC IDENTITY

$\mathbf{W}$e are living in a time when people have a growing sense of ethnic identity. The sense of belonging to a racial or cultural group is a powerful force. Indeed, it is producing political conflicts across the globe, as ethnic groups seek recognition and even independence. At the same time, many cultural groups are learning to better understand each other as their interaction increases.

Setting Goals

In this chapter you will learn how to:

◈ recognize classification words.

◈ pay attention to how an author uses pronouns.

◈ cultivate a multicultural outlook by exploring your own cultural attitudes.

What other goals do you have for this chapter? Write one or two of them here.

_____

_____

 **Getting Started**

The writers in this chapter present four topics related to ethnic identity. Look at the titles of the readings and answer the questions that follow.

Readings:

"Ethnic Boundary Markers"

"Types of Ethnic Groups"

"The Problem of Stateless Nationalities"

"Stages of Cultural Growth"

1. What is a *boundary marker*? What would you guess is an *ethnic boundary marker*?

   _____

   _____

2. What is an *ethnic group?* Which *ethnic group* or groups do you belong to?

   _____

   _____

3. What do the words *stateless* and *nationality* mean? What do you think the words mean when they are put together?

   _____

   _____

4. What do you think *cultural growth* means?

   _____

   _____

5. Preview the photos and charts in the chapter. What do these tell you about the topics of the readings?

   _____

   _____

 **Getting Ready to Read**

Read the following definition of *ethnic group*, taken from a college textbook. Then, list the names of ethnic groups that you know from your native culture and other cultures. Share your list with classmates.

What is an ethnic group? First, it is necessary to realize that all peoples, not just minority populations, have a feeling of ethnicity and an ethnic group identity. In essence, an ethnic group is a

named social category of people based on perceptions of shared social experience or ancestry. Members of the ethnic group see themselves as sharing cultural traditions and history that distinguish them from other groups.

From *Humanity: An Introduction to Cultural Anthropology,* Fourth Edition (Wadsworth, 1997), by James Peoples and Garrick Bailey

Vocabulary Check

Check the words you already know. Work with a partner to find the meanings of new words. Use a dictionary, if necessary. You can add any new words you learn to your Vocabulary Log.

_____ overt _____ assimilating _____ transcends

_____ denote _____ encompass _____ adornment

_____ indicator _____ affiliation _____ homogenization

_____ antagonistic _____ constitute _____ brevity

_____ conversely

Reading 1: Ethnic Boundary Markers

1   Every ethnic group has a way of determining or expressing membership. **Overt** factors used to demonstrate or **denote** group membership are called ethnic boundary markers. Ethnic boundary markers are important not only to identify the members to one another, but also to demonstrate identity to and distinctiveness from nonmembers. Because they serve to distinguish members from all other groups, a single boundary marker seldom is sufficient. A marker that might distinguish one ethnic group from a second group may not distinguish it from still another group. Thus, combinations of markers commonly are used. Differences in language, religion, physical appearance, or particular cultural traits serve as ethnic boundary markers.

2   Language frequently serves as an ethnic boundary marker. The native language of an individual is the primary **indicator** of ethnic group identity in many areas of the world. In the southwestern United States, Hopi and Navajo members are readily distinguished by their language alone. However, just because two populations share a common language does not mean they share a common identity, any more than the fact that two populations speak different languages means that they have two distinct identities. For example, the Serbs and Croats of what was Yugoslavia speak Serbo-Croatian. They are, however, distinct and historically

antagonistic ethnic groups. **Conversely,** a person may be Irish and speak either Gaelic or English as his or her native language. The German government grants automatic citizenship to all ethnic German refugees from Eastern Europe. A difficulty in **assimilating** these refugees is that many speak only Polish or Russian. Thus, one does not have to speak German to be an ethnic German.

3   Like language, religion may serve as an ethnic boundary marker. The major world religions such as Christianity, Islam, and Buddhism **encompass** numerous distinct ethnic groups, so that religious **affiliation** does not always indicate ethnic affiliation. But in many cases, religion and ethnic group more or less correspond. The Jews may be categorized as either a religious or an ethnic group. Similarly, the Sikhs in India **constitute** both a religious and an ethnic group. In still other situations, religious differences may be the most important marker of ethnic identity. As we mentioned earlier, the Serbs and Croats speak the same language; the most important distinction between these two groups is that the Serbs are Eastern Orthodox and the Croats are Catholic. Conversely, the Chinese ethnic identity **transcends** religious differences; a person is still Chinese whether he or she is a Muslim, Christian, Taoist, Buddhist, or Marxist atheist.

4   Physical characteristics, or phenotypes, can also (at times) indicate ethnic identity. It is impossible to identify Germans, Dutch, Danes, and other northern European ethnic groups by their physical characteristics. A similar situation is found in those regions of the world in which populations have been in long association with one another. Thus, physical characteristics do not distinguish a Zulu from a Swazi, a Chinese from a Korean, or a Choctaw from a Chickasaw Indian. However, with the massive movements of people, particularly over the past few hundred years, physical characteristics have increasingly emerged as a marker of ethnic identity. Members of the three major ethnic groups in Malaysia—Malays, East Indians, and Chinese—are readily distinguishable by their physical appearance. The significance or lack of significance of physical characteristics in ethnic identity may also vary with the level of ethnic identity. The American identity includes almost the full range of human physical types. However, at a lower level of identity—Euro-American, African-American, and Native American—physical characteristics do serve as one marker of ethnic identity. Yet within these groups, physical characteristics alone cannot be the only marker. Some Native Americans physically appear to be Euro-Americans or African-Americans, and some African-Americans would be identified as Euro-Americans or Native Americans on the basis of physical appearance alone.

5   A wide variety of cultural traits, clothing, house types, personal **adornment,** food, technology, economic activities, or general lifestyle may also serve as ethnic boundary markers. Over the

past 100 years, a rapid **homogenization** of world material culture, food habits, and technology has erased many of the more overt cultural markers. Today, you do not have to be Mexican to enjoy tacos, Italian to eat pizza, or Japanese to have sushi for lunch. Similarly, you can dine on hamburgers, the all-American food, in Japan, Oman, Russia, Mexico, and most other countries. Cultural traits remain, however, the most important, diverse, and complex category of ethnic boundary markers. For the sake of **brevity,** we will limit our discussion to one trait—clothing.

6   Clothing styles have historically served as the most overt single indicator of ethnic identity. In the not-too-distant past, almost every ethnic group had its own unique style of dress. Even today, a Scottish-American who wants to overtly indicate his ethnic identity wears a kilt, and a German-American may wear his *lederhosen*. Similarly, on special occasions, Native Americans wear "Indian clothes" decorated with beadwork and ribbonwork. These are not everyday clothing, and they are worn only in social situations in which people want to emphasize their ethnic identity. In many regions of the world, however, ethnic clothes are still worn every day. In highland Guatemala, clothing, particularly women's clothing, serves to readily identify the ethnic affiliation of the wearer. Guatemalan clothing styles actually indicate two levels of ethnic identity. If a woman wears a *huipil,* a loose-fitting blouse that slips over the head, she is a Native American. Non-Native American women, called *Ladinas,* dress in Western-style clothes. The style, colors, and designs on the huipil further identify the particular Native American ethnic group the woman is from: Nahuala, Chichicastenango, Solola, or one of the other hundred or so Native American groups in highland Guatemala.

Members of Some Major World Religions, 1999

Christianity 2 billion
Islam   1 billion
Judaism   12 million

SOURCE: *BRITISH BROAD-CASTING CORPORATION*

◈After You Read

A. Analysis: Discuss the following questions with a small group of classmates. Share your group's answers with your entire class.

1. Make a list of the types of ethnic markers this reading presents:

   _____   _____

   _____   _____

   _____   _____

2. According to the reading, which of these ethnic boundary markers are still the strongest indicators of ethnic identity? Find some examples of these markers in specific cultures from the reading.

3. When do ethnic boundary markers less accurately indicate a person's ethnic identity? Find examples from the reading.

4. What conclusion can you reach about ethnic markers and ethnic identity after reading "Ethnic Boundary Markers"? Write a

statement to tell this conclusion. Compare your statement with others in your group.

B. Distinguishing Fact from Opinion: Divide Reading 1 into parts so that each of your group members rereads a different section of the reading. As each of you reads, think about this question: Is the information presented in the section *fact* or *opinion*? Be prepared to explain your answer to the group.

LANGUAGE LEARNING STRATEGY

Recognize the way that certain words help organize or classify important ideas, things, or people. Identifying these special words will help you better understand what you are reading.

Academic writing is commonly characterized by classification, a pattern of text organization in which general ideas are placed into groups. In classification texts, one or more general ideas are classified into groups. A classification sentence introduces the general idea and its categories and generally includes a "group" word. For example, Reading 1, "Ethnic Boundary Markers," classifies ethnic boundary markers by type. The first two sentences of the reading are the classification sentences and include a "group" word (in bold-faced type).

Every ethnic group has a **way** of determining or expressing membership. Overt **factors** used to demonstrate or denote group membership are called ethnic boundary markers.

Logical connectors introduce each category in later sentences and allow you to predict the ideas that will appear next. This logical type of organization clearly presents the relation among ideas and is useful in your own writing, too.

Apply the Strategy

Read the following "group words" that commonly appear in classification sentences. Reread the passages from Reading 1 reprinted after the chart. Underline the classification sentence in each passage and circle the "group" word. Be prepared to explain what general idea is being classified and the word used to represent the groups or categories.

Common "Group Words" Used in Classification Sentences			
types	reasons	traits	categories
ways	groups	characteristics	levels
factors			

1. The American identity includes almost the full range of human physical types. However, at a lower level of identity—Euro-American, African-American, and Native American—physical characteristics do serve as one marker of ethnic identity. Yet within these groups, physical characteristics alone cannot be the only marker. Some Native Americans physically appear to be Euro-Americans or African-Americans, and some African-Americans would be identified as Euro-Americans or Native Americans on the basis of physical appearance alone.

2. In many regions of the world, however, ethnic clothes are still worn every day. In highland Guatemala, clothing, particularly women's clothing, serves to readily identify the ethnic affiliation of the wearer. Guatemalan clothing styles actually indicate two levels of ethnic identity. If a woman wears a *huipil,* a loose-fitting blouse that slips over the head, she is a Native American. Non-Native American women, called *Ladinas,* dress in Western-style clothes. The style, colors, and designs on the huipil further identify the particular Native American ethnic group the woman is from: Nahuala, Chichicastenango, Solola, or one of the other hundred or so Native American groups in highland Guatemala.

◆ Getting Ready to Read

Read the title and first paragraph of Reading 2. What general idea will be classified in this reading? Which is the classification sentence in the first paragraph? What do you think is the meaning of each of the groups mentioned in this sentence?

Vocabulary Check

Are the following words familiar? Put check marks next to the words that you already know. Look up new words in your dictionary. Work with a partner to choose the appropriate dictionary definition that best relates to the topic of ethnic groups. Add new words to your Vocabulary Log.

_____ exclusive	_____ subordinate
_____ implicit	_____ subset
_____ assumption	_____ hence
_____ inherent	_____ asserting
_____ autonomy	_____ collective
_____ self-determination	_____ conquest
_____ distinct	_____ rightfully
_____ sovereignty	_____ implications

Read

Reading 2: Types of Ethnic Groups

1 The term *ethnic group* covers a range of social groupings. In general, ethnic groups fall into two main categories: national and subnational.

2   A nationality is an ethnic group with a feeling of homeland, a geographical region over which they have **exclusive** rights. **Implicit** in this concept is the **assumption** of an **inherent** right to political **autonomy** and **self-determination.** In contrast, subnationalities lack a concept of a **distinct** and separate homeland and the associated rights to separate political **sovereignty** and self-determination. A subnational group sees itself as a dependent and politically **subordinate subset** of a nationality.

3   Although it is easy to define the difference between ethnic nationalities and subnationalities, sometimes it is far more difficult to classify particular groups. The ethnic groups in the United States demonstrate some of the difficulties in classification. With some ethnic groups, there is no doubt about their classification. Italian-Americans, German-Americans, Polish-Americans, Scottish-Americans, and Irish-Americans are all subnational groups. At a higher level of identity, the same is true for African-Americans. None of these groups has a concept of a distinct and separate geographical homeland within the United States. **Hence,** they are subnational groups who, together with many other groups, collectively constitute the American ethnic nationality.

4   There are other ethnic groups within the United States whose status is not as clear. What is the status of Native American groups such as the Navajo, the Hopi, the Crow, the Cheyenne, the Cherokee, and the Osage, to name only a few? These groups have a concept of homelands within the United States. They also have histories quite distinct from that of other Americans. In recent years, they have been **asserting** increased political sovereignty and self-determination within their reservations (homelands). Although there is disagreement, many Native American individuals and groups still see themselves as distinct nationalities. The U.S. government does recognize most American Indian groups as national groups with **collective** legal and political rights. No other ethnic groups in the United States have officially recognized governments and limited rights of self-determination. There is also some question about the ethnic status of Spanish-speaking peoples in the southwestern United States. Until the mid-nineteenth century, Texas, New Mexico, Arizona, and California were part of Mexico. The United States acquired this region through military **conquest.** Most of the native Spanish-speaking people in this region think of themselves

as Mexican American or Spanish American, a subnational group. There is, however, a small group who see themselves as "Mexicans" living in a land that is **rightfully** part of Mexico, a region they call "Atzlan."

5   The distinction between nationality and subnationality is important because of their different political **implications.** The demands of subnational groups for equal rights and treatment have long been a source of conflict.

After You Read

A. Recognizing Classification of Ideas: Discuss these questions with a group of classmates: What is the main classification in Reading 2? What is the definition of the two categories of ethnic groups, according to the reading?

B. Reactions: Discuss the following questions with classmates:

1. The author of Reading 2 describes U.S. ethnic groups as being *subnational.* Do you agree that the ethnic groups he mentioned are distinct ethnic groups? Why?

2. Should the author have mentioned other ethnic groups in the U.S.? If so, which ones?

3. In your native culture, do subnational ethnic groups exist? If so, which ones? What conflicts arise among ethnic groups, if any?

4. Do subnational ethnic groups have a right to be recognized as separate ethnic groups? Why or why not?

Getting Ready to Read

With a group of classmates, discuss the following questions before reading "The Problem of Stateless Nationalities":

1. Think about the title of the reading. The word *stateless* means "not having a state," yet the word *nationality* means "belonging to a particular nation or group." How can an ethnic group be a *nationality* but *stateless*?

2. What problems might arise from members of *stateless nationalities*? Make a list of possible problems, and mentally check your list as you read.

3. Preview the first paragraph of the reading. Who is the author speaking to when he says "*our* common perception"? In other words, who is *we*? Why do you think the author addresses this particular audience?

Vocabulary Check

Put checks next to the words you already know. Find the words you don't know in a dictionary, and record them in your Vocabulary Log. With a partner, discuss which words might relate to the subject of nationalities. Share your ideas with your entire class.

to compare 2 things in importance (meaning value)

_____ equating

_____ *determined* resolvable

_____ reparable

_____ bitter

_____ evicted

_____ partitioned

_____ guerrilla

_____ ambushes

_____ assassinations

_____ rival

_____ hostile

_____ integral

_____ inalienable

_____ proclaimed

_____ legitimate

_____ tenuous

_____ volatile

_____ vividly

_____ nationalist

_____ rational

_____ magnitude

_____ encompass

_____ homogeneous

_____ legacies

_____ indigenous

_____ polyglot

_____ endemic

 Read

Reading 3: The Problem of Stateless Nationalities

1 For the most part, the ethnic groups in the United States are sub-nationalities, not nationalities. Thus, from our common perception, a Russian is a person from Russia, a Nigerian is a citizen from Nigeria, and so forth. Falsely **equating** country of origin with ethnic nationality, we view ethnic conflicts in other regions of the world as comparable to conflicts between subnational groups within the United States. Ethnic problems within a country are thought to be the result of social or economic discrimination—**resolvable** and **reparable** by reforms—and their political significance is minimized. However, the ethnic conflicts in most countries are not between subnational groups but between distinct nationalities.

2 The ethnic conflicts in Northern Ireland and in Israel and Palestine have proved particularly **bitter.** In 1922, after several centuries of British colonial domination and periodic rebellions by the native Irish, the Irish Free State (now the Republic of Ireland) was established. However, not all of Ireland was given indepen-

dence. In the seventeenth century, to control the Irish, the British **evicted** Irish farmers from the northernmost portion of the island and colonized the region with Scottish **Presbyterians,**[1] who became known as the *Scotch-Irish*. The Scotch-Irish did not identify themselves as Irish and had no desire to become part of an independent Ireland. Recognizing the wishes of the Scotch-Irish, at independence the British **partitioned** the island. The northern six counties became Northern Ireland and remained part of the United Kingdom. Many Irish did not and do not accept the legality of this partitioning of Ireland. To them, Northern Ireland is part of the Irish homeland and thus should be part of the Republic of Ireland. Since 1968, the Irish Republican Army, a secretive **guerrilla** army that is illegal in the Republic of Ireland, has been actively waging a war with the object of reuniting Northern Ireland with the Republic of Ireland. Bombings, **ambushes,** and **assassinations** have claimed the lives of more than 2,200 persons, and no end appears in sight. The news media frequently report the problems in Northern Ireland as conflict between the British and the Irish or between Catholic and Protestants; in reality, it is neither. The root of the problem is the conflicting claims of two **rival** and **hostile** nationalities: the Irish and the Scotch-Irish. The Scotch-Irish have emerged over the past 400 years as a distinct nationality who claim the northern part of Ireland as their homeland. In contrast, the Irish see the area as an **integral** and **inalienable** part of the Irish homeland.

3   After an absence of almost 2,000 years, the Jews began returning to their historic homeland in Palestine in 1882. During the early twentieth century, Jewish settlements in Palestine grew, and in 1948 the state of Israel was **proclaimed** by the Jewish settlers. For the past forty-five years, conflict between Israelis and Palestinians has been constant, varying only in the intensity and form of violence. The problem is similar to that in Northern Ireland, in that two nationalities—Israelis and Palestinians—claim the same geographical region as their **legitimate** homeland. While some progress has been made recently toward peaceful settlements of the conflicts in Northern Ireland and between Israelis and Palestinians, such agreements are **tenuous.** These situations remain extremely **volatile.** In Israel, it is impossible to resolve this conflict to the satisfaction of both nationalities.

4   These two conflicts **vividly** illustrate the strength of **nationalist** sentiments. In both cases, we see groups of educated, **rational** human beings who are willing to sacrifice their lives and economic well-being in unending conflicts for what they consider to be their nationality's legitimate rights.

---

[1]**Presbyterians:** a denomination (group) within the Christian religion

5   Such conflict is more common in the modern world than most of us realize. To understand the **magnitude** or potential magnitude of this problem, one need only realize that the world is divided into less than 200 countries and between 3,000 and 5,000 distinct ethnic nationalities. As a result, the populations of most countries **encompass** a number of distinct nationalities. China officially recognizes fifty-six distinct nationalities. Some estimates are as high as 300 ethnic nationalities in Indonesia. Ethiopia has at least 70 nationalities. Only a handful of countries are peopled by members of a single nationality and are thus ethnically **homogeneous.**

6   The ethnic nationality problem is further complicated because current political boundaries for most of the world are **legacies** of European colonialism and expansion. During the nineteenth century, the European powers divided most of the geographical regions and peoples of the world among themselves. In 1884-1885, at the Berlin Conference, European leaders sat at a table and with pens and pencils drew lines on a map of Africa, dividing the resources and peoples of that continent among themselves. Through this agreement, the English, French, Germans, Belgians, and other European powers assumed sovereignty over lands they had never traveled and over peoples who had never seen a white man. Nor was Africa the only continent to have boundaries imposed by Europeans. The national boundaries of most of the world were drawn by Europeans for their own interest, with little regard for the interest of any **indigenous** peoples or the boundaries of the ethnic groups affected. As a result, most European colonial possessions were a **polyglot** of ethnic groups, many of whom had long histories of hostilities toward one another. In other instances, an ethnic group found its land and people divided between two or more European colonies. To make matters worse, colonial powers frequently moved people from one colony to another to supply labor, introducing still other ethnic groups to new areas. For example, the British settled Indian laborers in Burma (Myanmar), Malaya (Malaysia), Fiji, Sri Lanka, Kenya, Uganda, South Africa, Trinidad, and British Guiana.

7   The end of the colonial period did not end the ethnic conflicts in the world but only signaled the beginning of the problems. As European powers granted independence to their colonies, they made little attempt to redefine political boundaries. In most cases, these newly independent countries had precisely the same boundaries and ethnic composition as the former colonies. Because these political divisions were imposed by European military power, some scholars have termed the former colonies artificial countries. In most cases, the basic colonial administrative and governmental structure was maintained after independence; the major departure from the colonial period was that native officials

replaced European officials. However, not all ethnic groups were equally represented in these new governments, and most former colonies quickly came under the domination of one or two of the more powerful ethnic groups. Thus, in many instances European domination was replaced by domination by one of another "native" ethnic group. With this in mind, the political problems **endemic** in much of the Third World become more comprehensible.

 **After You Read**

A. Expressing the Main Idea: Write one sentence to express the main idea of Reading 3. Include the *topic* and *what the reading says about the topic* in your statement. Compare your sentence with other classmates'.

B. Recognizing Classification of Ideas: Reading 3 classifies stateless nationalities by explaining *reasons* why they exist. Scan the reading to find the major reasons given for the existence of stateless nationalities. In the chart below, briefly state each reason and the paragraph number in which you found it. Compare your answers with classmates'.

Reasons Why Stateless Nationalities Exist	Par. #

C. Creating a Time Line: Reading 3 presents two examples of stateless nationalities: the Scotch-Irish in northern Ireland and the Palestinians in Israel. In order to better remember the historical details, create a time line of the dates and events associated with each group. Place important dates on a horizontal line and briefly describe key events above or below the line. Compare your time line with classmates'.

TUNING IN: "Malaysia Aborigines"

A. Pre-Viewing

Discuss these questions with classmates before viewing "Malaysia Aborigines," a CNN video clip.

© CNN

1. What do these words mean? How do the words apply to people?

   original   indigenous   aboriginal   non-aboriginal

2. What rights do you think aboriginal people should have? How do their rights compare to non-aboriginal inhabitants of the same land?

3. Where is Malaysia? What do you know about this country?

B. Discussion

Read the following questions. Find the answers or think about the ideas as you view the video clip. Discuss your responses after you view.

1. What are the complaints of the aboriginal people of Malaysia?

2. What is happening to the land they inhabit?

3. What should be done to correct this problem?

4. Do aboriginal groups exist in your native culture or a culture that you know well? Do they have problems similar to the Malaysian aborigines?

Getting Ready to Read

Before you read "Stages of Cultural Growth," discuss these key points with a group of your classmates:

1. What does the term *ethnocentrism* mean? What does it mean for a person to be *ethnocentric*?

2. What does it mean for a society to be *multicultural*? How can a person have a *multicultural* outlook?

Vocabulary Check

[handwritten: ethnocentric (adv) they think their culture is the best]

Are the following words and expression familiar? Put check marks next to the ones you already know. Look up new words in your dictionary. Write them and their meanings in your Vocabulary Log. Discuss the vocabulary with classmates and your instructor before you begin reading.

_____ dominant

[handwritten: hộp chất] _____ composite

[handwritten: related to belief in the superiority of one's own people & culture] _____ ethnocentric, ethnocentrism

[handwritten: to make rich or richer] _____ enriched

_____ multicultural

_____ sting

_____ worldview

_____ concession

[handwritten: under, lower in quality] _____ inferior

_____ radicalization

Read

Reading 4: Stages of Cultural Growth

For persons of a **dominant** culture (for example, white males in the United States or wealthy people in a poor community), the change from an **ethnocentric** to a **multicultural worldview** can involve three stages:

1. **Ethnocentrism**   My culture is best; all others are **inferior.** I don't like people who are different from me—never have, never will. I was born and raised that way. If it was good enough for my parents and grandparents, it's good enough for me.

2. **Understanding**   As I have more contact with people of other cultures and learn more about them, I can see why they act the way they do. Their ways and customs are OK for them. In fact, I've already learned to like some of their food, clothing, music. I respect their right to be different. **Live and let live.**[1]

3. **Multiculturalism**   My lifestyle is a **composite** of the best things I have seen in other cultures, and I've seen a lot. These things have **enriched** my life, even though I'm still me. I feel comfortable around all kinds of people. I'm open to new experiences, and I continue to grow in positive ways.

  For persons in groups who have felt the **sting** of discrimination all their lives, the pattern of growth may be somewhat different:

1. **Concession**   I'm what the dominant culture says I am. I wish I could be more like them. But at least I'm not like those other minority groups.

2. **Radicalization**   They're just trying to put me down. I accept the way I am—in fact, I think I'm just great. Those other cultures are OK too, even though they're not part of mine. We've all got to stick together against the dominant culture. Eventually we'll pay them back for the way they've treated us.

3. **Multiculturalism**   My lifestyle is a composite of the best things I have seen in other cultures, and I've seen a lot. These things have enriched my life, even though I'm still me. I feel comfortable around all kinds of people. I'm open to new experiences, and I continue to grow in positive ways.

[1]**Live and let live:** Live the way you want, and allow others to do the same. (idiom)

> **Mind is actually internalized culture.**
>
> —EDWARD T. HALL

◆ **After You Read**

Every text is written for a particular audience (a group or groups of readers) and for a specific purpose or purposes (for example, to inform, to persuade, or to create emotions). Reread "Stages of Cultural Growth," and discuss the following questions with a group of classmates:

1. What do you think is the authors' intended audience? In other words, which groups are the authors speaking to?

2. What is the authors' main purpose? In other words, what effect do the authors want to produce in the readers' minds? Is there more than one purpose?

ACADEMIC POWER STRATEGY

Cultivate a multicultural outlook to help you thrive in the college community—and in the world. People generally feel more secure in their native cultures, so it's natural that at times, they are ethnocentric. However, today's colleges and universities are increasingly multicultural. Typical college classrooms illustrate this cultural diversity, as students from many cultures work side-by-side to reach common goals. If you are "open" to students of different cultures, you can learn together and help each other navigate your ways through college. "We must prepare ourselves for a future in which all cultures and nations will, of necessity, depend on each other for survival," write college success experts Robert Holkeboer and Laurie Walker. "By being open to other cultures, we soon discover people are more alike than different."

Apply the Strategy

Reread the section of "Stages of Cultural Growth" that applies to you (as a member of a dominant or a minority cultural group). Discuss these questions with a group of classmates:

1. Which stage of cultural growth are you in? Explain.

2. Have you felt that other students were prejudiced toward you because of your culture? Explain what happened.

3. Which stage of cultural growth is the best? Why?

4. Do you have a multicultural outlook? In what ways?

5. Is there anything about your cultural attitudes that you would like to change? Explain.

LANGUAGE LEARNING STRATEGY

Pay attention to how an author uses pronouns—this can help you detect the author's purpose. The personal pronouns in Reading 4 are features of writing that communicates interactively. Through the use of pronouns, the writer can "talk" to the reader in an intimate, personal way. Writers use *we, us,* or *our* to communicate shared experiences or beliefs. When writers use *you* or *your,* they are speaking directly to the reader, often to persuade. These pronouns differ from *they, them,* or *their* pronouns, which commonly appear in writing that informs rather than persuades. Being aware of how an author uses pronouns will help you become more aware of the author's meaning and purpose. You will recognize when a writer is trying to persuade you or create certain emotions. As your knowledge of English increases, you will become increasingly "tuned in" to the ways in which writers use language to interact with their audience.

Apply the Strategy

Read the following passages, taken from the chapter readings. Circle the pronouns. Discuss with a small group of classmates how the writer may be using the pronouns to communicate with the audience and achieve a particular purpose. Who is the writer referring to with the pronouns? What is the writer's purpose? Is the writing intended to persuade? To create a certain emotion? Share your group's answers with your entire class.

1. For the sake of brevity, we will limit our discussion to one trait—clothing. (Reading 1, par. 5)

2. For the most part, the ethnic groups in the United States are subnationalities, not nationalities. Thus, from our common perception, a Russian is a person from Russia, a Nigerian is a citizen from Nigeria, and so forth. Falsely equating country of origin with ethnic nationality, we view ethnic conflicts in other regions of the world as comparable to conflicts between subnational groups within the United States. (Reading 4, par.1)

3. These two conflicts vividly illustrate the strength of nationalist sentiments. In both cases we see groups of educated, rational human beings who are willing to sacrifice their lives and economic

(continued on next page)

well-being in unending conflicts for what they consider to be their nationality's legitimate rights. Such conflict is more common in the modern world than most of us realize. (Reading 3, pars. 4–5)

4. My culture is best; all others are inferior. I don't like people who are different from me—never have, never will. I was born and raised that way. If it was good enough for my parents and grandparents, it's good enough for me. (Reading 4, par. 1)

> I celebrate myself, and sing myself. And what I assume you shall assume. For every atom belonging to me as good belongs to you.
>
> —WALT WHITMAN, AMERICAN POET

PUTTING IT ALL TOGETHER

Write

Write a paragraph or short composition related to the ideas in the Chapter 9 readings. Answer *one* of the following questions:

1. Describe an ethnic group that you know well. Have any of the ethnic boundary markers of this group changed over the years? In what ways?

2. Do you show your ethnic identity? What ethnic boundary markers distinguish you from members of other ethnic groups? Explain.

3. Are you ethnocentric or multicultural in your worldview? What do you do that makes you ethnocentric or multicultural? Explain with specific examples of your behavior.

Vocabulary Building

Review your Vocabulary Log entries for Chapter 9. Test your knowledge of the vocabulary by studying the following vocabulary words. Find each of the words in the chapter readings. Discuss with a partner how the words are used in the reading. Discuss problem words with your classmates. Then, take turns testing your partner on the definitions of the words.

final exam

Reading 1 Vocabulary:

overt	assimilating
indicator	encompass
antagonistic	affiliation
conversely	

Reading 2 Vocabulary:

assumption	autonomy
inherent	

Reading 3 Vocabulary:

rival	nationalist
hostile	homogeneous
integral	indigenous
volatile	

Reading 4 Vocabulary:

dominant	multicultural
ethnocentric	

Final Project

Complete one of the projects listed below on your own, with a partner, or with a group of classmates.

A. Description of an Ethnic Minority Group

Find at least *two* readings that describe one minority ethnic group. You might start by consulting a computerized encyclopedia like *Encarta*. Also look in books, scholarly journals, or magazines in your library, or on the Internet. Try to find basic information about the group: population, country(ies) of residence, language, and other ethnic boundary markers.

B. Description of Ethnic Groups within One Country

Find at least *two* readings that describe the ethnic populations of one country. You may want to start by reading a short article from a printed or computerized encyclopedia, and this may lead you to articles about the individual ethnic groups. Find basic information about the country, such as total population, percentage of population of each ethnic group, geographic location, and language(s). Include data on each ethnic group: population, country(ies) of residence, language, and other ethnic boundary markers. Note any conflicts that exist in the country among ethnic groups.

Share the information that you gained from your research in a brief presentation to your classmates. Answer the following questions about your classmates' reports:

1. What is your reaction to the information from the readings?
2. Do you want to know more about this subject? If so, what?
3. What did you learn from this presentation?

Test-Taking Tip

Don't panic if you do not know the answer to a question. Use all the knowledge you do have about the material and your own reasoning ability to try to analyze the question and decide on a logical answer. If it is an essay examination, write whatever you do know about the topic and you may at least receive partial credit. If it is a multiple choice, fill in the blank, or matching test and you have no idea of the answer—guess!

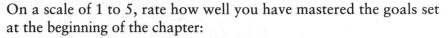
CHECK YOUR PROGRESS

On a scale of 1 to 5, rate how well you have mastered the goals set at the beginning of the chapter:

1 2 3 4 5   recognize classification words.

1 2 3 4 5   cultivate a multicultural outlook by exploring your own cultural attitudes.

1 2 3 4 5   pay attention to how an author uses pronouns.

If you've given yourself a 3 or lower on any of these goals:

- visit the *Tapestry* web site for additional practice.
- ask your instructor for extra help.
- review the sections of the chapter that you found difficult.
- work with a partner or study group to further your progress.

L ook at the photo. Then discuss these questions with your
classmates:

• Which career interests you? Why?

• What qualities are important to you in a job?

• How do you plan to reach your career goals?

THE JOB PUZZLE

Choosing a meaningful career is like putting together a puzzle. First, you think about yourself—your interests, strengths, goals. Then, you research the job market. Finally, you explore your options. The pieces of this problem-solving process are discussed in this chapter's readings.

Setting Goals

In this chapter you will learn how to:

◈ annotate, or mark, texts.

◈ recognize generalizations and examples.

◈ research the job market to predict the best careers.

What other goals do you have for this chapter? Write one or two of them here.

_____

_____

◆ **Getting Started**

The writers in this chapter present three topics related to careers. Look at the titles of the readings and answer the questions that follow.

Readings:

"Solving the Job Puzzle" by Anne W. Clymer and Elizabeth McGregor

"Tomorrow's Jobs"

Occupational Outlook Handbook: "Computer Scientists, Computer Engineers, and Systems Analysts"

1. Is finding a career a *puzzle* for you? Why or why not?

   _____

   _____

2. What areas do *you* think most of tomorrow's jobs will be in?

   _____

   _____

3. What do computer scientists do? Computer engineers? Systems analysts?

   _____

   _____

4. Preview the photos and charts in the chapter. What do these tell you about the topics of the readings?

   _____

   _____

◆ **Getting Ready to Read**

A. Read the following statements. Each describes one factor that people generally consider when choosing a career. Think about your *own* career goals or choices. Rank each statement from 1 to 8, with 1 being *the most important* factor in your career choice and 8 being *the least important*. Discuss your answers with a group of classmates.

_____ I want a career with a high salary.

_____ The work has to be enjoyable.

_____ I want to feel that I am helping people in my job.

_____ My job should not require much physical work.

_____ The work must be mentally challenging.

_____ I want a job where I work closely with other people.

_____ My work hours should be regular.

_____ I want a job that lets me move up to higher positions.

B. Before you read, discuss these questions with classmates:
Read paragraph 1. What does this quotation mean? What does the quotation suggest about job choices?

Vocabulary Check

Which of these words do you already know? Check the words you already know. Work with a partner to find the meanings of new words. Use a dictionary, if necessary. Record the new words and definitions in your Vocabulary Log.

_____ diversities	_____ assessing	_____ crucial
_____ occupations	_____ clientele	_____ stockroom
_____ attributed	_____ substantially	_____ inventory
_____ devote	_____ open-minded	_____ interpersonal
_____ extensive	_____ respiratory	_____ apparel
_____ undertaking	_____ invoke	_____ assembly line
_____ stimulating	_____ misconceptions	_____ compensated
_____ fulfilling	_____ strenuous	_____ garments
_____ expectations	_____ adaptability	

LANGUAGE LEARNING STRATEGY

Annotate, or mark, texts to highlight important ideas that will be useful for further study. One of the best ways to remember what you read is to annotate the reading. You can do this by underlining or circling important ideas in the lines of the reading. Even better, you can write notes or marks in the reading margins next to important ideas. Stars or exclamation points in margins clearly indicate key ideas. Highlighting with bright markers is another useful way to note important ideas. You can develop your own method for annotating readings; the important thing is to use this strategy to help you remember the most important ideas in what you read.

Apply the Strategy

As you read the following reading, annotate ideas that you feel are important. Use whichever method (underlining, circling, or margin notes) that works best for you.

Read

Reading 1: Solving the Job Puzzle

by Anne W. Clymer and Elizabeth McGregor

1 "I am myself reminded that we are not alike; there are **diversities** of natures among us which are adapted to different **occupations**." These words, which Plato **attributed** to Socrates, are still true today.

2 Choosing a career is one of the hardest jobs you will ever have. You should **devote extensive** time, energy, and thought to make a decision with which you will be happy. Even though **undertaking** this task means hard work, view a career as an opportunity to do something you enjoy, not simply as a necessity or as a means of earning a living. Taking the time to thoroughly explore career options can mean the difference between finding a **stimulating** and **fulfilling** career or hopping from one job to the next in search of the right job. Finding the best occupation for you also is important because work influences many aspects of your life—from your choice of friends and recreational activities to where you live.

3 Choosing a career is work that should be done carefully. As you gain experience and mature, however, you may develop new interests and skills which open doors to new opportunities. Work is an educational experience and can further focus your interests or perhaps change your career preferences. The choice you make today may not be your last. In fact, most people change occupations several times during their careers. With careful consideration of the wide range of occupations available, you should be able to find the right career.

4 There are many factors to consider when exploring career options and many ways to begin solving your job puzzle. Everyone has certain **expectations** of his or her job—these may include career advancement, self-expression or creativity, a sense of accomplishment, or a high salary. Deciding what you want most from your job will make choosing a career easier.

5 Identifying your interests will help in your search for a stimulating career. You might start by **assessing** your likes and dislikes, strengths and weaknesses. If you have trouble identifying them, consider the school subjects, activities, and surroundings that appeal to you. Would you prefer a job that involves travel? Do you want to work with children? Do you like science and mathematics? Do you need flexible working hours? Does a particular industry, such as health services, appeal to you? These are just a few questions to ask yourself. There are no right or wrong answers, and only you know what's important. Decide what job characteristics you require, which ones you prefer, and which ones you would not accept. Then rank these characteristics in order of importance to you.

6   Perhaps job setting ranks high on your list of important job characteristics. You may not want to work behind a desk all day. Many diverse occupations—from building inspectors, to surveyors, to real estate agents—require work away from an office. Or maybe you always dreamed of a job that involves instructing and helping others; in this case, child care workers, teachers, and physicians are among the occupations that might interest you.

7   Geographic location may also concern you. If so, it could influence your career decision because employment in some occupations and industries is concentrated in certain regions or localities. For example, aerospace jobs are concentrated in three states—California, Texas, and Washington—while advertising jobs are concentrated in large cities. If you choose to work in one of these fields, you probably will have to live in one of these states or in a large city. Or, if you live in Denver or the Southeast, for instance, you should learn which industries and occupations are found in those locations. On the other hand, many industries such as hotels and motels, legal services, and retail trade, as well as occupations such as teachers, secretaries, and computer analysts, are found in all areas of the country.

8   Earnings potential varies from occupation to occupation, and each person must determine his or her needs and goals. If high earnings are important to you, look beyond the starting wages. Some occupations offer relatively low starting salaries, but earnings substantially increase with experience, additional training, and promotions. In the end, your earnings may be higher in one of these occupations. For example, insurance sales workers may have relatively low earnings at first; after years of building a **clientele**, however, their earnings may increase **substantially.**

9   Job setting, working with a specific group of people, geographic location, and earnings are just a few occupational characteristics that you may consider. Be **open-minded.** Consider occupations related to your initial interests. For example, you may be interested in health care, and certain qualities of nursing may appeal to you, such as patient care and frequent public contact. Exploring other health occupations that share these characteristics—including doctors, **respiratory** therapists, and emergency medical technicians—may stimulate your interest in a health field other than nursing.

10   Don't eliminate any occupation or industry before you learn more about it. Some occupations and industries **invoke** certain positive or negative images. For some people, fashion designers produce a glamorous image, while production occupations in manufacturing industries bring to mind a less attractive image.

11   However, jobs often are not what they first appear to be, and **misconceptions** are common. Exciting jobs may have dull aspects, while less glamorous occupations may interest you once you learn about them. For example, the opportunity to travel makes a flight attendant's job seem exciting, but the work is **strenuous** and tiring; flight attendants stand for long periods and must remain friendly when they are tired and passengers are unpleasant. On the other hand, many people consider automotive assembly work dirty and dull; however, production workers in the motor vehicle manufacturing industry are among the highest paid in the nation.

Skills

12   One way to choose an occupation is to examine the skills required to perform the job well. Consider the skills you already have or your ability and interest in obtaining the skills or training required for specific occupations. Some occupations that require mechanical ability, for instance, include elevator installers and repairers and automotive mechanics. If you do not plan to attend college, consider occupations that require less formal education. If you are interested in engineering, for example, but do not want to pursue a college degree, drafters and engineering technicians are two occupations you can enter with 1 or 2 years of post-secondary training.

13   Some skills—analysis, persuading, and mechanical ability, for example—are specific to certain occupations. However, certain skills are needed, in varying degrees, in virtually all occupations, from factory workers to top executives.

Skills Common to All Jobs

14   As the marketplace becomes increasingly competitive, a company's ability to succeed depends upon its workers' skills—in particular, basic skills in reading, writing, and mathematics. These skills allow workers to learn and adapt to rapid technological advances and changing business practices in their jobs. This **adaptability** is **crucial** to one's survival in the job market.

15   Reading skills are essential to perform most jobs. Workers must often read and understand text, graphs, charts, manuals, and instructional materials. Writing skills are necessary to communicate thoughts, ideas, and information in written forms such as memorandums, invoices, schedules, letters, or information requests. Many jobs require basic mathematical skills to take measurements and perform simple calculations.

16   Lack of these skills can lead to many problems, including poor quality products and missed deadlines. These problems can then

result in a decline in sales and increased customer complaints. Reading, writing, and mathematical skills are as important for a research scientist as they are for occupations that require little formal education, such as a **stockroom** clerk at a manufacturing plant. Although a computer system may be designed to track **inventory** by electronically recording all transactions, the clerk is responsible for verifying the information. The clerk must be able to read and do simple calculations to confirm that stockroom inventory matches what the computer registers. Any inaccuracies in counting, computing, or recording of this inventory could result in a slowdown in production.

17   Workers also need good listening and speaking skills to interact with others. Greater interaction among workers is evident in factories, offices, and laboratories. Problems often are solved through communication, cooperation, and discussion, and workers must be able to listen, speak, and think on their feet. When dealing with customers, workers must listen and understand customers' needs and communicate solutions and ideas. It is not good enough to merely take a customer's order; workers must provide customers with useful information.

18   Good **interpersonal** skills are critical, as the workplace becomes more team-oriented. **Apparel** plants, for instance, are replacing the traditional **assembly line** with modular manufacturing. On the traditional assembly line, workers performed a specific task independent of other workers and were **compensated** accordingly. Today, groups of workers, called modules, work as a team to produce **garments,** solve problems as they occur, and make suggestions to improve production or working conditions. Group interaction is important because an individual's earnings are based upon the group's performance.

19   Workers at all levels must be willing to learn new techniques. Computers, for instance, were once found primarily in office settings; today, computers are found in every work setting from factories to classrooms. The introduction of computers into the manufacturing process is transforming many craft and factory occupations; many of these jobs now require the use of computer-controlled equipment. For example, most elevators are computerized and electronically controlled. In order to install, repair, and maintain modern elevators, elevator repairers need a thorough knowledge of electronics, electricity, and computer applications. Even though a high school education is the minimum requirement for entering this field, workers with post-secondary training in electronics usually have better advancement opportunities than those with less training. As technological changes continue, retraining will be essential for workers in many fields.

After You Read

A. Expressing the Main Idea: Write one sentence that tells the main idea of Reading 1. In the sentence, include the name of the article (in quotation marks), the *topic* of the reading, and *what the reading says about the topic*. Compare your sentence with other classmates'.

B. Annotating a Text: With one or more classmates, compare your annotation of important ideas in the reading. Discuss why you marked certain ideas. Revise or add to your markings, if necessary.

LANGUAGE LEARNING STRATEGY

Recognize how generalizations and examples are used in readings, and use them in similar ways to enhance your *own* writing.

Generalizations—statements of general truths or beliefs—are common features of academic writing. For example, in the history texts in Chapter 8, the writers make the generalization that the Olmec culture influenced many native American cultures. In order to "prove" that this general statement is indeed true, the writers support the general statement with several examples of ways in which the Olmec culture affected other cultures. Likewise, in Reading 1 of Chapter 10, the authors describe many skills that workers need. To convince readers that these skills are, in fact, essential, the writers include examples of job situations requiring the skills. Students can follow this model of stating generalizations and supporting them with examples in their own academic writing assignments. An ideal way to learn how generalizations and examples are used is to analyze a reading that contains them. The generalization, which contains a broad, *general* idea, precedes the example, which relates a less broad, *specific* idea. Expressions like *for instance* or *for example* commonly introduce an example. However, such expressions are not always present.

Apply the Strategy

With a partner, reread the following passages from Reading 1. Underline the generalization(s) and circle the example(s) in each passage. Discuss your answers with classmates.

1. Perhaps job setting ranks high on your list of important job characteristics. You may not want to work behind a desk all day. (par. 6)

2. Don't eliminate any occupation or industry before you learn more about it. Some occupations and industries invoke certain positive or negative images. For some people, fashion designers produce a glamorous image, while production occupations in manufacturing industries bring to mind a less attractive image. (par. 10)

3. If you do not plan to attend college, consider occupations that require less formal education. If you are interested in engineering, for example, but do not want to pursue a college degree, drafters and engineering technicians are two occupations you can enter with 1 or 2 years of post-secondary training. (par. 12)

4. Workers also need good listening and speaking skills to interact with others. Greater interaction among workers is evident in factories, offices, and laboratories. (par. 17)

TUNING IN: "Hot Jobs"

A. Pre-Viewing

Discuss these questions about the CNN video clip "Hot Jobs," before you view.

1. In the list below, put a check mark next to the college majors (fields of study) that you think offer college graduates the best chances of getting good jobs.

_____ Engineering	_____ Theatre
_____ Computer science	_____ Journalism
_____ Nursing	_____ Psychology
_____ Sociology	

2. Have you considered any of these majors for yourself?

3. Do you think the job situation in the field that interests you is better or worse *now* than it was five years ago? Why?

B. Discussion

1. As you view, check whether your predictions about majors with good job potential were accurate.

2. Why did students have a difficult time finding jobs 5 to 7 years before the report?

3. Which jobs pay the highest starting salaries and the biggest bonuses? Why?

4. Why do liberal arts majors have a difficult time finding jobs?

5. Will this information influence your choice of a college major?

◆**Getting Ready to Read**

A. In Reading 2, researchers at the U.S. Bureau of Labor Statistics make predictions about the jobs of the future. Read the following statements, and discuss their meaning with your instructor and classmates. Make your *own* predictions by marking the statements True or False, based on the changes *you* think will occur in jobs in the U.S. through the year 2006.

_____ 1. Between now and 2006, the number of jobs will grow faster than in the last ten years.

_____ 2. More women will be working in the future.

_____ 3. Unemployment will rise.

_____ 4. More job growth will occur in service areas than in goods-producing areas.

_____ 5. On the average, workers will be younger in the future.

_____ 6. The greatest number of new jobs will be in the health care industry.

_____ 7. The greatest number of new jobs will be in computer-related areas.

_____ 8. Most future jobs will come from hiring new workers rather than replacing retiring workers.

_____ 9. The fastest-growing job areas of the future will require at least a bachelor's degree.

B. Asking Questions: Preview the headings in Reading 2, "Tomorrow's Jobs." Make a list of questions that you have about the information presented in the headings. Compare your questions with those of other classmates.

Vocabulary Check

Are these words familiar? Check the words that you already know. Look the others up in the dictionary, and write the definitions in your Vocabulary Log. Discuss any "problem" words with your instructor and classmates. Add new words to your Vocabulary Log.

_____ ultimately	_____ relatively	_____ shifted
_____ constrains	_____ numerical	_____ offset
_____ surged	_____ sector	_____ enhanced
_____ anticipating	_____ steady	_____ comprise
_____ projects (verb)	_____ innovative	_____ attainment

Read

Reading 2: Tomorrow's Jobs

1   Making informed career decisions requires reliable information about opportunities in the future. Opportunities result from the relationships between the population, labor force, and the demand for goods and services. Population **ultimately** limits the size of the labor force—individuals working or looking for work—which **constrains** how much can be produced. Demand for various goods and services determines employment in the industries providing them. Occupational employment opportunities, in turn, result from skills needed within specific industries. Opportunities for registered nurses and other health-related specialists, for example, have **surged** in response to the rapid growth in demand for health services. Examining the past and **anticipating** changes in these relationships are the foundation of the **Occupational Outlook Program.**[1]

The labor force will grow more slowly.

2   The **Bureau of Labor Statistics**[2] (BLS) **projects** that the labor force will grow to 14.9 million between 1996 and 2006. This is

[1]**Occupational Outlook Program:** U.S. government agency that projects job growth

[2]**Bureau of Labor Statistics:** U.S. government agency that collects data about work and workers

1.2 million less than the previous 10 years, reflecting a slower growth in the population 16 years of age and older. Growth was much faster from 1976 to 1986, when the baby boomers were entering the labor force.

3   The labor force will grow 11 percent between 1996 and 2006, slightly slower than during the 1986-96 period but only half the rate of growth during the 1976-86 period. The labor force will continue to grow faster than the population rate as a result of an increase in the percentage of the population working or looking for work. Between 1996 and 2006, employment will increase by 18.6 million or 14 percent. This is slower than during the 1986-96 period, when the economy added 21 million jobs.

4   Wage and salary worker employment will account for 94 percent of this increase. In addition, the number of self-employed workers is expected to increase to 11.6 million in 2006, while the number of unpaid family workers will decline.

The labor force will become increasingly diverse.
....

5 The labor force growth of Hispanics, Asians, and other races, will be faster than for blacks and white non-Hispanics. The projected labor force growth of these ethnic groups stems primarily from immigration. Despite **relatively** slow growth, white non-Hispanics will have the largest **numerical** growth between 1996 and 2006.

6   Between 1996 and 2006, women's share of the labor force is projected to slowly increase from 46 to 47 percent, continuing a pattern since 1976. The participation rate for women will continue to increase for those 20- to 65-years old. The number of men in the labor force will grow at a slower rate than in the past, in part reflecting declining employment in well-paid production jobs in manufacturing, and a continued shift in demand for workers from the goods-producing **sector** to the service-producing sector. Participation rates for men will decline for all age groups below age 45 except for 16–19; the rates for those 16–19 will remain **steady** at 53 percent. Rates for age groups 45 and above will increase.

The labor force will become older.
....

7 Workers over age 45 will account for a larger share of the labor force as the baby-boom generation ages. Two age groups with large numbers of baby boomers will grow by more than 30 percent—people 45 to 54 and those 55 to 64. Only the trailing edge of the baby boomers, those born from 1962 to 1964, will be younger than 45 in 2006.

> In 1830, 70.5% of workers in America worked on farms. By 1980, this figure was 2.2%.
>
> —U.S. BUREAU OF THE CENSUS

8   The very large group of workers aged 35 to 44, which is about one-fourth of the labor force, will change hardly at all during the period. The 25- to 34-year old group will decline by 3.0 million, a result of falling birth rates in the late 1960's. Those 16 to 24 will increase by more than 3.0 million, making this group the largest it has been in 25 years. Industry employment growth is projected to be highly concentrated in service-producing industries.

9   Employment in service-producing industries will increase faster than average, with growth near 30 percent. Service and retail trade industries will account for 14.8 million out of a total projected growth of 17.5 million wage and salary jobs.

Business, health, and education services will account for 70 percent of the growth within the service industry.

10 Health care services will increase 30 percent and account for 3.1 million new jobs, the largest numerical increase of any industry from 1996-2006. Factors contributing to continued growth in this industry include the aging population, which will continue to require more services, and the increased use of **innovative** medical technology for intensive diagnosis and treatment. Patients will increasingly be **shifted** out of hospitals and into outpatient facilities, nursing homes, and home health care in an attempt to contain costs.

11 Educational services are projected to increase by 1.8 million jobs between 1996 and 2006. Most jobs will be for teachers, who are projected to account for 1.3 million jobs.

12 Computer and data processing services will add over 1.3 million jobs from 1996-2006. The 108 percent increase is due to technological advancements and the need for higher skilled workers. The high percent increase makes this the fastest growing industry over the projection period.

13 Growth in goods-producing industries will be restrained by declines in manufacturing and mining.

14 Projected employment growth in the construction and agriculture industries will be **offset** by a decline in manufacturing and mining jobs. Manufacturing will account for 13 percent of total wage and salary worker employment in 2006, compared to 15 percent in 1996.

15 Construction employment will grow one-fourth slower than during the previous 10-year period.

16 Within the agriculture, forestry, and fishing industry, growth in agriculture services and forestry will more than offset the projected declines in crops, livestock, and livestock related products, and fishing, hunting, and trapping.

Replacement needs will account for three-fifths of the 50.6 million projected job openings between 1996 and 2006.

17 Job growth can be measured by percent change and numerical change. The fastest growing occupations do not necessarily provide the largest number of jobs. A larger occupation with slower growth may produce more openings than a smaller occupation with faster growth.

18 Job opportunities are **enhanced** by additional openings resulting from the need to replace workers who leave the occupation. Some workers leave the occupation as they are promoted or change careers; others stop working to return to school, to assume household responsibilities, or retire.

19 Replacement needs are greater in occupations with low pay and low training requirements with a high proportion of young and part-time workers. Service and professional specialty occupations will provide about 2 out of every 5 job openings—primarily due to high replacement needs.

Employment in professional specialty occupations is projected to increase at a faster rate and have more job growth than any major occupational group.

20 Within professional specialty occupations, computer-related occupations and teachers will add 2.3 million new jobs, accounting for 15 percent of all new jobs from 1996 to 2006. Professional specialty occupations **comprise** the only group that will have a majority of job openings stemming from growth.

21 Little or no change is expected in employment in agriculture, forestry, fishing, and related occupations. All job openings in this cluster will stem from replacement needs.

22 Office automation will significantly affect many individual administrative and clerical support occupations. Overall, these occupations will increase more slowly than average, though some are projected to decline.

23 Precision production, craft, and repair occupations and operators, fabricators, and laborers are projected to grow slower than average, due to continuing advances in technology, changes in production methods, and overall decline in manufacturing jobs.

Of the 25 occupations with the largest and fastest employment growth, high pay, and low unemployment, 18 require at least a bachelor's degree.

24 These 25 occupations are somewhat concentrated, with 5 occupations in computer technology, 4 in health care, and 5 in education.

The 25 occupations with the largest and fastest growth in employment, as well as higher than average pay and lower than average unemployment, will account for 5 million new jobs, or 27 percent of all job growth. The fastest growing occupations reflect growth in computer technology and health care services.

25   Computer engineers and systems analysts jobs are expected to grow rapidly in order to satisfy expanding needs of scientific research and applications of computer technology. The three fastest growing occupations are in computer-related fields.

26   Many of the fastest growing occupations are concentrated in health services, which are expected to increase more than twice as fast as the whole economy. Personal and home care aides, and home health aides, will be in great demand to provide personal care for an increasing number of elderly people and for persons who are recovering from surgery and other serious health conditions. This is occurring, as hospitals and insurance companies require shorter stays for recovery to reduce costs.

Job growth varies widely by education and training requirements.
••••••••••••••••••••••••••••••••

27 Five out of the six education and training categories projected to have the fastest growth require at least a bachelor's degree, and the sixth requires an associate's degree. All categories that do not require a college degree are projected to grow slower than average.

28   Occupations usually requiring short-term on-the-job training accounted for 53.5 million jobs in 1996, more than any other education and training category. Occupations requiring a bachelor's degree or more education accounted for 22 percent of all jobs. Occupations in the four education categories not requiring post-secondary education accounted for about 70 percent of all jobs.

29   Occupations that require a bachelor's degree are projected to grow the fastest, nearly twice as fast as the average for all occupations. All of the 20 occupations with the highest earnings require at least a bachelor's degree. Engineering and health occupations dominate this list.

30   Education is essential in getting a high-paying job. However, many occupations—for example, registered nurses, blue-collar worker supervisors, electrical and electronic technicians/technologists, automotive mechanics, and carpenters—do not require a college degree, yet offer higher than average earnings.

31   Labor force groups with lower than average educational **attainment** in 1996 will continue to have difficulty obtaining a share of the high-paying jobs unless they raise their educational

attainment. Although high-paying jobs will be available without college training, most jobs that pay above average wages will require a college degree.

After You Read

A. Expressing the Main Idea: Write one sentence that tells the main idea of Reading 2. Begin the sentence with the name of the article (in quotation marks), and include both the *topic* and *what the reading says about the topic* in the sentence. Share your sentence with classmates.

B. Comparing Ideas: In the Getting Ready to Read activity on page 212, you made predictions about tomorrow's jobs. Were your predictions the same as those made by the U.S. Bureau of Labor Statistics? Review the statements which you marked True or False on page 212. Which information surprised you? Discuss the statements with classmates.

C. Asking Questions: Try to find answers to the questions you wrote in the Asking Questions activity as you read. Compare your questions and answers with a small group of classmates.

ACADEMIC POWER STRATEGY

Research the job market in order to predict the best careers for the future. This will help you decide what college classes and majors to consider in preparation for your chosen field.

When you choose a career, you should certainly consider whether you are interested in the work you will do. However, you must also think about the future of the field. For example, if you want to become a marine biologist, how strong is the demand for jobs in that field now? Will marine biology be a growth area in the future? Or will there be fewer jobs in this field in the next 10 years? The job market is constantly changing, so in order to make an informed decision about your career path, you need to do some research. Your college library, college professors, and the Internet are important resources for finding out more about careers that interest you. Think about two or more careers of interest in order to give yourself more than one career option. In this way, you can make a wise career choice and start taking appropriate classes to prepare you for your chosen career.

Apply the Strategy

With one or more of your classmates, decide on two career fields that you find interesting and exciting. Research the careers by using the library or Internet resources suggested below, or by consulting your instructor, a librarian, or a professor at your college. For each career, fill in the chart below. Identify the job title or titles (i.e. "Accountant") and the academic field (i.e. "Accounting"). Describe what a person does in this job. Also find out about the salaries and the future potential for growth in the number of jobs in this field. Write a short conclusion to tell whether you think this is a good career choice or not. Here are some resources you may wish to use:

Occupational Outlook Handbook, published by the U.S. Bureau of Labor Statistics (available in print in the reference section of libraries or on the Internet at www.bls.gov).
Career-related Internet sites: Career Resource Center (www.careers.org), The Catapult on JobWeb (www.jobweb.org/catapult), or CareerForward (www.careerforward.com).

Share your research results by giving a brief oral report about each career field to your entire class.

Job Title(s) _____

Academic Field _____

Duties of Job _____

Future Job Growth _____

Salary Range _____

Conclusion _____

When you have decided on a field which you think has a promising future, begin to explore college classes and majors related to this field.

◆**Getting Ready to Read**

A. Have you considered a career in computers? If so, you should familiarize yourself with computer-related job titles. Check your knowledge of computer jobs by matching the job titles on the left with a short description on the right. Discuss the computer-related terms used in the descriptive sentences below, and share your ideas with classmates.

_____ 1. Computer scientists

_____ 2. Computer engineers

_____ 3. Systems analysts

_____ 4. Database administrators

_____ 5. Computer support specialists

a. work with database management systems software

b. study business, scientific, or engineering data processing problems and design new solutions using computers

c. interpret problems and provide technical support

d. apply the theories and principles of science and mathematics to the design of hardware, software, and networks

e. design computers and the software that runs them

B. Annotating a Text: Check your understanding of the five computer-related jobs you discussed as you read the following text. Highlight, underline, or circle sentences that introduce the work done by professionals in each of these jobs.

Vocabulary Check

Are these words familiar? Put checkmarks next to the words you know. Look up the others in your dictionary, and write the words and definitions in your Vocabulary Log. Discuss any terms that do not appear in your dictionary with your instructor and classmates.

_____ virtually

_____ prerequisite

_____ theoretical

_____ innovation

_____ prototypes

_____ crossover

_____ devices

_____ clients

_____ devising

_____ harness

_____ database

_____ implementation

_____ configure

Read

Reading 3: Computer Scientists, Computer Engineers, and Systems Analysts

1   Computer scientists, computer engineers, and systems analysts are expected to be the top three fastest growing occupations and among the top 20 in the number of new jobs as computer applications continue to expand throughout the economy.

2   A bachelor's degree is **virtually** a **prerequisite** for most employers. Relevant work experience also is very important. For some of the more complex jobs, persons with graduate degrees are preferred.

3   The rapid spread of computers has generated a need for highly trained workers to design and develop new hardware and software systems and to incorporate technological advances into new or existing systems. This group includes a wide range of professional computer-related occupations.

4   The title "computer scientist" can be applied to a wide range computer professionals who generally design computers and the software that runs them, develop information technologies, and develop and adapt principles for applying computers to new uses. Computer scientists perform many of the same duties as other computer professionals throughout a normal workday, but their jobs are distinguished by the higher level of **theoretical** expertise and **innovation** they apply to complex problems and the creation or application of new technology.

5   Computer engineers also work with the hardware and software aspects of systems design and development. Whereas computer scientists emphasize the application of theory, computer engineers emphasize the building of **prototypes,** although there is much **crossover.** Computer engineers generally apply the theories and principles of science and mathematics to the design of hardware, software, networks, and processes to solve technical problems. They often work as part of a team that designs new computing **devices** or computer-related equipment, systems, or software.

6   Computer hardware engineers generally design, develop, test, and supervise the manufacture of computer hardware. Software engineers, on the other hand, are involved in the design and development of software systems for control and automation of manufacturing, business, and management processes.

7   Software engineers or software developers also may design and develop both packaged and systems software or be involved in creating custom software applications for **clients.** These professionals also possess strong programming skills, but they are more

concerned with analyzing and solving programming problems than with simply writing the code for the programs.

8   Far more numerous, systems analysts use their knowledge and skills to solve computer problems and enable computer technology to meet the individual needs of an organization. They study business, scientific, or engineering data processing problems and design new solutions using computers. This process may include planning and developing new computer systems or **devising** ways to apply existing systems' resources to additional operations. Systems analysts may design entirely new systems, including both hardware and software, or add a single new software application to **harness** more of the computer's power. They work to help an organization realize the maximum benefit from its investment in equipment, personnel, and business processes.

9   Most systems analysts generally work with a specific type of system, depending on the type of organization they work for—for example, business, accounting, or financial systems, or scientific and engineering systems. Companies generally seek business systems analysts who specialize in the type of systems they use.

10   Other computer professionals include **database** administrators and computer support specialists. Database administrators work with database management systems software, coordinating changes to, testing, and implementing computer databases. Since they also may be responsible for design **implementation** and system security, database administrators plan and coordinate security measures. Computer support specialists provide assistance and advice to users. They interpret problems and provide technical support for hardware, software, and systems. Support specialists may work within an organization or directly for a computer or software vendor.

11   Network or systems administrators may install, **configure**, and support an organizations systems or portion of a system. Telecommunications specialists generally are involved with the interfacing of computer and communications equipment. Computer security specialists are responsible for planning, coordinating, and implementing an organizations' information security measures. These and other growing specialty occupations reflect the increasing emphasis on client-server applications, the growth of the Internet, the expansion of World Wide Web applications and Intranets, and the demand for more end-user support. An example of this is the growing number of job titles relating to the Internet and World Wide Web such as Internet and Web developers, or Webmasters.

After You Read

A. Comprehension: How well did you understand the computer jobs you discussed in the Getting Ready to Read activity on page 220? Discuss some differences between the jobs with classmates.

B. Reactions: Make a list of the careers with the best potential in the near future. With a small group of classmates, discuss which careers interest you. Share information you know about these careers. Then, make a list of your personal "top three" career choices and your reasons for choosing them. Share your list with classmates.

PUTTING IT ALL TOGETHER

Vocabulary Building

Check your knowledge of the vocabulary you have studied in this chapter. Match the vocabulary words on the left with the short definitions on the right.

_____ 1. stimulating

_____ 2. clientele

_____ 3. substantially

_____ 4. misconception

_____ 5. crucial

_____ 6. interpersonal

_____ 7. surged

_____ 8. sector

_____ 9. steady

_____ 10. shifted

_____ 11. prerequisite

_____ 12. evolve

_____ 13. specialization

a. customers

b. extremely important

c. change over time

d. between people

e. misunderstanding

f. considerably

g. rose suddenly

h. requirement before something

i. division

j. subject which someone knows a lot about

k. firm, stable

l. increasing energy or activity

m. changed from one position to another

Average Weekly Salaries in the U.S.:

$444 – with vocational training

$639 – with associate degree

$686 – with bachelor's degree

SOURCE: U.S. BUREAU OF LABOR STATISTICS

Final Project

Work with a partner to research one career. Include information on these and other areas: job title, description of the work, educational requirements, and salary range. Follow these steps:

A. Conduct an Internet search to learn more about the career. Consult the guide, "Evaluating Web Sites" in Appendix B on page 227. Find two articles. Read them and identify the main ideas.

B. If Internet access is unavailable, conduct the same research using print resources from a library. Use your library's databases to search for magazine or journal articles or books. Also, use the *Occupational Outlook Handbook* published by the U.S. Bureau of Labor Statistics. Consult your instructor for information about using your college library. Find two articles. Read them and find the main ideas. Share the information that you gained from your research in a brief presentation to classmates. Answer the following questions about your classmates' reports:

1. What is your reaction to the information from the readings?

2. What did you learn from this presentation?

Test-Taking Tip

Learn from your mistakes on tests. After you get your graded test back, analyze the answers you got wrong. Try to understand why you made the mistakes you made. Did you misread the question? Did you not study material related to the question? Did you leave yourself too little time to answer the question? Evaluate the cause of mistakes to help you avoid similar problems on future tests.

CHECK YOUR PROGRESS

On a scale of 1 to 5, rate how well you have mastered the goals set at the beginning of the chapter:

1 2 3 4 5   annotate, or mark, texts.

1 2 3 4 5   recognize generalizations and examples.

1 2 3 4 5   research the job market to predict the best careers.

If you've given yourself a 3 or lower on any of these goals:

- visit the *Tapestry* web site for additional practice.
- ask your instructor for extra help.
- review the sections of the chapter that you found difficult.
- work with a partner or study group to further your progress.

APPENDIX A: READING RATE CHART

Use the chart below to record your reading rate for the timed readings in the book and other timed readings that you do in your class or outside class. The ideal reading rate is 150 words per minute. If you like, reread a text to improve your reading speed.

Date	Title of Reading	Words per Minute

APPENDIX B:
USING THE INTERNET AS A READING SOURCE

Evaluating Web Sites

As you know, the Internet is a giant network of millions of computers across the globe. These computers "talk to" each other by telephone and other types of electronic signals. There is an incredible amount of information on the popular Internet application, the World Wide Web ("the Web"). But is all this information accurate? Not always.

To evaluate information on the Web, first examine the address of the Web source. Each Web site has an address that tells you the name and kind of organization where the information comes from.

Here's an example:
www.ccp.cc.pa.us

Here, the name **ccp** indicates "Community College of Philadelphia," **cc** means "community college" and **pa** and **us** identify the geographic location of the site as "Pennsylvania, U.S.A."

Other common types of Internet sites contain the following abbreviations in their addresses. The abbreviations tell you that the site is owned and run by these kinds of organizations:

.com	some kind of **com**mercial business
.edu	**edu**cational institution (schools, colleges, universities)
.gov	local, state or federal **gov**ernment
.org	nonprofit **org**anizations, and
.mil	**mil**itary.

When you access the information on an Internet site, examine whether the site is owned by a commercial business or an educational institution. Is the site owned by a business which is trying to sell you something? Are they providing information free of charge? For example, in this group of ESL sites, which one is a commercial business? Which site is run by an educational institution?

Linguistic Funland
www.linguistic-funland.com/tesl.html

English Grammar for ESL Students
www.gl.umbc.edu/~kpokoy1/grammar1.htm

Sometimes, access to sites is free; however, often, Web sites charge you for their information.

Once you know the source of the information on the Web site, you should also consider the accuracy of the information. If you are doing research on a topic, you need to know whether the information on the Web site is **objective** (free of bias or opinion) or whether it is **subjective** (containing opinion). Which organization owns the site? Is their information accurate? Do they have a reason to present an opinion or bias? Do they present only one side of an issue? How old is the information?

Identifying the source of information on the Web will allow you to evaluate the purpose, the accuracy, and the reliability of the Web site.

Web Sites for English Language Learners

There are many useful Web resources for English language learning. Some sites include readings for ESL students, such as news articles, comics, jokes, and even movie scripts. Other sites help you build vocabulary, do grammar exercises, or play games. Many of these sites are **interactive,** so that you interact with the computer by answering language questions and getting "instant" answers.

As you explore some of the sites listed here, you will find that many sites have **links** which point you to other sites with language learning materials. Unfortunately, you may also find that some of the sites have disappeared. That's because the World Wide Web is a "work in progress" that changes constantly. You can develop your own personal list of favorite sites.

Here's a list of sites for students and teachers of English:

Activities for ESL Students
http://www.aitech.ac.jp/~iteslj/s/

Alice's House of EFL, ESL, ETC.
http://AD.Walker.org/

Bruce Laidlaw's Literacy and ESL Programs
http://pip.com.au/~abestuds/mac.html
(for Macintosh users)
or http://pip.com/au/~abestuds/win.html
(for Personal Computer users)

Centre for Language Training and Assessment
http://www.cita.on.ca

Dave's ESL Café
http://www.eslcafe.com

EFL Playhouse (for younger learners)
http://members.tripod.com/ESL4Kids/index.html

English as a Second Language@Cegep.Quebec
http://www.goecities.com/CollegePark/Library/
4777/

English Tests and Quizzes
http://www.englishlearner.com/tests/test.html

English as a Second Language Home Page
http://www.lang.uiuc.edu/r-li5/esl/

ESL Interactive
http://www.iaic.wsu.edu/eslint/eslindex.html

ESL Hub
http://www.soltect.net/esltutor/

ESL Loop
http://www.webring.org/cgi-bin/
webring?index&ring=esloop

ETC: ESL Teacher Connection
http://www-personal.si.umich.edu/~jarmour/etc/
etchome.html

Grammar Central
http://www.cita.on.ca/grammar.htm

Grammar Safari
http://deil.lang.uiuc.edu/web.pages/grammarsafari.
html

**Kaplan's Train Your Brain:
Vocabulary (interactive flashcards)**
http://www.kaplan.com/garnes/vocab/

Le Rosey English Link Site
http://www.geocities.com/Athena/Agora/9749/
index. html

On-line English Grammar
http://www.edunet.com/english/grammar/toc.cfm

Pop-Up Grammar
http://www.brownlee.org/durk/grammar/

Professor TOEFL's Fun Page
http://www.slip.net/~caa

Purdue University's On-line Writing Lab
http://owl.english.purdue.edu/

Randall's ESL Cyber Listening Lab
http://www.esl-lab.com/

Sarah and John's TEFL Pitstop
http://www.lingolex.com/jstefl.htm

Taiwan Teacher's Games
http://www.geocities.com/Athens/Delphi/1979/
games.html

TESL: Teaching English as a Second Language
http://www.quik13.com/mher/tesl/

**TOPICS: An Online Magazine by and for
Learners of English**
http://www.rice.edu/projects/topics/Electronic/
Magazine.html

Volterre's Web Links for Teachers of English
http://www.wfi.fr/volterre/weblinktch.html

Practice

Activity: With a partner, find and use two Web sites that contain information and/or activities to help ESL students. (Be sure to type in the address of the site carefully.) Then, evaluate the two sites. With your partner, write complete sentences to answer each of the following questions about each site. Present your answers to your classmates. Write the name and Web address of each site on the blackboard.

1. What is the content of the Web site? Briefly describe the information and/or activities on the site.
2. Is the Web site owned by a commercial business or an educational or nonprofit institution?
3. Does the Web site try to sell a product or products?
4. Is the information free? If not, what is the charge?
5. Do you think the information on the site is objective or subjective? Explain why.
6. How old is the information? Is the information still up-to-date? Explain why.
7. Would you recommend this site to ESL students? Why or why not?

SKILLS INDEX

TEXT CREDITS

• •

[Chapter 1]

Page 7, "Reading for Pleasure Versus Reading for Learning." From *Commuter Student, 1st edition,* by C.M. Wahlstrom and B.K. Williams. Copyright 1997. Reprinted with permission of Wadsworth Publishing, a division of Thomson Learning. Fax 800-730-2215.

Page 11, "What Do You Know about the Reading Process?" From *Commuter Student, 1st edition,* by C.M. Wahlstrom and B.K. Williams. Copyright 1997. Reprinted with permission of Wadsworth Publishing, a division of Thomson Learning. Fax 800-730-2215.

Page 16, "Ten Tips for Reading College Textbooks" From *College Study Skills: Becoming a Strategic Learner, 2nd edition,* by D. Van Blerkom. Copyright 1997. Reprinted with permission of Wadsworth Publishing, a division of Thomson Learning. Fax 800-730-2215.

[Chapter 2]

Page 25, *The Road Ahead.* From *The Road Ahead* by William Gates. Wheeler Publishing, 1996. Fair use.

Page 29, "Site Seeing on the Internet." 1999. Federal Trade Commission.

[Chapter 3]

Page 44, "Survival at Sea" by Ariane Randall.

Page 53, *The Story of the Titanic:* "A Night to Remember" by Gary Arnold.

Page 57, *The Story of the Titanic:* "Abandon Ship" by Gary Arnold.

[Chapter 4]

Page 70, "Microbes and Food Safety." From *Nutrition Concepts and Controversies, 7th edition,* by F.S. Sizer and E.N. Whitney. Copyright 1997. Reprinted with permission of Wadsworth Publishing, a division of Thomson Learning. Fax 800-730-2215.

Page 76, "Can Your Kitchen Pass the Food Safety Test?" by Paula Kurtzweil, 1998, U.S. Food and Drug Administration.

Page 83, "In Street Vendors' Smorgasbord, Threat of Sickness Lurks" and "Cooking Curbside: A Consumer's Guide." Copyright 1998 by *The New York Times.* Reprinted by permission.

[Chapter 5]

Page 96, "Traditional Sex Role Expectations." From *Introduction to Social Work and Social Welfare, 6th edition,* by C. Zastrow. Copyright 1996. Reprinted with permission of Wadsworth Publishing, a division of Thomson Learning. Fax 800-730-2215.

Page 100, "The Sex-Role Revolution." From *Introduction to Social Work and Social Welfare, 6th edition,* by C. Zastrow. Copyright 1996. Reprinted with permission of Wadsworth Publishing, a division of Thomson Learning. Fax 800-730-2215.

Page 107, "Median Weekly Earnings of Full-Time Workers." 1998, U.S. Bureau of Labor Statistics.

Page 110, "The New Majority," From *Your College Experience, 3rd edition,* by J.N. Gardner and A.J. Jewler. Copyright 1998. Reprinted with permission of Wadsworth Publishing, a division of Thomson Learning. Fax 800-730-2215.

[Chapter 6]

Page 118, "The Culture War." From *United States History: In the Course of Events, 1st edition,* by M. Downey, J.R. Glese, and F.D. Metcalf Copyright 1997. Reprinted with permission of South-Western Educational Publishing, a division of Thomson Learning. Fax 800-730-2215.

Page 124, "The Entertainment Media and the Social Construction of Crime and Justice," From *Media, Crime, and Criminal Justice, 2nd edition,* by R. Surette. Copyright 1998. Reprinted with permission of Wadsworth Publishing, a division of Thomson Learning. Fax 800-730-2215.

Page 127, "Voluntary Movie Rating System." Motion Picture Association of America.

Page 128, "Parental Guide Television Ratings." TV Parental Guidelines Monitoring Board Ratings.

Page 130, "Cannes Loves to Hate Censorship," Reprinted with permission of Associated Press, 50 Rockefeller Plaza, New York, NY 10020.

[Chapter 7]

Page 143, "Does Economic Growth Improve Human Morale?" Taken from *A Consuming Passion* edited by Rodney Clapp. Copyright 1998 by Christianity Today, Inc. Used by permission of InterVarsity Press, P.O. Box 1400, Downers Grove, IL 60515.

Page 150, "Keeping the American Dream" by Nha Dominic Cao Bui.

[Chapter 8]

Page 161, "The First Americans." From *United States History: In the Course of Events, 1st edition,* by M. Downey, J.R. Glese, and F.D. Metcalf Copyright 1997. Reprinted with permission of South-Western Educational Publishing, a division of Thomson Learning. Fax 800-730-2215.

Page 165, "Ways of Life Change." From *United States History: In the Course of Events, 1st edition,* by M. Downey, J.R. Glese, and F.D. Metcalf Copyright 1997. Reprinted with permission of South-Western Educational Publishing, a division of Thomson Learning. Fax 800-730-2215.

Page 169, "Trading Networks." From *United States History: In the Course of Events, 1st edition,* by M. Downey, J.R. Glese, and F.D. Metcalf Copyright 1997. Reprinted with permission of South-Western Educational Publishing, a division of Thomson Learning. Fax 800-730-2215.

Page 171, "Ancient Mound Builders." From *United States History: In the Course of Events, 1st edition,* by M. Downey, J.R. Glese, and F.D. Metcalf Copyright 1997. Reprinted with permission of South-Western Educational Publishing, a division of Thomson Learning. Fax 800-730-2215.

[Chapter 9]

Page 183, "Ethnic Boundary Markers." From *Humanity, 4th edition,* by J.G. Peoples and G. Bailey. Copyright 1997. Reprinted with permission of Wadsworth Publishing, a division of Thomson Learning. Fax 800-730-2215.

Page 188, "Types of Ethnic Groups." From *Humanity, 4th edition,* by J.G. Peoples and G. Bailey. Copyright 1997. Reprinted

with permission of Wadsworth Publishing, a division of Thomson Learning. Fax 800-730-2215.

Page 190, "The Problem of Stateless Nationalities," From *Humanity, 4th edition,* by J.G. Peoples and G. Bailey. Copyright 1997. Reprinted with permission of Wadsworth Publishing, a division of Thomson Learning. Fax 800-730-2215.

Page 195, "Stages of Cultural Growth." From *Right from the Start, 3rd edition,* by R. Kolkeboer and L. Walker. Copyright 1999. Reprinted with permission of Wadsworth Publishing, a division of Thomson Learning. Fax 800-730-2215.

[Chapter 10]

Page 206, "Solving the Job Puzzle" by Anne W. Clymer and Elizabeth McGregor, 1998, U.S. Bureau of Labor Statistics.

Page 213, "Tomorrow's Jobs," 1998, U.S. Bureau of Labor Statistics.

Page 221, "Computer Scientists, Computer Engineers, and Systems Analysts." From *Occupational Outlook Handbook,* 1998, U.S. Department of Labor.

PHOTO CREDITS

• •

2, 11 & 22: Photographs by Jonathan Stark for the Heinle & Heinle Image Resource Bank. 40: CORBIS/Jim Sugar. 52: CORBIS/Hulton. 64 & 70: Photographs by Jonathan Stark for the Heinle & Heinle Image Resource Bank. 87: CORBIS/Catherine Karnow. 92: CORBIS/George Hall. 99: CORBIS/Bettmann. 103, 107, 114 & 121: Photographs by Jonathan Stark for the Heinle & Heinle Image Resource Bank. 136: CORBIS/Owen Franken. 142: CORBIS/Gail Money. 146: CORBIS/Richard T. Nowitz. 150: CORBIS/Danny Lehman. 174: CORBIS/Catherine Karnow. 181: Peter Mendel/Stock Boston. 198: Robert Brenne/PhotoEdit. 202: CORBIS/Ted Streshinsky. 210 & 218: Photographs by Jonathan Stark for the Heinle & Heinle Image Resource Bank. 223: CORBIS/Owen Franken.